# Using the
# ORACLE®
## Toolset

# Using the
# ORACLE®
# Toolset

## Mike Krohn

ADDISON-WESLEY PUBLISHING COMPANY

WOKINGHAM, ENGLAND • READING, MASSACHUSETTS • MENLO PARK, CALIFORNIA • NEW YORK
DON MILLS, ONTARIO • AMSTERDAM • BONN • SYDNEY • SINGAPORE
TOKYO • MADRID • SAN JUAN • MILAN • PARIS • MEXICO CITY • SEOUL • TAIPEI

Cover designed by Designers & Partners of Oxford and printed by The Ethedo Press, High Wycombe, Bucks.
Typeset by Ian Kingston Editorial Services, Nottingham.
Printed in Great Britain at the University Press, Cambridge

First printed 1992. Reprinted 1993 and 1994 (twice).

**British Library Cataloguing in Publication Data**
A catalogue record for this book is available from the British library

**Library of Congress Cataloging-in-Publication Data**
Krohn, Mike.
    Using the oracle toolset / Mike Krohn.
        p.  cm.
    Includes index.
    ISBN 0-201-56538-2
    1. Application software.  2. Oracle toolset.  I. Title.
    QA76.76.A65K76      1993
    005.75'65--dc20

                                                           92-36525
                                                              CIP

# Preface

While I was planning and preparing this book, I kept looking round the technical bookshops to see what other books on Oracle were available, to see what the competition was like. There are quite a number and they all approach the subject from their own particular direction, with their own emphases and idiosyncrasies.

So what makes this one different? What are its emphases and idiosyncrasies? The answer is important to the prospective buyer. It will govern his or her choice of book. So, in keeping with the rest of this book, let's be straightforward about it....

■ Most importantly, **this is a practical book**. The original spur to write the book was seeing all the job advertisements in the computer technical press looking for people with Oracle skills. There is clearly a shortage of qualified people. So this book is intended to impart these practical skills. In general, it does not dwell on theory.

■ It is tailored to the **needs of people who will implement Oracle-based systems**. There are many excellent books on systems analysis and design, methodologies and so on. This is not one of them. My audience is the people who need to be able to implement Oracle-based systems. That is not to say that it is not relevant to systems analysts and designers. Quite the contrary; those people need to understand how to implement the systems before they set about designing them. But the emphasis is on the routine skills needed at the implementation stage. So the development tools are more important than the mechanics of the database management system.

■ **It is comprehensive**. Of course, there are degrees of comprehensiveness. The full set of Oracle manuals fills nearly a metre of my bookshelf and the thickness of this book is only a few centimetres. But within its chosen scope, it covers all the topics needed to an appropriate level of detail. The most important tools, used every day by an implementor of Oracle-based systems, are covered in detail. They are put into context by less detailed treatments of the rest of the products.

■ **It is up to date**. Oracle products are changing at a hectic pace and it is a constant battle for a book such as this to keep up. The book deals with the very latest versions of the toolset, delivered with version 6 of the database. This includes the new procedural extensions to SQL and the new graphical user interface supporting bit-mapped screens.

■ **It is primarily a tutorial book** rather than a reference one. Topics are
structured so that you are led in gently with plenty of examples. The idea
is to impart an understanding of how everything works rather than to give
a specification of every detail of the products. A single, realistic business
scenario is used throughout the book to give a practical slant to all the
examples and exercises. So you can read the book from start to finish,
working through the exercises, and you should have acquired the basic
skills necessary to build Oracle systems.

To get the most from the book, readers should already have some experience
of the development of commercial computer applications, database systems
and the use of third-generation languages such as COBOL, C, PL/1 etc. or
fourth-generation development tools (4GLs). Complete beginners may find it
rather hard going.

## Outline

Part 1 provides an introduction to the subject. There is a brief recap on
database management systems, the role of SQL and fourth-generation
software development trends. This is followed by a survey of the complete set
of Oracle products. We then home in on three important areas:

■ The Oracle implementation of **SQL and SQL extensions**. This a comprehensive treatment of interactive SQL and includes Oracle's proprietary
procedural extensions to the language, PL/SQL.

■ The development of **screen-based applications** using SQL*Forms and
SQL*Menu. SQL*Forms is probably the most important of Oracle's
software development tools and it is covered thoroughly. The latest
version (version 3), which implements a new style of user interface, is
covered as well as version 2.3 which is still in quite widespread use.

■ **Report writing**. There are two products described here. SQL*Report-
Writer is the latest report-writing product and this is described in detail.
The old report writer, SQL*Report, which is still relevant for some complex
report requirements and batch jobs, is also covered.

Notice that the Oracle end-user and decision support tools are given only a
brief mention, as are the more specialized products to do with text retrieval,
office automation and Oracle's application packages.

## How to use the book

If you are new to Oracle systems, you can read the book from start to finish
and it will progressively take you through all the relevant topics. The case
study used throughout the book is described in Chapter 1 and Appendix A. I

recommend that readers familiarize themselves with it before studying any of the examples or exercises. The other appendices contain reference information.

Each chapter can stand on its own, so if, for instance, you already know SQL, you may want to skip Chapter 4. You may already know the old version of SQL*Forms and want to catch up with the new version, in which case you can skip the first part of Chapter 6. But, wherever you are going to dip in, I would still recommend that you read Chapters 1 and 2 first.

## Acknowledgements

T he book is developed from a training course which I prepared for The Instruction Set Ltd, Hoskyns Open Systems division. My thanks to them for letting me convert and expand the material into book form. Throughout the preparation of the book, I have had unstinting help from Oracle UK. As a result, the book is more accurate and up to date than it would otherwise have been. Thanks particularly to John Spiers, Phil Slater and Steve Cave. Some of the early detail work on which the book is based was done by Greg Spence, one-time chairman of the Oracle UK User Group. His knowledge of the details of the products is based on many years experience and is quite formidable. My thanks to him, as well. Stan Blethyn of Bristol Polytechnic has contributed to the section on SQL*ReportWriter and has made many improvements to the rest of the text. Any mistakes (as they always say) are my own.

*Mike Krohn*
*Nettleton Mill*
*November 1992*

# Contents

## Trademarks

Aegis Domain™ is a trademark of Apollo

AIX™, MVS™, OS/2™, PC-AT™, PC-DOS™, Presentation manager™, PS/2™, QMF™ and VM™ are trademarks of International Business Machines Corporation

ALL-IN-1™, ULTRIX™, VAX™ and VMS™ are trademarks of Digital Equipment Corporation

AOS/VS™ and DG/UX™ are trademarks of Data General

Easy\*SQL®, ORACLE®, SQL\*Calc®, SQL\*Forms®, SQL\*Menu®, SQL\*Plus® and SQL\*Report® are registered trademarks and CASE\*Method™, CASE\*Dictionary™, CASE\*Designer™, CASE\*Generator™, Oracle Card™, Oracle Data Lens™, Oracle Data Query™, Oracle\*Mail™, PL/SQL™, SQL\*QMX™, SQL\*ReportWriter™ and SQL\*TextRetrieval™ are trademarks of Oracle Corporation UK Limited

CTIX™ is a trademark of Convergent

DYNIX™ is a trademark of Sequent Computer Systems Incorporated

GCOS™ is a trademark of Groupe Bull

HP/UX™ is a trademark of Hewlett-Packard Company

HyperCard™ and Macintosh™ are trademarks of Apple Computer, Inc.

IDMS™ is a trademark of Cullinet Corporation

Lotus 1-2-3® is a registered trademark of Lotus Development Corporation

MS-DOS® and Xenix® are registered trademarks and Windows™ is a trademark of Microsoft Corporation

NOS/VE™ is a trademark of Control Data Corporation

OS3™ is a trademark of Sun Microsystems, Inc.

OSx™ is a trademark of Nixdorf Computers Limited

Primos™ is a trademark of Prime Computer

SINIX™ is a trademark of Siemens AG

Sintran™ is a trademark of Norsk Data

UNIX™ is a trademark of AT&T

VOS™ is a trademark of Harris

# Part 1

*Introduction and
background*

# One

# The example company and applications

All the examples and exercises in the book are built around a single imaginary business. This first chapter, therefore, contains a short background to the company and a description of its database so that you can understand the business environment as you study the examples and exercises. A detailed specification of the database and its components is contained in Appendix A.

## 1.1   50K Cars Ltd

The example company is a car hire company called 50K Cars Ltd. 50K Cars rent expensive cars at expensive rates. The average price of their cars (to buy) is £50,000; hence the company name. Because they aim at an exclusive and rich clientele (people who are used to getting the very best service), 50K Cars are obsessed with providing flawless service to their clients.

They have an administrative headquarters and a sales office on Park Lane in central London. They also have a sales office at Heathrow airport and expect to open another shortly at Gatwick. Each of the offices has its own fleet of cars under its own control, though they do occasionally help another office which has run out of cars by lending one.

Each branch office is largely autonomous and keeps its own accounts on its own local computer. Clients, of course, may rent from different offices at different times. So a register of clients, past and current, is held on a central computer at the HQ in Park Lane. Each of the sales offices has links to this computer to access the client information. The HQ accountants can access branch office data on revenue, costs and so on.

Branch offices use their database system for applications in all areas of their business. In this book, we will be looking at the following application areas:

- **Reservations**. Customers reserve cars by telephone or in person. The system allocates the cars.

- **Collection and return of cars**. Cars are booked out when the customers come to collect them, noting the miles on the clock and so on. When the car is brought back, the system prepares the bill.

- **Invoicing**. Invoices and statements of account are prepared for account customers.

- **Vehicle maintenance**. The system schedules routine maintenance for the cars and tracks the reporting and fixing of any faults. These may be small faults or breakdowns.

- **Depreciation accounting**. The system calculates the written down value of the cars for the financial accountants.

- **Marketing**. Promotional mailshots are produced to be sent to people who have rented before.

- **Personnel**. The system at each branch office keeps personnel records and does payroll for their staff.

## 1.2 The database

The extract of the company's database used for the examples holds information about the cars available for hire, the customers and the bookings made by customers. The detailed structure of the database and its component tables is in Appendix A.

A populated database is available in machine-readable form for you to practice on (see Appendix A for details of how to get a copy). Many of the examples and exercises assume that there is a sensible amount of valid data in the database – for instance, that there are always enough cars to fulfil all bookings.

### 1.2.1 Cars

The information about the company's cars is split between several database tables. Structuring the data like this avoids redundant data and is known as normalization.

Cars fall into a number of rental groups which define the rental rates for the cars, all the cars in a group having the same rates. Thus there is a table of **car groups**, identified by a group name, which defines the rental rates for the group. Individual cars are of a particular model and there is a table of **car models**, identified by a model name which contains details of the rental group the model falls into, a description of the model and how often this model of car needs to be serviced. Finally, there is a table of **individual cars**, identified by the car registration number, which contains details specific to an individual car like original cost, date bought, miles to date etc.

## 1.2.2 Customers and bookings

It is not necessary to have any complicated structure for customer or booking records. There is a single table of all customers, each identified by a customer number. It holds name, address, payment method etc.

Similarly, there is a table of bookings, each identified by a booking number. A single booking record follows the progress of the rental. It starts when the booking is first made; a car model will be allocated to the booking but not a specific car. When the rental commences, a car is allocated and the car mileage at start of rental is recorded. At the end of the rental period, the return mileage is recorded and the cost of the rental is calculated. Finally, an indicator is set when the bill for the rental is paid.

## 1.2.3 Employees

Each branch of 50K Cars keeps its own personnel records in an employees table. This table contains details of the employee's name, address, job title and salary. Salary has a commission element and this is derived from a monthly scan of the bookings table. Staff can be paid weekly or monthly and the payroll system automatically keeps track of the cumulative amount paid so far during the current financial year.

*Two*
# The world according to Oracle

Oracle has a clear view of what the IT world is like and what its customers want or, at any rate, need. This view both governs and is implicit in the architecture and characteristics of the Oracle products. So, as an introduction to the Oracle products, this chapter provides a quick review of database systems, SQL and fourth-generation applications development techniques. This review pretty closely reflects Oracle's own views.

There is then a description of the complete Oracle product set. Some of these products – the ones of mainly specialist interest – are not dealt with in detail elsewhere in the book, but they are included here so that you can see how the complete set of products relate to one another.

Readers are assumed to have already had some exposure to relational database management systems and fourth-generation software development tools, and thus the principles and philosophy are not dealt with in any detail. Some important concepts are outlined and relational database systems are contrasted with other types.

## 2.1  The relational difference

Over the years, many different sorts of software system have been called database systems. As the software industry has matured, a consensus has appeared as to the important characteristics of a database management system:

- It must provided a single source of data for multiple applications.

- The applications should not need to worry about the physical storage of the data.

- The applications should be able to work with their own view of the data. This view or version of the data should automatically be drawn from the totality of the data.

- Perhaps most important of all, the database system must protect the data from the conflicting requirements of multiple users.

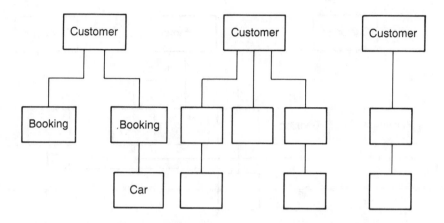

**Figure 2.1**  Hierarchical database structure.

There are, of course, many other important factors: performance, ease of use, flexibility to encompass changes to the data content and to the ways in which the data is to be used and so on.

Several generic types of database system have been identified according to the strategies they use to satisfy all these requirements and the trade-offs they make. The classes of database are named after the strategy they use.

**Hierarchical** systems (Figure 2.1) first appeared in the early 1970s. They put the data in a predefined hierarchy. The structure of the hierarchy defines the relationships between the items of data. At each level in the hierarchy, the higher level item (parent) can be linked to many lower level items (children) but each child can only be linked to one parent. All the linking is vertically through the hierarchical tree structure; no cross linking is allowed. IBM's IMS is the most famous of this class.

This structure was often found to be too restrictive when trying to model the relationships between data in real companies. So **Network** or **CODASYL** systems (Figure 2.2) extended this structure to allow cross links. Cullinet's IDMS is the most famous of this class.

These are the two most commonly used strategies. There are other systems which use strategies particularly suitable for certain classes of application. Inverted file structures for bill-of-materials processing is a well-known example.

The major characteristic of all these systems is that the relationships between the items of data is defined in the structure with which the database is set up. The structure (and therefore the relationships) are defined right at the beginning and they become very difficult (expensive) to modify later on. A company using these systems has to analyse very carefully how it expects to use the data over quite a long time frame so that the database can be set up correctly and then not changed.

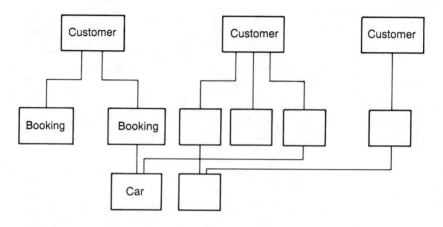

**Figure 2.2**   Network database structure.

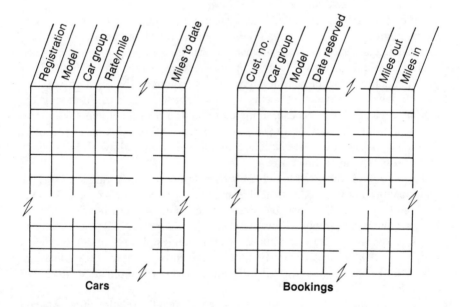

**Figure 2.3**   Relational tabular structure.

The problem, of course, is that the world is not that tidy. Business circumstances may change radically over quite short time frames. Whole new areas of computer applications may open up. Look, for instance, at how the deregulation of financial markets radically changed computing in the finance sector.

**Relational** database management systems (RDBMSs) are aimed at solving this problem. As well as satisfying the basic requirements of a DBMS, their primary concern is to provide the flexibility to change both the content of the database and the way in which it can be used. As you would expect, there is usually a penalty to be paid for this flexibility. It is in performance.

Relational systems do not use the structure of the database to define the relationships in the data. The only logical structure imposed on the data is that of treating it as a series of two-dimensional tables (Figure 2.3). In non-relational terminology, the columns represent fields and the rows represent records. Relationships between tables are established by relating the values in the columns of the tables. Commonly a data item appears in more than one table specifically to allow links to be established, based on the value of the data item. In the example database, for instance, the car registration number appears in both the cars table and the bookings table.

The relationships in the data only become apparent when the data is used and they are deduced by looking at the values of the data items. As an example, details of all the employees of a company who work in the same department are not grouped together by the structure of the database. But, when a query to extract all the employees in a department is executed, then, by looking at the values of the data in the database, the relevant employee details are grouped together.

## 2.2 Application areas

Since they put a premium on flexibility, relational systems were originally most often to be found in management information systems and other similar application areas. The inherent unpredictability of the sorts of analyses that would be needed and the usual absence of tight time constraints meant that relational systems were ideal.

Advances in software technology are constantly improving the performance of RDBMSs. More and more, as the performance of RDBMSs approaches that of the other DBMSs and as the rate of business change accelerates, relational systems are being used for routine corporate data processing jobs. Going with this gradual change of emphasis is the movement of relational systems from their original home on minicomputers to mainframes. Relational systems are also the only ones capable of providing a real distributed database. Relational databases and distributed systems are becoming more popular together.

In spite of the claims of the RDBMS vendors, though, the performance of relational systems does not yet match that of the major hierarchical and network systems. So for routine jobs, where the nature of the job is not going to change and where the response time must be minimized, non-relational systems still hold their own.

## 2.3  SQL

SQL, Structured Query Language, is now established as the standard language for accessing and managing relational database systems. It was originally developed as part of a research programme by IBM. In spite of the name, SQL (often pronounced as 'sequel') is not just concerned with querying. It also deals with other aspects of data manipulation, like inserting, updating and deleting. SQL is also used to look after the administration of the database, setting up tables, defining the access rights of the various users and so on.

Like any language, SQL is not perfect. The most important criticism is that it has only very rudimentary features for defining integrity rules for data, that is, what constitute valid values for the data items and how the existence of one data item and its range of valid values relate to other data items.

It is not surprising that a language coming from a research project and thrust into the commercial world would be found to be in need of modification and extension. This has indeed been the case with SQL. The major problem was the lack of standards. Many dialects grew up before any standard variant of SQL was defined. The initial ANSI SQL standard was weak. Slow to appear, it was little more than the lowest common denominator of the SQL implementations from the major suppliers – too little, too late. Meanwhile, all the vendors went ahead with their own proprietary extensions. They were, of course, mutually incompatible.

More recently, the dialects of SQL have tended to converge and the standardization process is beginning to get ahead of the suppliers' development programmes. In the USA there is now a test procedure to verify that an implementation of the SQL language does conform to an ANSI standard. Such conformance will help users to move an application from one database system to another, though portability like this, of course, will require more than just the use of a standard SQL. Conformance is not usually a simple yes or no; there are several component standards covering different aspects of SQL usage. Thus everyone can probably still claim some sort of conformance. The most important standard to meet is level 2 of ANSI SQL89 which includes data integrity aspects. Version 6 of Oracle does not conform to the data integrity aspects of this standard but does conform to the other elements. A pre-release version 7 of Oracle has been tested and shown to conform to all aspects of the standard.

The problem of standards is by no means resolved, however. Though SQL is approaching a useful standard, all the database suppliers have developed procedural extensions to SQL to widen the range of application of their systems. There has been no significant standardization here.

## 2.4 Fourth-generation software development

At about the same time that relational database systems were being developed, there was also a major change going on in the way in which software systems were being implemented. 4GLs are the best known aspect of this, but CASE tools, non-procedural applications generators and end-user computing are all part of the same trend.

The aim is, firstly, to apply the discipline of a more rigorous, engineering approach to the development of applications and, secondly, to allow the people who need the results of the system to participate in its development. The RDBMS vendors were quick to surround their database systems with their own range of fourth-generation development tools, and the 4GL, report-writer and CASE vendors interfaced their products to the relational database systems.

## 2.5 The Oracle product set

The Oracle product set is a wide-ranging one and is being extended all the time. The most prominent products are summarized here, grouping them according to their function. First, though, we will look at one of Oracle's main strengths, portability.

### 2.5.1 Hardware platforms

Oracle products are available on a very wide range of different styles and sizes of hardware. Within the limits set by the hardware itself, the implementations of the products on all these platforms are identical. The differences in the capabilities of terminals are the main obstructions to all the implementations being totally identical.

This portability has obvious benefits to organizations which have a mix of different types of hardware. It also means that it is quite possible, and usual, to develop applications on one machine, often a PC, and then simply carry it across to another machine, which could be a big mainframe.

Table 2.1 shows a list of the most prominent platforms on which Oracle is available. The list is constantly being extended. Not all the products are available on all the platforms and the picture of what is available on what is constantly changing.

### 2.5.2 The Oracle RDBMS

The RDBMS is at the heart of the whole product set. It is the component responsible for the storage and manipulation of the data and all the other products interface with it.

**Table 2.1** Hardware support for Oracle. All implementations are, for practical purposes, identical.

| Supplier | Operating system(s) |
|----------|---------------------|
| AT&T | Unix System V |
| Altos | Unix System V |
| Amdahl | MVS, VM |
| Apollo | Aegis Domain |
| Bull | GCOS, Unix System V |
| Comparex | MVS, VM |
| Control Data | NOS/VE |
| Convergent | CTIX |
| Dansk Data | Unix System V |
| Data General | AOS/VS, DG/UX |
| DDE | Unix |
| DEC | VMS, Ultrix |
| Edge | Unix |
| Encore | Unix |
| Gould | Unix |
| Harris | VOS, Unix System V |
| Hewlett-Packard | HP/UX |
| IBM | MVS, VM, AIX |
| ICL | VME, Unix System V |
| Nixdorf | OSx |
| Norsk | Sintran |
| Olivetti | Unix System V |
| PCS | Unix System V |
| Plexus | Unix System V |
| Prime | Primos, Unix |
| Pyramid | OSx |
| Sequent | Dynix |
| Siemens | Sinix |
| Stratus | VOS |
| Sun | OS3.x |
| Unisys | Unix System V |
| Wang | VS |
| | |
| IBM PC-AT, PS/2 and compatibles | PC-DOS, MS-DOS, Xenix, OS/2 |

Version 6 is the current RDBMS version and is now sold on all hardware platforms. Some established users will not have upgraded and will still be using version 5, which is quite different internally but similar externally. Version 7 is scheduled for release soon. Version 6 involved a major re-write of the innards of the RDBMS in order to provide much higher performance than previous versions and it is specifically aimed at the routine production systems in a company's data processing applications. That implies transaction processing.

A set of enhancements for transaction processing, called the Oracle transaction processing option (tpo) is available as an optional extra with version 6. It consists of:

- a set of major extensions to SQL called PL/SQL. This is intended to provide a procedural capability to optimize the throughput of transactions in transaction processing systems.

- an improved procedure for minimizing the interference between multiple users all trying to update data. Contention is reduced by locking data at row level and this improves throughput.

Routine maintenance and administration of the database is carried out using SQL*Plus and SQL*DBA. There are also a number of utilities for importing data into the database, for exporting it and for loading data from flat files.

### 2.5.3 Applications development products

Viewing them in terms of the applications development process, the applications development tools start with a set of CASE (computer-aided software engineering) products (Figure 2.4).

CASE*Method is not really a product in that its physical manifestation is as part of Oracle's training material and as a series of books. It is a set of methods and procedures for analysing the business need behind the development of an application system and for governing the design and implementation of the system.

CASE*Dictionary is a product that manages all the information derived during the analysis, design and implementation of a system. Definitions of all the functions, entities, and even data definitions are held in the dictionary. CASE*Dictionary has its own built-in forms-based interface to enter and extract the information. Alternatively, there is a graphical interface to the dictionary, called CASE*Designer, which allows the analyst to use quite sophisticated graphics techniques to define the characteristics of the target system.

Oracle places great importance on its CASE products. CASE*Dictionary runs on almost all of the hardware that runs Oracle, including PCs. CASE*Designer currently runs on various workstations under Unix with X Window and its derivatives and on PCs under OS/2 and Presentation Manager.

These so-called *upper-CASE* products provide a discipline for specifying the requirements of the target system. The benefit they provide derives as much from the way that they enforce consistency and completeness in the system specification as from any reduction in the analyst's workload. More emphasis is now being placed on the next stage of the development process where *lower-CASE* products take over much of the detailed work of building the

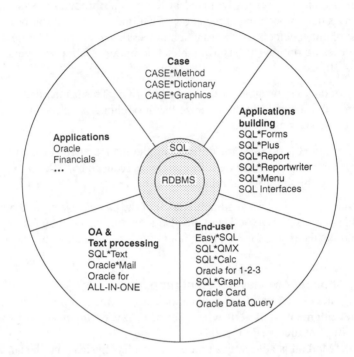

**Figure 2.4**   The Oracle product set.

application to meet the specification. A whole raft of CASE*Generator products is imminent which will take the system specification, maintained by CASE*Dictionary, and automatically generate complete applications using SQL*Forms, SQL*ReportWriter, SQL*Menu and so on.

For the moment, these products are used manually. SQL*Forms produces interactive, forms-based applications. SQL*ReportWriter and SQL*Report are used to produce reporting applications and a whole structure of forms, reports and other programs can be tied together with menus generated by SQL*Menu. SQL*TextRetrieval is a development system for building applications that process large amounts of textual information.

There are often jobs which cannot be tackled by SQL*Forms and the other high-level tools. For these Oracle provides a number of interfaces from third-generation languages to the RDBMS. Ada, C, COBOL, FORTRAN, Pascal and PL/1 are all supported.

### 2.5.4   End-user computing products
Getting the end-users of an application system to build their own systems was part of the move away from traditional third-generation development methods.

Oracle's products in this area (Figure 2.4) fall into two groups. The first group consists of what Oracle describe as 'mature' products. They were all developed some time ago and are not now being developed further. They are quite widely used but are being replaced by more capable alternatives. They include:

- **Easy*SQL** lets the user build simple applications by 'point-and-select' from windows rather than by writing SQL statements. It is available on DEC VAX/VMS and several Unix platforms. Easy*SQL has its own built-in graphics package to display the results of queries as colour graphics.

- **SQL*QMX** looks and feels like IBM's QMF, a mainframe query management facility. QMF is a popular IBM product and SQL*QMX was developed as part of Oracle's move into the IBM mainframe marketplace where there would be a lot of users who would know how to work it. It is good at reporting, but not so good at querying. It is available on PCs, VAX/VMS, IBM VM and IBM MVS.

- **SQL*Calc** is a spreadsheet program, superficially very similar to Lotus 1-2-3. In effect it uses the spreadsheet as the user interface to the database system. Cells can contain numbers, formulæ, etc. like any spreadsheet. They can also contain SQL statements so, when the spreadsheet is evaluated, data is automatically extracted from the database into the spreadsheet. The database can be updated, too. SQL*Calc is available on VAX/VMS, several Unix platforms and on PCs.

- **The Oracle add-in for Lotus 1-2-3** serves much the same purpose as SQL*Calc. This time, though, it is an Oracle interface embedded in the real Lotus 1-2-3, not a lookalike. It is available only on PCs and works with Lotus 1-2-3 version 2.

The second group of products are all under active development and they reflect the revised requirements, environments and styles of working employed by end-users nowadays:

- **Oracle Card** is available only on the Macintosh or on IBM PC with Windows but is designed to work with either a local database on the PC or a remote database. It provides a simple, point-and-select interface to create tables, enter data, query data, prepare reports and so on. It operates through an object-oriented scripting system which appears to be a close clone of the Macintosh Hypercard system and which allows complete applications to be built.

- **Oracle Data Query** in effect replaces SQL*QMX and most of the functions of Easy*SQL. It provides users with a very simple way of specifying queries and producing reports, which can be saved and re-run. The system runs on VAX, most Unix platforms, IBM VM and PCs.

- **Oracle Data Lens** for Lotus 1-2-3 provides an Oracle interface for version 3 of Lotus 1-2-3.

### 2.5.5   Applications packages

Oracle are moving more and more into applications packages. They have a number of products covering an ever-widening range of application areas. They are all built using Oracle development tools and are relatively easily tailored to a customer's specific needs. The range includes a number of accounting systems, a personnel management system and a number of packages for specific vertical markets.

For some time, Oracle have provided interfaces to the most popular office automation systems, like DEC's ALL-IN-1 and Uniflex. There is also an electronic mail system, Oracle*Mail. A complete office system is now under development which extends Oracle*Mail with a whole range of office automation functions. This is expected to be released soon.

*Part 2*

*SQL and
SQL extensions*

*Three*
# Oracle and SQL

O racle pioneered the use of SQL and the language is fundamental to all Oracle products. It is used for all aspects of data handling: to define or modify database structure and content, to define users, to access data in the database, to insert new data and so on.

## 3.1  Aspects of SQL

T here are two main elements of SQL: a *Data Definition Language* (DDL) and a *Data Manipulation Language* (DML). Both components operate within the same language structure and syntax so the distinction between the two is a conceptual one rather than one which is immediately apparent in the various language statements. DDL is used to define the structure of the data. It specifies what columns appear in the tables, what indexes are maintained, users' access rights, how the tables are stored on disk and so on. DML deals with retrieving data, inserting, updating and deleting data, and various associated issues, such as protecting the data from multiple concurrent updates from several users. There is a third category of commands in Oracle's implementation of SQL. These *Embedded SQL* statements are used when SQL is embedded in a procedural language.

Old versions of Oracle (version 5 and previous) used SQL as the sole interface between application programs, including the Oracle tools like SQL*Plus, and the database management system. Later versions of Oracle (version 6 and higher) have a number of important changes, intended to increase performance and to make the system suitable for on-line transaction processing applications. Foremost among these is a set of extensions to the interface to the RDBMS, called PL/SQL.

One of the strengths of SQL is that it is a declarative and non-procedural language. The structure of the database and the relationships between data items are defined as a set of rules and not as a specification of how the rules are to be applied. Each statement of the language is executed without any regard for statements which may have been executed previously. More than anything else, it is these characteristics that have distanced SQL from the incompatibilities of proprietary systems and allowed it to reach its pre-eminent position as a standard language for database management systems.

But there are penalties. The first is in performance. Although improved software technology has produced perhaps a one hundred-fold increase in performance since relational systems first appeared, relational databases which are based strictly on SQL are still not as fast as non-relational systems for many applications. There are many underlying factors which govern the achievable performance of any database system: I/O throughput, locking strategies, memory management and so on. But it is the flexibility provided by the non-procedural approach which complicates these underlying factors and so imposes the performance penalty.

The second problem is that the real world of business is sometimes just too complex to be defined in a declarative way. It is fairly easy to use the declarative approach to specify, for example, that it is not allowed to have order information without having information for the corresponding customer. But real-life data integrity rules are often much more complicated than this and are simply beyond the scope of the declarative approach, at least as far as SQL is concerned. The only way is to specify such rules in terms of the procedure to be carried out to enforce them.

All the relational database suppliers have been aware of these problems for some time. They all have developed, or are in the process of developing, extensions to the SQL language to provide the procedural capability. PL/SQL is Oracle's answer.

## 3.2   Interface to the RDBMS

The database management system itself accepts SQL (and PL/SQL) commands via a number of system calls. A program communicates with the DBMS through an inter-program communication interface, in effect sending SQL commands and getting data or some other response back. The interface can operate within one machine or across several machines, over a network. The detail of how the interface works depends on the characteristics of the hardware and operating system software being used.

The program sending the SQL commands could be a specially written user program, written in a third-generation language and developed using one of the sets of program interface routines provided by Oracle's PRO*... series of products. More commonly, it can be one of the Oracle application development tools.

The Oracle product which provides users with interactive access to the database is SQL*Plus. In simple terms, its function is to accept SQL commands from users on terminals, to send the commands to the RDBMS and to pass the response back to the user.

## 3.3   The next two chapters

The next chapter describes the Oracle implementation of SQL and how to access it with SQL*Plus. Oracle's implementation is a superset of ANSI SQL. SQL*Plus also provides a number of its own commands. In the following chapters, little distinction is made between what is in standard SQL and what is an Oracle extension; when using Oracle it does not really matter much which is which. SQL*Plus, as opposed to SQL, commands are identified as they are introduced.

At the end of the chapter, you should have a good knowledge of the underlying SQL language and of the Oracle extensions. You should be able to use SQL*Plus for data manipulation, setting up tables, controlling access rights and so on – all the major functions of the SQL language, in fact. There is a lot of material and the approach is to take you in gradually, starting with the simplest features and progressively building on them. If you have the Oracle software running as you work through the section, you will find that you can practice using the examples and exercises.

There follows Chapter 5 on Oracle's procedural extensions to SQL, PL/SQL. Because it is a procedural language, PL/SQL is not commonly used in a conversational, interactive way. It is available in SQL*Plus but it is only really useful in predefined command files which are then invoked from SQL*Plus.

The most important use for PL/SQL is in SQL*Forms, the interactive applications generator described in Part 3. There are examples and exercises in Chapter 5 but you will get most practice in its use during Chapter 7, on SQL*Forms version 3.

# Four

# SQL*Plus: interactive SQL

## 4.1 SQL basics

### 4.1.1 Basic syntax

SQL has a simple consistent grammar and syntax. It can be said to be 'English-like' in the same way that COBOL or PL/1 is English-like. Each SQL statement consists of one or more clauses. Each clause is introduced by a keyword. It may be a command like SELECT or another keyword like FROM or WHERE. Keywords like this are reserved words in the language. There are other reserved words, too – see Appendix B for a complete list.

Clauses are separated by the appearance of a reserved word and arguments within clauses are separated by commas. Statements are terminated by a semi-colon. Case is not treated as significant by the software but it can be used to enhance readability. In particular, throughout this book upper case is used to show SQL reserved words. You are recommended to follow this standard.

A statement may be written on several lines, with indentation if desired. This often has a marked benefit in the readability of the code. For example:

```
SELECT model_name,
    date_bought,
    cost
FROM cars;
```

Some statements may be nested within statements. There may be up to 16 levels of nesting – far more than you are likely to need. Nesting is discussed later; an example:

```
SELECT model_name, date_bought, cost
FROM cars
WHERE registration = (SELECT registration
        FROM bookings
        WHERE booking_no = 502);
```

### 4.1.2 Comments

Comments are started by /* and terminated by */. They can be as long as you like, spanning several lines, and they can appear anywhere in the SQL code. Alternatively, single line comments may be introduced by the keyword

REMARK or just REM. For example:

```
/* Comments, too, can benefit from indentation.
   Remember: (1) The solidus is on the outside
             (2) REM or REMARK are alternatives
        but  (3) slash-star form is most useful
*/
```

### 4.1.3  SQL syntax – the SELECT statement

The SELECT statement is the most widely used SQL statement. It extracts data from a database. In this section, we use it to illustrate simple SQL syntax.

A SELECT statement must have at least two clauses (though this is not always the case for other statements). As a minimum, the columns to be selected must be specified, along with the table to get them from. The simplest form is to select everything (designated by an asterisk, meaning all columns) from a table. Thus:

```
SELECT * FROM cars;
```

will extract and display every column for each row of the cars table. Individual columns to be selected are specified by listing their names as arguments to the SELECT verb. For example:

```
SELECT registration, cost
FROM cars;
```

will display just the registration and cost of each car in the table.

Unless specified otherwise, the SELECT statement will return all the rows (i.e. records) of the table. There are a number of ways of limiting the number of rows returned. The simplest of these is the WHERE clause. For example:

```
SELECT model, cost
FROM cars
WHERE cost > 35000;
```

will select only cars whose original cost is greater than £35,000.

The ORDER BY clause can be used to re-order the selected data. Use the ASC or DESC qualifier to specify ascending or descending sequence. If no qualifier is used in the ORDER BY clause, the rows are returned in ascending order. It is possible to order by more than one column, each column being either ascending or descending. For example:

```
SELECT model, cost, car_group
FROM cars
WHERE cost > 35000
ORDER BY car_group_name, cost DESC;
```

will select the same cars as the previous example, but will present them in descending order of original cost within ascending order of car group.

### 4.1.4   Nulls

Null values are an important concept in any database system. The value of an item of data is said to be *NULL* when it is undefined or not relevant. For example, 50K Cars' employees table has columns which hold the commission element of an employee's pay. This data item is relevant for sales people but it is not relevant for anyone who is not on the commission scheme, and for them it will be null. Similarly, an item of data that has not yet been input to the system will usually be set null to mean 'not known'.

Old systems often gave a zero value to such data items so that the arithmetic of totals would still work (though averages would be calculated wrongly). But this is clearly an unsatisfactory solution as it does not distinguish a true value of zero from a null value. Other types of data, like character strings, can, of course, also have a null value.

SQL uses the concept of null values and Oracle implements a true null value, quite distinct from any other value. All arithmetic and other sorts of data manipulation automatically operate correctly with nulls. Various special functions are provided for processing nulls.

Nulls can make things more complicated, particularly when doing logical operations on null values. A test for equality between two values, for instance, can have three outcomes: true, false or null. The outcome will be null if either of the two values is null. This is very easily overlooked.

### 4.1.5   Getting started with SQL*Plus

To start SQL*Plus, type SQLPLUS at the operating system prompt (or sqlplus if, like Unix, the operating system command processor is case-sensitive). SQL*Plus will then prompt for a username and password. Once these have been checked it will display the SQL*Plus prompt, SQL>. It is now ready for you to enter SQL commands. This sign-on procedure can be shortened by specifying the username and password as parameters when SQL*Plus is invoked:

    SQLPLUS USER1/PASS1

SQL commands can be entered on several lines. The command is not executed until terminated with a semi-colon followed by a carriage return. At each carriage return until then, SQL*Plus saves the line just entered and prompts for the next line of the command by displaying the line number. For example:

    SQL> SELECT *
      2 FROM
      3 cars;

When SQL*Plus starts up, it executes the commands in its start-up file, called LOGIN.SQL. This file sets various environment variables, such as line width and page size; you can edit it to change any of them, including the SQL prompt. To leave SQL*Plus, type EXIT or QUIT when at the SQL> prompt. If you make a mistake while entering a line of a command, use the destructive backspace key and re-enter. Mistakes in some SQL commands are often most easily corrected just by re-entering the correct version of the command.

### 4.1.6 Access rights

In order to be able to log on, your username must already have been set up by the database administrator. Different privileges can be given to different users. Unless you are explicitly given access, you cannot see data belonging to other users. Not only can you not access other users' tables, you cannot even know of their existence. Any tables you create yourself can, of course, be accessed by you, but they cannot be accessed by other users until you give permission. The system provides a list of the tables available to you. To see the list of tables and other objects available to you:

```
SELECT table_name
FROM user_objects;
```

The name in the FROM clause, user_objects, is actually a *view* rather than a table. Views are described in detail later on. In this case it represents that subset of all the tables and other objects in the database which you can access.

Oracle keeps a whole range of information about the database, its structure, the tables and data in the database, users, their privileges and lots more in a series of system tables known collectively as the data dictionary. The user_objects view is just one aspect of the data dictionary. Oracle maintains the dictionary automatically and only the database administrator has unrestricted access to it.

### 4.1.7 The line editor

SQL*Plus stores all the lines of a SQL statement in a buffer, called the SQL buffer. There is a line editor to modify the contents of the buffer to correct mistakes or to change SQL commands. The editor is simple but effective. You use editor commands to get to the line of your SQL command that you want to edit, then you use other editor commands to change the line and re-execute the SQL command. The editor commands available are shown in Table 4.1.

When you list the SQL buffer with the L command, the editor indicates which line it is currently operating on (the current line) with an asterisk. The commands A, C, DEL and I all operate on or after the current line.

You can get SQL*Plus to use your normal system editor with the ED command. By itself, the command will invoke the system editor to edit the

**Table 4.1**   SQL*Plus line editor commands.

| Command | Action |
| --- | --- |
| A | Add text to the end of a line |
| C/old/new | Change text in a line from old to new |
| C/text/ | Delete text from a line |
| CL BUFF | Clears all lines from the buffer |
| DEL | Delete complete line |
| I | Add (insert) a number of lines in front of the current line pointer. The editor stays in insert mode until a blank line is entered |
| I text | Add text as a new line in front of the current line pointer |
| L | List all lines in the buffer |
| L n | Go to and list line number *n* |
| L m n | List line numbers *m* to *n* |
| R or / | Execute the SQL statement in the buffer |

current contents of the SQL buffer. You can also use it to edit specific command files.

## 4.1.8   Saving and running commands

The contents of the SQL buffer can be saved in an operating system file for later use. Use the SAVE command with the format:

    SAVE filename

The filename you use can be any filename which is considered valid by the operating system you are using. You can specify the filetype if you like. If you do not, it will default to .SQL. Examples:

    SAVE COMMAND1
    SAVE COMMAND2.TST

SAVE commands like these will not overwrite an existing file. To do this, you must use the keyword REPLACE after the filename.

To run such a saved command use the START command. If the filetype is not .SQL, you must specify it. Examples:

    START COMMAND1
    START COMMAND2.TST

## Summary: SQL basics

☐ SQL is a command-oriented language with a straightforward, English-like grammar.

☐ Statements are made up of clauses, each introduced by a verb or other keyword, and are terminated by a semi-colon.

☐ Spread your SQL statements over several lines, and use indentation and upper case to help make your code more readable.

☐ The concept of a null value is important in RDBMSs. It means not relevant or not known. Null is a distinct value and is not the same as zero or blank.

☐ SQL*Plus provides an interactive SQL environment. It accepts SQL commands and displays the results. It has a simple line editor to edit and re-run SQL commands.

---

**EXERCISE 4.1**

1. Enter the following (incorrect) command using the lines exactly as shown. Then correct it and re-run it.

```
SELECT
*
FRUM cars;
```

2. Write a select statement to extract registration number, model and rental price per day for all cars in the cars table. Present them in descending order of original cost.

---

## 4.2  Naming and datatypes

### 4.2.1  Naming rules

Before we can start to explore the power of SQL, we need to set up some tables to use in the examples. Tables, like other database objects, have to be named. There are rules for the formation of valid names. They govern names for tables, views, synonyms, columns, indexes and user variables; certain other things (user and database names, for instance) have slightly different rules.

Names must not be longer than 30 characters and must:

- begin with a letter

- contain only numbers, letters, $ (dollar), # (hash) and _ (underscore)

- not be a reserved word

- not duplicate the name of another database object of the same type.

Do not forget that the system makes no distinction between upper and lower case letters. So names must be unique irrespective of the case of their letters. Some valid names are:

```
Cars, CaRs, Customers, money_$, customer#, t107,
this_is_a_table
```

Some invalid names are:

```
#_of_accounts, date, 1989, customer(debit),
this-is-a-table-name, file_name.type
```

**Table 4.2**  Oracle's basic datatypes.

| Datatype | Meaning |
|---|---|
| CHAR(n) | A character string up to $n$ characters long.  Maximum size is 240 characters. |
| NUMBER(n,m) | A signed decimal number $n$ digits wide including $m$ decimal digits. The value of $m$ can lie in the range $-84$ to $+127$, while $n$ must be in the range 1 to 38. $m$ does not have to be specified and $m$ may not be specified alone. If $n$ is not specified, it defaults to 38. There are thus variants of this datatype: NUMBER, NUMBER(n). A variety of input and display formats are supported, including scientific notation (e.g. 1.63E2 which is 163). |
| DATE | A date and/or a time of day. A single column of datatype DATE can hold both together. Dates can be input and displayed in a wide variety of European and US formats. Times can be on either a 12- or 24-hour clock. |
| RAW(n) | Raw binary data $n$ bytes long. Maximum size is 240 bytes. |
| LONG | Character data of variable size, from 1 to 64K chars long; usually used to hold unstructured text. A table may have only one LONG column and there are restrictions on the use of LONG columns. |
| LONG RAW | Raw binary data to a maximum of 64K bytes long. There are the same restrictions on LONG RAW as on LONG. |

**Table 4.3** Oracle's additional datatypes.

| Datatype | Meaning |
|---|---|
| `VARCHAR(n)` | The same as `CHAR` |
| `LONG VARCHAR` | The same as `LONG` |
| `NUMBER(*)` | The same as `NUMBER`, length parameters not allowed |
| `DECIMAL` | The same as `NUMBER`, length parameters not allowed |
| `FLOAT` | The same as `NUMBER`, length parameters not allowed |
| `INTEGER` | The same as `NUMBER`, length parameters not allowed |
| `SMALLINT` | The same as `NUMBER`, length parameters not allowed |

### 4.2.2 Datatypes

Every column in a table has a datatype associated with it. This defines the format, style and interpretation of the contents of the column. The basic datatypes recognized by SQL*Plus are shown in Table 4.2. Oracle also recognizes a number of other datatypes which it maps on to one of the datatypes above. These extra datatypes are provided for compatibility with other RDBMSs, notably DB2 and SQL/DS. They are shown in Table 4.3.

## Summary: Naming and datatypes

☐ All database objects are named according to simple rules. Oracle does not distinguish between upper and lower case in names.

☐ Columns in a table are given a datatype when the table is set up. `CHAR` holds character strings, `NUMBER` holds numbers of all sorts and `DATE` holds date and time of day.

☐ Other less commonly used datatypes hold raw binary data and long unstructured character strings. There are restrictions on the use of these datatypes.

☐ Oracle also provides various other datatypes so as to provide compatibility with other systems. It maps these on to its own datatypes.

---

**EXERCISE 4.2**

1. Which of the following database object names are legal and which are illegal? Why?

   (a) `cow`
   (b) `_last_variable`

    (c) `no_@_10p_per_unit`
    (d) `gross_profit_this_year`
    (e) `character`
    (f) `P71$`
    (g) `gross_profit_to_date_plus_gross_profit_this_year`

2. Write down a valid constant for each of the following datatypes:

    (a) `char(10)`
    (b) `number`
    (c) `number(9,4)`
    (d) `number(5)`

## 4.3   Tables and indexes

### 4.3.1   Creating a table

The CREATE command is used to create a database object and to define its properties. CREATE TABLE is used to set up a table and to define its content. Before creating a table, decide on a table name, the column names, their datatypes, widths and other formatting information. All names must conform to the naming rules. For example:

```
CREATE TABLE maintenance
    (registration CHAR(8) NOT NULL,
    date_last_serviced DATE NOT NULL,
    miles_done NUMBER(5));
```

creates a table called `maintenance` with three columns. Note that the first two columns have the optional parameter NOT NULL. This tells the system that these columns may not be left empty when data is inserted into the table. This is the way of ensuring that key values are always supplied. Oracle will allow null values to be entered in columns defined without the NOT NULL qualifier.

NOT NULL is just one of a number of possible *constraints* which may be defined for a column or for a whole table. These constraints all restrict the range of valid values for the columns of the table. Eventually, all SQL statements which change the values in the table will be checked against the constraints. In version 6, though, any constraints specified are checked and stored but are not actually enforced; later versions enforce constraints. NOT NULL is the only exception to this; it is actually enforced in version 6. We will return to constraints at the end of this chapter.

If you need to create a table which has columns of the same characteristics as columns in an already existing table, you can reduce typing and the likelihood of error by using the AS clause. The column names are specified without a datatype or constraints. Following them is a SELECT to retrieve the corresponding columns from the existing table. For example:

```
CREATE TABLE cars_to_sell
(reg, model,
    date_bought, miles_to_date)
    AS SELECT
        registration, model_name,
        date_bought, miles_to_date
    FROM cars;
```

The characteristics of each column in the new table are set to be the same as those of the corresponding column of the SELECT statement. Obviously there must be the same number of columns in each case.

There are a number of other clauses which optionally can follow the specification of the columns. They govern where and how the table is to be stored, how much free space to allow for expansion and the maximum number of transactions that can concurrently access each data block of the table. These sorts of things are not usually decided by the application developer. Any sizeable Oracle installation will have a database administrator who will establish standards to be followed.

### 4.3.2  Altering or deleting a table

Once a table definition has been created, it can be changed at any time using the ALTER TABLE command. It is possible to modify the definition of a column and add columns. For example:

```
ALTER TABLE maintenance
MODIFY (miles_done NUMBER(6));
```

extends the length of the miles_done column to six digits. The column width can be increased whether there is data in the column or not. The column width can only be decreased or the datatype changed if the column is empty (i.e. contains only nulls).

This example:

```
ALTER TABLE maintenance
ADD(next_maintenance_due NUMBER(9));
```

adds a new column to the table. The column is defined in the same way as in CREATE TABLE. When adding a column, the NOT NULL parameter can only be used if the whole table is empty.

To examine a table definition, use the SQL*Plus DESCRIBE command. This can be abbreviated to DESC; for example:

```
DESC maintenance
```

will show all the column definitions and datatypes of the table maintenance. A table can be renamed with the RENAME command. For example:

```
RENAME maintenance TO car_maintenance;
```

and to delete (or drop) a table from the database, use the DROP TABLE command. For example:

```
DROP TABLE maintenance;
```

will remove the table called maintenance and all its data from the database.

### 4.3.3   Indexing tables

Indexing a table is similar to indexing a book. The index helps you to find information much more quickly. Without the index, you would have to scan the entire book to find the bit you wanted. Similarly, an index on a table allows Oracle to find the rows you are interested in much more quickly, without having to scan the whole table.

Indexes can extend to several levels, particularly for tables with a large number of rows (see Figure 4.1). Indexing techniques can be quite complicated, but the mechanisms are not generally of interest to the Oracle user. Once you have created an index, the system looks after building, updating and optimizing it.

Indexing is a feature of the Oracle database system, rather than of SQL\*Plus. Queries executed by other products using the tables will get the benefit of indexes you set up.

### 4.3.4   Creating an index

To create an index on a table, use the CREATE INDEX command. Indexes are given names according to the naming rules. More than one index can be created on a single table, but each index must be created separately. An index can be created on one or more columns. An index on more than one column is called a *concatenated* index.

SQL\*Plus will automatically use an index (if one exists) to satisfy any query if the SELECT statement refers directly to an indexed column. Indexes are not explicitly referenced in SELECT (or other) statements.

Indexes can be created and dropped dynamically without affecting any related queries, except in terms of performance. An index can be defined as being *unique*, in which case the system will not allow duplicate key values in the index or in the table itself. The default is a non-unique index which will allow duplicate values. Some examples:

```
CREATE INDEX cars_ind
        ON cars(registration);
```

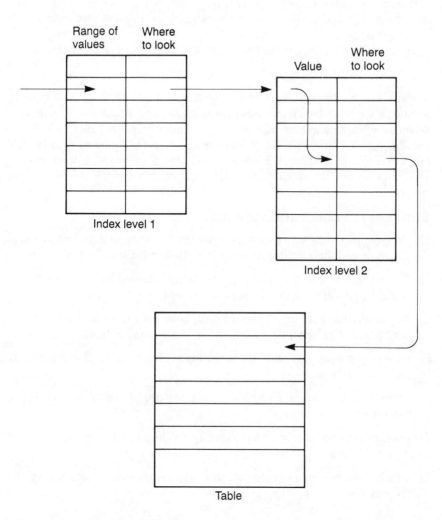

**Figure 4.1**  Index structure.

will create an index named `cars_ind`, which indexes the cars table on the registration column. It will be a non-unique index, allowing duplicate values.

```
CREATE UNIQUE INDEX cars_indx
      ON cars(registration);
```

is a more realistic example, because it would not allow duplicate values for registration.

```
CREATE INDEX bookings_ind
      ON bookings(cust_no, car_group_name);
```

will create an index named `bookings_ind`, which indexes the bookings table on the combination (i.e. concatenation) of `cust_no` and `car_group_name`.

To remove an index, use the DROP INDEX statement. For example:

```
DROP INDEX car_indx;
```

There can be disadvantages to having an index on a table. It will occupy additional space on disk. It may make inserting and updating data a little slower. When inserting data into an indexed table, the index is updated after each record and this can be very wasteful. If you need to do a bulk load of data into an indexed table, for instance, it is usually quicker to drop the index, load the data and then re-create the index.

## Summary: Tables and indexes

☐ Variants of the CREATE command are used to set up tables and indexes. Columns and their datatypes are specified when the table is first created.

☐ The content of a table can be altered without it having to be taken off-line and without it having to be rebuilt in any way.

☐ To ensure that keys are always entered, columns can be defined as being NOT NULL. Oracle will not allow a null value in the column.

☐ Dropping a table gets rid of the table, together with all its contents and its indexes. Beware!

☐ Indexes are used to speed up access to the contents of a table. A single index can use one or more keys.

☐ Indexes may be defined as having unique values for the keys or allowing duplicate values.

☐ Oracle uses any existing indexes to a table automatically, when it thinks there is benefit from doing so.

---

### EXERCISE 4.3

1. Create a table called `cars_to_sell` containing the following columns:

   ```
   registration char(8)
   model        char(8)
   date_bought  date
   ```

2. Index the cars table on the registration. What sort of index should be used?

---

3. Index the cars table on model. What sort of index should be used?

4. Drop both these indexes.

5. Drop the table `cars_to_sell`.

## 4.4 SELECT with a WHERE clause

Unless its scope is limited, a SELECT statement (and other SQL statements) will operate on all rows of the table. The WHERE clause is one way to limit the scope by specifying the conditions which must be satisfied for the SELECT to operate. The conditions are defined using arithmetic and logical operators, operating on columns and constants.

### 4.4.1 Constants

Character string and date constants are enclosed in single quotes. Use two single quotes to indicate a single quote within the string. For instance: `'O''Brien'`. Numeric constants are written directly, without quotation marks. Some examples:

```
SELECT registration, model_name
FROM cars
WHERE car_group_name = 'A1';
```

or:

```
SELECT cust_no, model_name
FROM bookings
WHERE date_rent_start > '01-JAN-91';
```

or:

```
SELECT model_name, registration
FROM cars
WHERE cost > 100000;
```

### 4.4.2 Arithmetic operators

The arithmetic operators which can be used are shown in Table 4.4. Multiplication and division have precedence over addition and subtraction. Parentheses can be used to override the default precedence of the arithmetic operators. For instance, suppose the first 10 000 miles are always maintenance-free. Then

**Table 4.4**  Arithmetic operators.

| Operator | Meaning |
| --- | --- |
| * | Multiplication |
| / | Division |
| + | Addition |
| – | Subtraction |

```
SELECT registration, model, miles_to_date
FROM cars
WHERE (miles_to_date-10000)/maint_int>2;
```

allows for this when selecting cars which should have had more than two services.

### 4.4.3  Logical operators

The basic logical operators which can appear in the WHERE clause and the operators to combine logical expressions are shown in Table 4.5.

Logical expressions can be tricky to specify correctly if they are at all complicated. Parentheses can be used to clarify the structure of the whole expression. Unless modified by parentheses, the NOT operator has the highest precedence and its expression is always surrounded by parentheses. AND takes

**Table 4.5**  Logical operators.

| Operator | Meaning |
| --- | --- |
| = | Equal to; tests for equality |
| IS | Test for the existence of a null value |
| != <br> ^= <br> <> | All three variants mean not equal to; tests for inequality |
| > and < | Greater than and less than |
| >= and <= | Greater than or equal to and less than or equal to |
| NOT | Reverses the result of a logical expression |
| AND | Combines logical expressions. The combined expression is true if all its component expressions are true. |
| OR | Combines logical expressions. The combined expression is true if any of its component expressions are true. |

precedence over OR. Nevertheless, it is sensible to use parentheses to ensure that the correct logical effect is achieved even if the default precedence means that they are not strictly needed. For example:

```
SELECT registration, model_name, car_group
FROM cars
WHERE date_bought<'01-JAN-88'
    AND(miles_to_date>20000 OR cost<30000);
```

BETWEEN and LIKE are less commonly used. This example of BETWEEN would select cars whose rental rate per day was between £200 and £300:

```
SELECT registration, model_name, rate_per_day
FROM cars
WHERE rate_per_day BETWEEN 200 AND 300;
```

Templates for LIKE and NOT LIKE are specified as literals. A per cent sign matches against any string of zero or more characters. An underscore matches against any single character. For example:

```
SELECT registration, model_name
FROM cars
WHERE model_name LIKE 'P%';
```

would select cars whose model code started with 'P' (like P911 TC or P944 T) and:

```
SELECT registration, model_name
FROM cars
WHERE model_name NOT LIKE 'P_1%';
```

would select cars whose model code did not start with 'P', something, '1'. So 'P944 T' would be selected, while 'P911 TC' would not.

Notice that NOT BETWEEN and NOT LIKE are operators in their own right, rather than a combination of an operator and NOT. Note also that neither per cent nor underscore will match when compared with a null string.

## Summary: The WHERE clause

☐ The WHERE clause is used to restrict the range of rows on which a SQL statement acts.

☐ It can use logical operators, arithmetic operators and constants to define the rows to be processed.

☐ Complex logical expressions can be built up. Use parentheses to ensure that you get the precedence of the operators correctly defined, and likewise with arithmetic.

☐ Number constants are written directly without quotation marks. Character string and date constants are enclosed in single quotation marks.

☐ Wildcards can be used with the LIKE operator to do imprecise matching of character strings. Wildcards do not match against a null value.

---

**EXERCISE 4.4**

Write SELECT statements for each of the following and decide for yourself which columns you should include in the SELECT clause:

1. Retrieve all the cars whose model is not equal to 'P911 TC' from the cars table.

2. Retrieve all cars, from the cars table whose miles_to_date is higher than 9000 miles and whose cost is lower than £70,000.

3. Retrieve all bookings which are on account (indicated by an 'A' in the pay method column) and have a rental start date before 1 January 1992, or those bookings for cash (indicated by payment method 'C') and rental start date before 1 March 1992.

4. Retrieve all cars whose daily rental is more than £150 and less than £350.

5. Retrieve all cars whose model name starts with 'MERC'.

---

## 4.5   Combining data from more than one table

Up to now, data has been selected from only one table at a time. Very often, you will want to correlate data held in different tables. There are a number of different ways of doing this. We deal with these starting with the simplest.

### 4.5.1   Joins

The *join* allows data to be selected from more than one table in a single statement. There are several types of join. They all involve the automatic matching of rows in one table with the corresponding rows in another table. You specify the column names that define the match in a WHERE clause. Notice that the matching is done when the join is executed and is not built into the structure of the database in any way. For example:

```
SELECT booking_no, cust_name,
    cargroups.model_name, description,
```

```
            date_reserved
    FROM bookings, cargroups
    WHERE bookings.model_name
         =cargroups.model_name;
```

will show the full description of each of the models for which there is a booking as well as other booking details. In doing so, it is matching the bookings table and the car groups table using the values of the model name (as shown in Figure 4.2). Information from both tables is displayed.

Column names do not have to be the same in each table, though they are in this example. Where they are the same, use the combination of the table name and column name to specify the column unambiguously. It is possible to reduce the amount of writing needed for this by using an alias for a table name. So

```
    SELECT booking_no, cust_name,
          c.model_name, description,
          date_reserved
```

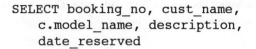

**Figure 4.2** Matching values with a JOIN.

```
FROM bookings b, cargroups c
WHERE b.model_name = c.model_name;
```

is exactly the same as the previous example but uses the alias 'b' for the bookings table and 'c' for the car groups table.

Tables can be joined on more than one column. The values in all the columns have to match in the two tables for the correlation to work.

### 4.5.2 Outer joins

What happens when there are some values of the joining column(s) which appear in one table but do not appear in the other? In the previous examples, there will usually be rows in the bookings table for which there are no corresponding rows in the cars table. These are the advance bookings which have not yet been allocated a car and old dead rentals for cars which may have been sold since.

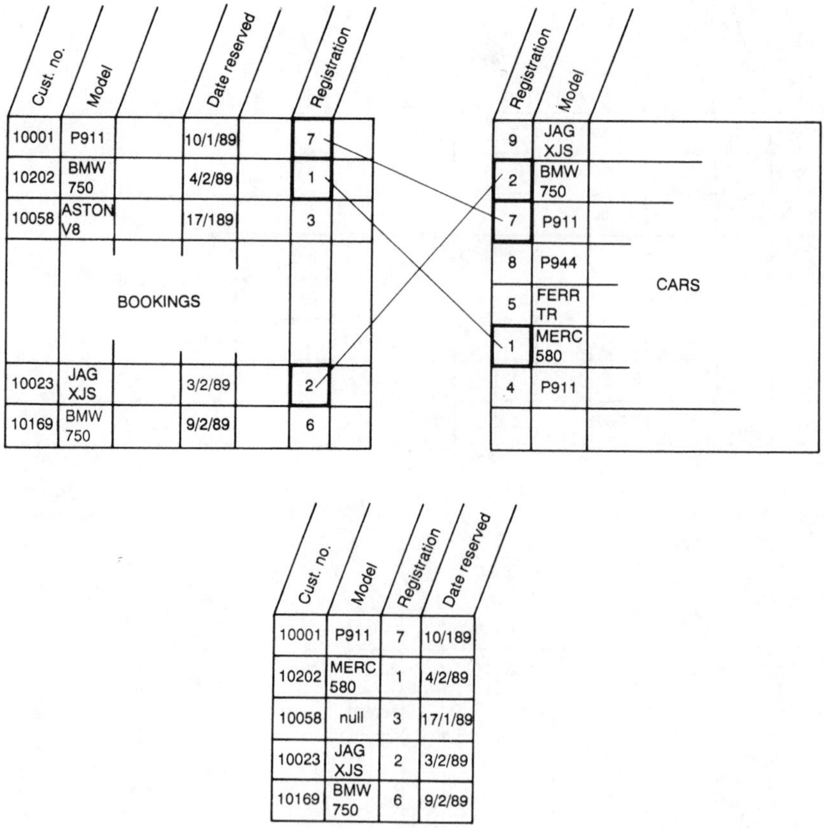

**Figure 4.3** Outer join.

Unless specified otherwise, these rows will **not** be returned by the join. But they can be selected as well by specifying an *outer join* by putting the outer join indicator, a plus sign, after the join relation in the WHERE clause (see Figure 4.3). In this case, the missing columns from the table which did not have the corresponding entry are set null. For example:

```
SELECT cust_no, c.model_name, b.registration,
    date_reserved
FROM bookings b, cars c
WHERE b.registration=c.registration(+);
```

will list all bookings ever made; most will have no information about a car. Those that are currently active (a car is out on rental) will have the car details displayed. The plus sign is always put on the potentially deficient side of the relation.

### 4.5.3   UNION, INTERSECT and MINUS
There are other ways of correlating tables that allow you to pick out rows depending on whether they appear in one or both tables. These are the three set operators, UNION, INTERSECT and MINUS (see Figure 4.4). The rows

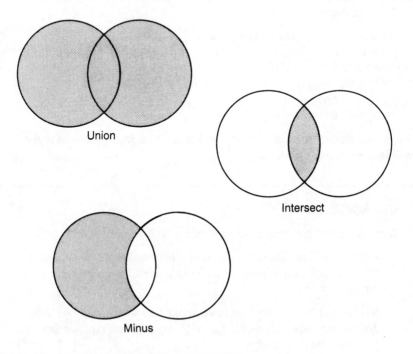

**Figure 4.4**  UNION, INTERSECT and MINUS.

returned can be those where each value of the joining columns appears either in table A or in table B or in both (UNION), or those which appear in both A and B (INTERSECT), or those which appear in A but not in B (MINUS). For example:

```
SELECT registration, model_name
FROM cars
UNION
SELECT registration, model_name
FROM bookings;
```

will return all cars whether they are in the current cars table or have booking details in the bookings table (the car may since have been sold).

If we were to use INTERSECT, the example would return all cars to be found in both the bookings and the cars tables, i.e. cars which have been booked. If we were to use MINUS, the example would return all cars to be found in the cars table but not in the bookings table, i.e. cars for which there have never been any bookings.

The columns selected in each of the component queries must be of the same datatype as the corresponding column in the other query, though they may be of different length. If the returned rows are to be ordered, use the ORDER BY clause at the end of the second query. The ORDER BY is slightly different, though, in that you do not need to specify the column name(s) to order by but the sequence number of the column as it appears in the select list.

For example

```
SELECT registration, model_name
FROM cars
INTERSECT
SELECT registration, model_name
FROM bookings
ORDER BY 2 DESC, 1;
```

will select all cars currently booked and order them in sequence of registration within descending model code.

---

**EXERCISE 4.5**

Write SELECT statements for each of the following:

1. Retrieve all customers who currently have car rental bookings. Display their customer number, name and address together with the rental start date.

2. Retrieve all customers who have booked a car in group 'A1' and display the customer number, model, registration, rate per day, rate per mile and date reserved.

3.  Retrieve the registration, group, model, rate per day, date reserved, date rental start, customer number, customer name and address for all customer bookings taken since 1 February 1992.

4.  Retrieve those customers who do not currently have any car rental bookings. Display their customer number, name, address and contact name.

5.  Retrieve model, registration, rate per day from the cars table, for those cars whose daily rate is less than the daily rate for model 'P924'.

6.  Retrieve those customers who appear in both the customers table and the bookings table (i.e. those customers who currently have bookings), displaying their customer number and name.

### 4.5.4  Subqueries

A subquery is a SELECT statement nested within another SQL statement. Subqueries are usually found within the WHERE clause of another SELECT statement, but they may appear in other types of statement as well. To understand how they work, consider this example:

```
SELECT registration, model_name, miles_to_date
FROM cars
WHERE miles_to_date > (SELECT miles_to_date
    FROM cars
    WHERE registration = 'H286 MHU');
```

The example extracts all rows from the cars table whose mileage is greater than the mileage of the car with registration number 'H286 MHU'.

In this case, both the main query and the subquery operate on the same table, but this need not be so. The subquery finds the mileage for the car with the specified registration and the main query finds the rows with greater mileage. Note that the subquery is enclosed in parentheses.

Subqueries can contain further subqueries. There is a limit to the number of levels of nesting allowed (16) but, in practice, if you need to go beyond two levels, there is probably something wrong with the way you are approaching the application. Subqueries can also return more than one column.

You should be able to see that many of the examples of subqueries can also be done with joins. The decision on whether it is more efficient to use a join or a subquery can be complex and is influenced by a number of factors: the size of the tables, the existence of indexes, and so on. Optimization issues like this are really beyond the scope of this book but they can have a dramatic influence on the performance of application systems; hence they are an important subject for more advanced study. A simple rule of thumb which is right more often than it is wrong is that Oracle is rather better at executing subqueries than it is at doing joins. So, given the choice, it may be better to use a subquery rather than a join, especially when handling big tables.

### 4.5.5   Using ANY and ALL

Subqueries can return many rows, each of which is used to process the main query. The way in which the returned values are to be used is specified in the WHERE clause. There are several ways of doing this. First we will look at ANY and ALL. They prefix the subquery to show how the values are to be used.

If the relation in the main query WHERE clause is a test for equality, the effect of ANY and ALL is exactly what you would intuitively expect. For ANY, the main query will look for any value returned by the subquery which satisfies the equality test (it will use the first one returned, in fact). For ALL, it will check that all the values returned by the subquery satisfy the equality test (see Figure 4.5).

| Cust. no. | Car group | Rental period | Miles in | Miles out | Miles used |
|---|---|---|---|---|---|
| 10082 | A1 | 10 | 20500 | 16000 | 4500 |
| 10136 | A1 | 2 | 30000 | 28000 | 2000 |
| 10211 | A2 | 30 | 25000 | 23000 | 2000 |
| 10009 | B1 | 7 | 50000 | 40000 | 10000 |
| 10173 | A1 | 4 | 50000 | 47000 | 3000 |
| 10092 | B1 | 8 | 44000 | 40000 | 4000 |
| | | | | | |

| Car group | Rental period | Miles in | Miles out | Miles used |
|---|---|---|---|---|
| A4 | 10 | 20500 | 16000 | 4500 |
| A4 | 2 | 30000 | 28000 | 2000 |
| A2 | 30 | 25000 | 23000 | 2000 |
| B1 | 7 | 50000 | 40000 | 10000 |
| A1 | 4 | 50000 | 47000 | 3000 |
| B1 | 8 | 44000 | 40000 | 4000 |
| | | | | |

| Cust. no. | Car group | Rental period |
|---|---|---|
| 10082 | A1 | 10 |
| 10009 | B1 | 7 |
| 10173 | A1 | 4 |
| 10092 | B1 | 8 |
| | | |

**Figure 4.5**   The effect of ANY and ALL.

So, for example, in this statement:

```
SELECT cust_no, model_name, date_reserved
FROM bookings
WHERE registration = ANY
                (SELECT registration
                    FROM cars
                    WHERE car_group_name = 'A4');
```

the subquery selects cars in group 'A4' and the main query will then return all the bookings for any of the cars in group 'A4'.

The next example:

```
SELECT cust_no, model_name, rental_period
FROM bookings
WHERE miles_in-miles_out > ANY
    (SELECT miles_in-miles_out
    FROM bookings
    WHERE model_name = 'P911 TC');
```

looks at how rental mileage varies with the group of car rented. The example will return all customers who travelled more miles than any customer who rented a Porsche 911. That is, more miles than the lowest mileage of any booking for a Porsche 911.

The subquery returns all values of the mileage where the car used was a Porsche 911. The main query will then return the rows whose mileage is greater than the lowest value from the subquery.

If we had used ALL instead of ANY in the second example, the main query would return all rows with a mileage greater than the highest mileage returned by the subquery.

### 4.5.6   Using IN and NOT IN

The operators IN and NOT IN are also used to combine the results of queries. They are similar to ANY and ALL. The IN section of the main query's WHERE clause will evaluate true if any of the values match. If you use NOT IN, it will evaluate true if none of the values match.

If you think about it, you will see that IN produces the same result as = ANY and NOT IN produces the same result as <> ALL. For example:

```
SELECT cust_name, address, town, county
FROM customers
WHERE cust_no IN (SELECT cust_no
                    FROM bookings
                    WHERE model_name = 'FERR TR');
```

will select the details of customers who have at least one booking for a Ferrari

Testarossa. The subquery selects the customers with a booking for a Testarossa and the main query extracts the details for these customers.

### 4.5.7   Testing for existence with subqueries

A subquery may be used to test for the existence of a row in a table and so control the processing of the main query dependent on whether a row is returned by the subquery or not. To do this, use the EXISTS operator. It returns a boolean value, true or false, depending on the existence of the required value. For example

```
SELECT model_name, car_group_name, cost
FROM cars
WHERE EXISTS
      (SELECT *
      FROM cars
      WHERE model_name = 'P944 T');
```

will only return any rows at all if there is at least one Porsche 944 in the cars table. If there is one, it will display model, group and cost for all the cars in the table.

The same result could be achieved with ANY or IN but EXISTS is more efficient as, unlike the other operators, it will stop searching as soon as a single matching row is found. EXISTS can be prefixed with NOT to reverse the effect.

## Summary: Combining data from different tables

☐ There are two main ways in which data can be extracted from two or more tables: *joins* and *subqueries*.

☐ For joins, a WHERE clause specifies the criteria for joining the tables. It very often specifies that the value of a column in one table should equal the value of a column in the other table.

☐ A normal join will return only the data from the rows in each table which satisfy the join criteria. Rows with values which appear in one or other tables can be retrieved as well using an *outer* join.

☐ If the same column name is used in both tables, use the table name and column name to specify the column you want. Reduce the amount of typing required for this by using aliases.

☐ A subquery is a SELECT statement within another SQL statement. It is used to extract a value (or set of values) which are then used in the main query.

☐ A subquery can, potentially, return a large number of rows to be handled by the main query. ANY, ALL, IN and NOT IN precede the subquery to show how the rows are to be used.

☐ The set operators UNION, INTERSECT and MINUS allow you to pick out rows depending on whether values appear in one or both tables.

---

**EXERCISE 4.6**

Write SELECT statements which incorporate a subquery for each of the following:

1. Select customer number, name, town, from the customers table for customers who have had their bookings taken by 'JAB'.

2. Retrieve model, registration, rental start date, customer number and town for all bookings made by customers who live in London, Bristol or Birmingham.

3. Display 'YES' by selecting the constant 'YES' from the bookings table if the customer 'James Taylor' exists.

---

# 4.6 Grouping and aggregates

## 4.6.1 Aggregate functions

Queries will usually return many rows, and often you will want to display aggregate characteristics (like average values) of the group of rows returned. There are a number of aggregating functions to achieve this, shown in Table 4.6. Some examples:

```
SELECT AVG(cost)
FROM cars;
```

returns a single value: the average cost of all the cars in the table.

```
SELECT MIN(miles_to_date), MAX(miles_to_date)
FROM cars;
```

returns two values: the mileage of the car that has done least miles and the mileage of the car that has done most miles.

All the aggregate functions ignore nulls in their calculations. For this reason, be careful when counting values. This example:

**Table 4.6**   Aggregate functions.

| Function | Effect |
|----------|--------|
| AVG | Calculates the average value of a column for each group defined |
| COUNT | Returns the number of values (hence rows) in a column or columns. So COUNT(model) will return the number of rows in the table with a non-null value for the model. The DISTINCT qualifier is used to exclude duplicate values. So COUNT(DISTINCT model) will return the number of distinct, non-null models. |
| MAX | Returns the highest value in a column |
| MIN | Returns the lowest value in a column |
| STDDEV | Returns the standard deviation, ignoring nulls |
| SUM | Returns the total of all the values in a column |
| VARIANCE | Returns the variance, ignoring nulls |

```
SELECT COUNT(model_name)
FROM cars;
```

will return the total number of values held in the model column, excluding any null values, while this example:

```
SELECT COUNT(*)
FROM cars;
```

will return a count of all rows in the table, including any null values. This is because at least one column of each row must be non-null.

Aggregate functions can be used in arithmetic expressions and may be placed in SELECT, WHERE and ORDER BY clauses. For example:

```
SELECT MAX(miles_to_date) - MIN(miles_to_date)
FROM cars;
```

will return a single value: the difference in mileage between the car that has done the most miles and the one that has done the least miles.

When using aggregate functions in the SELECT clause, you must not mix expressions or columns which potentially return many values with ones that return a single value. For instance,

```
SELECT model_name, AVG(miles_to_date)
FROM cars;
```

is wrong because selecting model_name will return many values, one for each car in the table, while selecting the average will return a single value, the average for all the cars in the table.

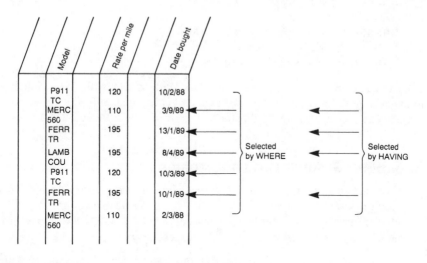

**Figure 4.6**  The effect of WHERE and HAVING.

## 4.6.2 Grouping rows returned

To get an aggregate of a column for groups of rows within a table, for instance for each model of car, use the GROUP BY clause. It groups rows into logical sets, depending on the values of specified columns. For example:

```
SELECT model_name, AVG(cost)
FROM cars
GROUP BY model_name;
```

will return the rows grouped by the value of the model code.

The GROUP BY must follow the WHERE clause or the FROM clause if the WHERE clause is missing. It can be used to group by a single column or multiple columns. The number of groups resulting will be the factor of the numbers of groups in each of the columns. Although the GROUP BY clause can reference any of the columns in the table, you will usually find that the GROUP BY columns are amongst those SELECTed and are not used with aggregate functions.

A WHERE clause can be used to restrict the rows on which the grouping operates. For example:

```
SELECT model_name, AVG(cost)
FROM cars
WHERE status <> 'A'
GROUP BY model_name;
```

will exclude unavailable cars.

A HAVING clause can be used to restrict the groups which are returned. A WHERE clause acts on the **rows** returned, the HAVING clause works on the **group**. For example:

```
SELECT model_name, AVG(cost)
FROM cars
WHERE date_bought > '01-JAN-91'
GROUP BY model_name
HAVING AVG(cost) < 60000;
```

will exclude any cars bought before 1 January 1991, so they will not be included in the averages. All models whose average cost is less than £60,000 will also be excluded as a group. Figure 4.6 illustrates the effects of WHERE and HAVING.

## Summary: Grouping and aggregates

☐ There are several aggregating functions which act on groups of rows. The main ones are AVG which calculates the average value of a column, COUNT which returns the number of values in a column, MAX and MIN which return the highest and lowest column values respectively.

☐ The GROUP BY command groups rows into logical sets. These sets can then be further refined by use of the HAVING clause, which eliminates those sets that do not meet the selection requirements. The GROUP BY must follow the WHERE clause, if present, or the FROM clause, if not.

☐ When using COUNT consider whether you require nulls to be included.

☐ When using aggregate functions such as AVG, you must not mix these with expressions that return individual rows.

---

**EXERCISE 4.7**

1. Write a SELECT statement to find the car which has the cheapest daily rate.

2. Write a SELECT statement to return the number of car groups in the cars table. Do not include duplicates.

3. Write a SELECT statement to return the total number of customers who have rented during 1989. Use the HAVING clause to exclude those customers who did not charge the rental to their account.

4. Write a SELECT statement which returns just the models, groups and maintenance intervals of the cars in the cars table. The rows should be returned in ascending order of car group and descending order of maintenance interval.

## 4.7 Data modification

The SELECT statement discussed so far is probably the most commonly used SQL command. It is used to get data out of the database. Just three more commands provide the facilities to manipulate the data. They are IN-SERT, UPDATE and DELETE.

### 4.7.1 INSERT

The INSERT statement inserts one or more rows into a table. Values to be inserted can be quoted directly or can be derived from a subquery. This example:

```
INSERT INTO cars VALUES ('H286 MHU','P911 TC',
    'A2',120,310,'10-FEB-91',
    63290,12000,15451);
```

will insert one row into the cars table. The values to go in each column are quoted in the order in which the columns have been defined. Null values can be quoted as NULL and, if not all the columns are given values, they will also be set null.

Suppose that we wanted to sell off all the cars that have done more than 100 000 miles and put their records in another (already existing) table. This could be achieved with this example:

```
INSERT INTO cars_to_sell
    (SELECT registration, date_bought
        FROM cars
        WHERE miles_to_date>100000);
```

This INSERT statement uses a subquery to extract the relevant records and then inserts them in the new table.

### 4.7.2 UPDATE

The UPDATE statement modifies the data values in one or more columns of one or more rows of a table. It must have at least two clauses, introduced by UPDATE and SET. For example:

```
UPDATE cars SET rate_per_mile = 200;
```

will update the mileage rate for all the cars in the cars table. Arithmetic expressions can be used in the SET clause. For example:

```
UPDATE cars SET rate_per_mile =
        1.1*rate_per_mile;
```

will increase the mileage rate by 10 per cent. The values to be used for the update are often derived using a nested SELECT statement.

A WHERE clause is often used to restrict the range of rows updated, as in this example:

```
UPDATE cars SET maint_int = 12000,
       car_group = 'A2'
WHERE model_name = 'P911 TC';
```

which only updates the maintenance interval and car group code for Porsche 911s.

### 4.7.3   DELETE

The DELETE command removes rows from a table. As with UPDATE and SELECT, a DELETE without a WHERE clause will act on all the rows in a table – so beware. Use a WHERE clause to restrict the scope. For instance:

```
DELETE FROM cars;
```

deletes all the rows in the cars table while

```
DELETE FROM cars
WHERE model_name = 'FERR TR';
```

limits the scope to Ferrari Testarossas and

```
DELETE FROM cars
WHERE registration = 'H126MHU';
```

restricts the scope to just the one car with that registration.

### 4.7.4   Making changes permanent

All data modifications resulting from the DML statements INSERT, DELETE and UPDATE do not, at first, permanently affect the database. The changes are made permanent by *committing* them. This can be done explicitly with the COMMIT statement or it can be done automatically by SQL*Plus. When a statement is executed, the 'hard' copy of the data in the database, held on disk, is not changed. Only a copy of the data held in memory is updated. When the changes are committed, then the database itself is changed. If you realize that you have made a mistake you may issue a ROLLBACK statement, rather than a COMMIT. This will restore the copy of the data held in memory to its original value. Figure 4.7 shows the effect of these statements.

For automatic commit, you must use the SQL*Plus SET command to set the environment variable AUTOCOMMIT:

```
SET AUTOCOMMIT ON
```

SQL*Plus will then automatically commit after every DML statement. You might well want to edit this command into your LOGIN.SQL file.

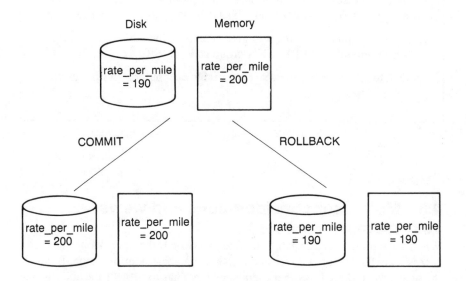

**Figure 4.7** The effect of COMMIT and ROLLBACK.

Note that commands to create, alter and drop tables are always automatically committed as soon as they are executed. They cannot be rolled back.

This process of committing changes may seem an over-complicated way of going about things. But it is a crucial part of the mechanism necessary to provide a consistent view of the data when there are many users accessing the database, all potentially modifying the data in an uncoordinated way.

## Summary: Data modification

☐ INSERT, UPDATE and DELETE are used to modify the database. Remember that they all operate on the whole of a table unless their scope is restricted by a WHERE clause.

☐ Subqueries are often useful when inserting data from one table into another.

☐ Modifications to the data do not become permanent until a COMMIT command is issued. Until then, the data can be restored to its original state by issuing a ROLLBACK command.

---

**EXERCISE 4.8**

1. Write an insert statement to insert all cars in group A4 into a table `ex_cars`. This table already exists and is empty.

2. Write an update statement to give all cars in the table `ex_cars` whose model is 'FERR TR' a group code of '99'.

3. Delete all cars from the `ex_cars` table except those with a group code of '99'.

---

# 4.8 Multi-user considerations and views

## 4.8.1 The GRANT command

When a database object, such as a table, is created, the only people who can access it are the person who created it and the database administrator. To allow the object to be shared by other users, the owner has to GRANT the appropriate privileges to those users. For example:

```
GRANT SELECT ON bookings TO Jones;
```

will allow the person with user ID 'Jones' to select rows from the bookings table. It will not allow Jones to do anything else to the table. If Jones wanted to update, insert or delete rows in the bookings table, further permissions would need to be granted. The possible privileges are shown in Table 4.7. Several permissions can be granted with a single GRANT statement. For example:

```
GRANT SELECT, UPDATE ON bookings
TO Jones;
```

will allow Jones both to select and update rows in the bookings table and

```
GRANT ALL ON bookings TO Jones;
```

will allow Jones to select, insert, update and delete rows in the bookings table, to alter the table and to create and drop indexes to the table.

If certain privileges are to be granted to all users of the system, then the pseudo-user PUBLIC can be used in the GRANT command. Thus

```
GRANT SELECT ON bookings TO PUBLIC;
```

allows everyone to select rows from the bookings table.

The user to whom a privilege is granted in this way is not normally able to grant privileges on the same object to other users. The WITH GRANT OPTION clause allows a user to do so:

**Table 4.7** Access permissions and privileges.

| Permission | Effect |
|------------|--------|
| SELECT | Allows a user to select data from a table |
| INSERT | Allows a user to insert data into a table |
| UPDATE | Allows a user to update data in a table |
| DELETE | Allows a user to delete data from a table |
| ALTER | Allows a user to alter a table definition |
| INDEX | Allows a user to create and drop indexes to a table |
| ALL | Allows a user to do all of the above actions on a table |

```
GRANT SELECT ON bookings
TO carruthers WITH GRANT OPTION;
```

The REVOKE ... FROM command revokes permissions from a user of an object. The variations are the same as the GRANT ... TO command. For instance:

```
REVOKE DELETE, UPDATE ON bookings
FROM Jones;
```

### 4.8.2 Referring to tables

If you are given access to another user's table with the GRANT command, you must refer to that table using a concatenation of the owner's user ID and the table name. User Jones would refer to Mike's table, for example, like this:

```
SELECT * FROM mike.cars;
```

This can get tedious, especially as you may not know who originally created the table. To deal with this, the database administrator may define a synonym which allows you to refer to the table with a simple name. For example:

```
CREATE PUBLIC SYNONYM cars FOR mike.cars;
```

allows anyone who has permission to access Mike's cars table to refer to it as just cars. Alternatively, you may set up your own synonyms, available only to yourself.

### 4.8.3 Creating views

The GRANT command allows a user other than the owner to access all the columns of a table. It may be the case that the owner wants to restrict access to the table to only a few columns. For example, it is likely that access to the employees table should be restricted so that employees' salary is not available to most users. This can be achieved using a *view*.

A view defines a range of columns and rows that are returned when the view is queried. With a few restrictions, a view is accessed just like a normal table. It is created using the CREATE VIEW command. The view is given a name and the columns to be available are specified. For example:

```
CREATE VIEW personal AS
    SELECT emp_no, name, address, town, county
    FROM employees;
```

creates a view, called personal, which shows employee number, name, address etc. from the employees table. Using this view, it is not possible to see any of the salary details.

Views can restrict the rows available as well as the columns. This is done using a WHERE clause. For example:

```
CREATE VIEW commissioned_staff AS
    SELECT emp_no, name, address, town, county
    FROM employees
    WHERE commission_ytd IS NOT NULL;
```

is similar to the previous example but only makes available details of employees who have earned some commission. Note that, through this view, you cannot tell how much commission they have earned, just that they have earned some commission. Views can also reference aggregate functions. The following example:

```
CREATE VIEW num_paytype AS
    SELECT COUNT(emp_no) num_emp, pay_type
    FROM employees
    GROUP BY pay_type;
```

creates a view which shows the number of employees paid weekly and paid monthly. Note that the aggregated column in the view must be given an alias name (num_emp in the example) so that it can be referred to when using the view. Similarly, the columns included in a view can be derived from arithmetic on the columns of the underlying table. In this case as well, the derived column must be given an alias name. For example:

```
CREATE VIEW salary_proportion AS
    SELECT emp_no,
        salary_ytd*100/(salary_ytd+commission_ytd)
            sal_percent
    FROM employees;
```

creates a view which shows the proportion of total wage coming from salary (as opposed to commission) for each employee. This derived column is called sal_percent.

Views can use data from several tables. The join criteria are specified in a WHERE clause. For example:

```
CREATE VIEW currently_renting AS
    SELECT cust_no, cust_name, registration,
        date_rent_start, rental_period
    FROM bookings b, customers c
    WHERE c.cust_no = b.cust_no
    AND SYSDATE BETWEEN date_rent_start AND
                date_rent_start+rental_period;
```

creates a view of the customers and bookings tables which shows information on the car and the customer only for those customers who currently have a car out on rental.

### 4.8.4   Using views

Views can be used in SELECT statements in exactly the same way as an ordinary table. For example:

```
SELECT * FROM currently_renting;
```

will select all rows that are returned by the view currently_renting. Users are often not even aware that they are using a view. There are, however, restrictions on using views in INSERT, UPDATE and DELETE statements:

* Rows can only be deleted if the view is based on a single table and does not reference any aggregate functions, GROUP BY nor DISTINCT.

* Rows can only be updated if these delete conditions are met and none of the columns in the view are defined as expressions.

* Rows can only be inserted if the update conditions are met and the view includes all the NOT NULL columns of the underlying table.

If you think about these restrictions for a moment, you will see that they are all eminently sensible. Only if the rules are followed can the system make any sense of what to insert, update or delete.

### 4.8.5   Altering tables used in views

Tables used in views can be altered (using the ALTER TABLE command) exactly as before. However, the renaming of a table, the adding or removing of columns etc. will not cause any views to be changed. So, if a table is renamed and that table is referred to by a view, then the view will no longer work. If a NOT NULL column is added to a table that is referred to by a view, then the view can no longer be used for inserting data.

In general, a user altering a table must be aware of all the views which refer to the table because the views may need to be amended as well. Views themselves are amended by being DROPped and reCREATEd with the appropriate changes.

Note also that, if a view is used only to restrict the rows available and is defined as SELECT * FROM tablename WHERE..., and the table is subsequently altered, then the view will fail when applied to the new version of the table. It is safer to list explicitly all the column names to be included in the view.

### 4.8.6   Using views with GRANT

We have already discussed how GRANT is used to restrict or allow different types of access to tables. GRANT can also be used with views. Hence it is possible to allow a user to see only certain columns of a table or combinations of tables, thus enforcing a degree of security over the data.

Using this technique, users can be restricted to accessing only the data that they need to know about. They need not be aware that they are using views rather than tables, they need not be aware that the data they are accessing may come from several tables and, indeed, they need not be aware even of the existence of any data other than that which they can access.

## Summary: Views and GRANT

☐ The GRANT command can be used to allow or restrict access to tables for users other than the owner of the table. Note, however, that only the owner of the table can drop it.

☐ A view can be thought of as a window on a table or set of tables. It shows the user only a subset of the total data in the table(s). It may be used to bring out just the relevant data or to hide the underlying tables from the user.

☐ Data can be selected from views in the same way as from tables. There are restrictions on INSERT, UPDATE and DELETE through views.

☐ GRANT can allow permissions on views as well as tables to provide a complete and transparent system of access control.

---

### EXERCISE 4.9

1.  Write a statement which creates a view of the bookings table to include customer number, car group, model, date reserved, reserved by, date rental start, rental period and pay method.

2. Modify the above statement to contain a column holding the total number of miles travelled during a rental period.

3. Write a statement to create a view from the customers, cars and bookings tables which contains customer number, customer name, contact, model, registration, date reserved, total number of miles travelled (derived from miles out and miles in columns), rate per mile, rate per day and cost.

4. Modify the statement you wrote in Question 3 to include the number of bookings for each car.

## 4.9  SQL functions

Calculations and manipulations are carried out within SQL commands using operators and functions. We have already looked at arithmetic and logical operators and some of the aggregating functions; this section deals with the rest of the functions.

Without being too precise about it, a function is something that operates on one or more arguments (or parameters), and returns a value. The square root function is an obvious example. It operates on a number and returns the square root of that number. There are a wide range of SQL functions; a complete list is given in Appendix B. Only the most common and useful ones are covered here. Note that functions associated with date handling are covered in a separate section on the whole topic of dates.

The syntax for all the functions is the same, with the arguments in parentheses and separated by commas. For instance:

```
SELECT GREATEST(miles_to_date, maint_int)
FROM cars;
```

will select whichever is greatest of the miles to date or the maintenance interval for each car in the cars table.

### 4.9.1  Numeric functions

All the arithmetic functions operate on and return numeric or date datatypes. The most common ones are ROUND, TRUNC, GREATEST, LEAST and NVL. You may also occasionally need others like SIGN and ABS for arithmetic sign handling or POWER, SQRT and MOD for calculations.

ROUND and TRUNC shorten a numeric value to a specified number of decimal places, rounding or truncating. For example:

```
SELECT registration,
        ROUND(rate_per_mile*miles_to_date/100,1)
FROM cars;
```

will select the total mileage revenue for each car, rounded to the nearest ten pence. The final argument (, 1 in this case) specifies the number of decimal places to which the rounding should be done. If omitted, it will default to zero decimal places (i.e. whole numbers).

GREATEST and LEAST have a variable number of arguments. They return the value of the argument which evaluates to be the greatest (least). Note that, if the arguments are of different datatypes, Oracle automatically converts the datatype of the parameters to match that of the first parameter in the list. For example:

```
SELECT registration, model_name
FROM cars
WHERE GREATEST(miles_to_date, maint_int)>20000;
```

will select cars where either the miles to date or the maintenance interval is greater then 20 000 miles.

NVL is important when dealing with columns which may be null. It returns the value of the first parameter if it is non-null. If the first parameter is null, it returns the value of the second parameter. For instance:

```
SELECT registration,
        NVL(miles_in, miles_out) - miles_out
FROM bookings;
```

will select the registration and, if the return mileage (miles_in) is non-null, the mileage used. If the return mileage is null because the rental has not been completed, it will return miles_out-miles_out, i.e. zero.

### 4.9.2  String handling

The string handling functions are shown in Table 4.8. Take special care when you use them. It is not that they are particularly difficult, just intricate. It is very easy to make a mistake. Remember that positions in a character string always start counting at one, rather than zero. For the examples, assume the field phrase contains 'The quick brown fox'.

String concatenation is achieved with the | | operator. For example:

```
SELECT 'Registration is: '||registration
FROM bookings
WHERE booking_no = 502;
```

will return Registration is: G123RMR.

**Table 4.8**  String handling functions.

| Function | Effect |
|---|---|
| SUBSTR(str,m,n) | This returns the string of characters within str, starting at character m and n characters long. n and its preceding comma may be omitted, in which case the substring is terminated at the end of str. For example, SUBSTR(phrase,5,7) will return 'quick b'. |
| LTRIM(str, chars) | This returns the string with the characters removed from the front up to (and excluding) the first character not found in chars. For example: LTRIM(phrase, 'quick Thebr') will return 'own fox'. |
| RTRIM(str, chars) | This returns the string with characters removed from the right starting after the first character not found in chars. For example, RTRIM(phrase, 'oxf') will return 'The quick brown'. |
| LPAD(str,n, chars) | This pads the left end of str to a total length of n inserting the characters in chars, replicated as many times as necessary. If chars and the preceding comma are omitted, padding is with blanks. For example, LPAD(phrase,31,'hello ') will return 'hello hello The quick brown fox'. If the required length is less than the original length of the string, the string will be truncated at the right-hand end. |
| RPAD(str,n, chars) | This pads the right end of str in the same way as above. For example, RPAD(phrase,27,' etc') will return 'The quick brown fox etc etc'. Again, if the required length is less than the original length of the string, the string will be truncated at the right-hand end. |
| INSTR(str, chars,n,m) | This returns the numeric position of the mth occurrence of chars in str. It starts its search at position n of str. n and m are optional and, if omitted, are assumed to be 1. For example, INSTR(phrase, 'o',1,2) will return 18. |

## 4.9.3  Character functions

There are a number of character handling functions to do with case and other miscellaneous jobs. They are shown in Table 4.9. For the explanations, assume again that the field phrase contains 'The quick brown fox'.

**Table 4.9**  Character functions.

| Function | Effect |
|---|---|
| LOWER(phrase) | This forces the whole of the contents of str into lower case. For example: LOWER(phrase) will return 'the quick brown fox'. |
| UPPER(phrase) | This forces the whole of the contents of str into upper case. For example, UPPER(phrase) will return 'THE QUICK BROWN FOX'. |
| INITCAP(phrase) | This forces the initial letter of each word into upper case. A new word is reckoned to start after any non-alphabetic character. For example: INITCAP(phrase) will return 'The Quick Brown Fox'. |
| ASCII(char) | This returns the numeric ASCII value of the first character of char. For example, ASCII(phrase) will return 84 (decimal), the ASCII value of 'T'. |
| CHR(n) | This returns the character with the ASCII value n. For example, CHR(83) will return 'S'. |
| LENGTH(str) | This returns a numeric value of the length of str, expressed as the number of characters in str. For example, LENGTH(phrase) will return 19. |
| SOUNDEX(chars) | This returns a character value of the sound of the word(s) in chars. The character value is, of itself, not much use, but it is useful sometimes to compare the SOUNDEX of one data item with that of another. For example:<br><br>SELECT cust_name FROM customers<br>WHERE SOUNDEX(cust_name) =<br>    SOUNDEX('SMYTH');<br><br>would find 'SMITH' and 'Shmif', as well as 'SMYTH' (assuming they existed in the database). |
| TRANSLATE(str, char1,char2) | This translates each character in str which appears in char1 into the corresponding character in char2. For example, TRANSLATE(phrase,'onk','alh') will return 'The quich brawl fax'. |
| USERENV(chars) | This returns information about the user as a character string. There are some esoteric variants of this and it is mainly used for auditing. One useful example is that USERENV('terminal') returns the user's terminal ID. |

**Table 4.10** Conversion functions.

| Function | Effect |
|----------|--------|
| TO_NUMBER (numeric_chars) | This returns a number with the same value as the numeric character string. |
| TO_CHAR(n, 'fmt') | This returns a numeric character string for the value of *n* in the format specified by *fmt*. The format spec is optional. |
| TO_DATE (char_string) | Converts to date datatype. See next section. |

### 4.9.4  Conversion functions

Conversion functions convert the datatype or the format of their arguments. They go from character string to date, from number to numeric character string etc. The most useful are shown in Table 4.10.

The format specification defines the format of the character representation of a number. It specifies the number of places before and after the decimal, how to show negative numbers and so on. For example, TO_CHAR(rate_per_mile, '999') returns a three character numeric string. There are many possible variations for format specification. A complete list of the possibilities is in Appendix B.

There are other functions of less general interest, for instance to convert from hexadecimal to binary and so on. See Appendix B or look in the Oracle manuals for more details.

## Summary: SQL functions

☐ SQL has a rich variety of functions for arithmetic, string and character handling, converting from one datatype to another. Anyone used to modern third-generation languages (like C or Pascal) will recognize many of them.

☐ Functions act on arguments to return a value. The arguments are enclosed in parentheses, separated by commas.

☐ Be specially careful when using the string handling functions. They are quite intricate. Remember that character positions are numbered starting at one, not zero.

☐ Functions which convert to character strings have a format specification as one of the arguments. This allows a wide range of formats to be used.

☐ Note that date handling functions are described in the next section.

---

**EXERCISE 4.10**

1. Write a SELECT statement to find out how much, to the nearest pound, it costs to rent a Silver Spirit for 3 days, doing 257 miles?

2. Select all rows from the customers table, converting the name to upper case.

3. Write a SELECT statement to display customer number and customer name for all cash customers. Prefix the customer name column with 'Customer is:'.

4. Update all rows in the customers table to convert the town column to lower case with initial capitals or to insert 10 asterisks if this column is null.

5. Select model and rate per mile for all cars in the cars table in group A1. Precede the rate with the text 'mileage rate is' and display the rate as a number of pounds with one digit before the decimal point and two after it.

---

## 4.10   Dates and times

The handling of dates can be very important in commercial applications. Oracle provides very comprehensive facilities and they are described in some detail in this section. There is a special datatype for dates and/or time of day. A column with the DATE datatype holds both date and time. Arithmetic works quite naturally on dates – you can subtract dates to find the number of days between them, for instance. There are also numerous functions for handling dates.

### 4.10.1   Date formats

Fields of DATE datatype are held in the database in Oracle's own special format. This internal format is quite separate from the external formats in which dates and time can be entered and displayed.

Oracle allows an enormous number of options for the external format. Some of these are illustrated in a moment using the two most common date conversion functions: TO_CHAR and TO_DATE. As well as converting a number to a numeric character string, TO_CHAR converts from the date datatype to a character string. TO_DATE goes the other way. Both use format specifications to describe the format of the character string. If dates are entered or displayed without using these functions, the default format produces dates like '31-MAR-92'. These functions have the date itself as the first argument and the format specification as the second argument. For example:

```
SELECT TO_CHAR(rental_start_date,'DD/MM/YY')
FROM bookings;
```

will display the date in a format like '31/03/92'.

Different formats of dates have different specifiers in the format specification. Years can be two-digit numbers, four-digit numbers, spelt out in letters, or prefixed with AD or BC. Months can be as numbers or names. Days can be named, number within month, number within year and so on. A full list is in Appendix B; here are some examples:

```
SELECT TO_CHAR(rental_start_date,'DD/MM/YY')
FROM bookings;
```

produces a date like '31/03/92'.

```
SELECT TO_CHAR(rental_start_date,'DD-MON-YYYY')
FROM bookings;
```

produces a date like '31-MAR-1992'.

```
SELECT TO_CHAR(rental_start_date,'DD MONTH YEAR')
FROM bookings;
```

produces a date like '31 MARCH NINETEEN HUNDRED AND NINETY TWO'.

```
SELECT TO_CHAR(date_reserved,'WW/YY')
FROM bookings;
```

produces a date like '13/92'.

```
SELECT TO_CHAR(date_reserved,'Dy, DD Month YY')
FROM bookings;
```

produces a date like 'Fri, 31 March 92'.

```
SELECT TO_CHAR(date_reserved, 'DD-MM-YY, HH:MI')
FROM bookings;
```

produces a date and time like '31-03-92, 02:31'.

## 4.10.2 Date functions

The functions TO_CHAR and TO_DATE are just two of a range of functions for manipulating dates. The others are summarized in Table 4.11. Some of the functions used on numeric fields are also relevant to dates and times. These are also shown in the table.

**Table 4.11**   Date manipulation functions.

| Function | Effect |
|---|---|
| `ADD_MONTHS` `(date,n)` | Adds a specified number of months to a date. For example:<br><br>`ADD_MONTHS(date_rent_start+`<br>`            rental_period,1)`<br><br>might be part of a system to send marketing material out one month after a customer brings a car back. |
| `LAST_DAY(date)` | Returns a number which is the date of the last day of the month of the date supplied as an argument. So if `date` contained 10-Feb-1992, the function would return 29. |
| `MONTHS_BETWEEN` `(date1,date2)` | Returns the number of months between two dates supplied as arguments. The result is positive if the first date is later than the second and negative if not. Note that this is not the number of 30 day periods between the two dates but the difference in the month element of the dates. So:<br><br>`MONTHS_BETWEEN('31-MAR-92','01-MAY-92')`<br><br>would return 2. |
| `NEXT_DAY(date,` `day-of-week)` | A date is supplied as the first argument and a day of the week as the second argument. The function returns the date of the same day of the week (second argument) that follows the date supplied (first argument). For example:<br><br>`SELECT NEXT_DAY(date_reserved, 'FRIDAY')`<br>`FROM bookings...`<br><br>will return the date of the first Friday after `date_` `reserved`. If it is already a Friday, it will return the date of that Friday, i.e. `date_reserved`. |
| `TO_DATE(date,` `fmt)` | Converts a character string containing a date in a specified format to produce a date value. |
| `NEW_TIME(date,` `zone1,zone2)` | Converts a date and time in time zone 1 to the contemporaneous date and time in a different time zone, zone 2. The zones are identified by various codes: 'AST' for Atlantic Standard Time to 'YDT' for Yukon Daylight Time. Refer to the Oracle manuals for details. |
| `ROUND(date)` | This rounds a date and time to the nearest whole day. |
| `TRUNC(date)` | This truncates a date and time to whole days only. |

**Table 4.11** *(cont.)*

| Function | Effects |
|---|---|
| GREATEST(date1, date2,date3, ...daten) | This returns the latest of the date and times supplied as arguments. |
| LEAST(date1, date2,date3, ...daten) | This returns the earliest of the date and times supplied as arguments. |
| TO_CHAR(date, fmt) | As discussed above, this converts a date to a character string of the format specified. |

### 4.10.3 Date comparison

All the normal operators for testing for equality, greater-than and less-than can be used quite happily with dates without having to worry about the date format. Later dates are considered greater than earlier dates. For instance,

```
SELECT cust_no, date_reserved
FROM bookings
WHERE date_reserved > '19-DEC-91';
```

will return rows with reservation dates of 20 Dec '91 and beyond.

```
SELECT cust_no, date_reserved
FROM bookings
WHERE date_reserved < '19-DEC-91';
```

will return rows with reservation dates of 18 Dec '91 and earlier.

### 4.10.4 Date arithmetic

Dates can be used in arithmetic involving addition and subtraction. You can add or subtract an integer number to/from a date or you can subtract two dates to give the number of days between them. For example, to calculate the date on which a rented car is expected to be returned, simply add the number of days rental to the start date, thus:

```
SELECT cust_no, date_reserved, date_rent_start,
      date_rent_start + rental_period
FROM bookings;
```

Note that it is not reliable to increase a date by one month by adding 31, 30 or 28, depending on the month. The reason is that this will not allow for leap years or other less frequent calendar adjustments. Instead, use the ADD_MONTHS function which does allow for leap years etc.

### 4.10.5 Using the system date

Oracle provides a special column, SYSDATE, which contains the current date and time, obtained from the operating system. SYSDATE is really a pseudo-column as it is not part of any real table.

SYSDATE can be used in exactly the same way as any other date field. To access the system date, select it as normal in a SELECT statement. The syntax of SQL requires that the SELECT command references a table and this is satisfied by using the dummy table dual.

On its own, SYSDATE produces a date in Oracle's default format. Use the TO_CHAR function to get other formats. For example:

```
SELECT TO_CHAR(SYSDATE,'DD/MM/YY HH:MI:SS')
FROM dual;
```

The arithmetic and date functions which can be used on other dates can also be used on SYSDATE. For example, to add 90 days to the system date, use the '+' operator, thus:

```
SELECT SYSDATE, SYSDATE+90
FROM dual;
```

### 4.10.6 Arithmetic using time of day

When using dates in arithmetical expressions, it is important to remember that a date column always also contains a time of day. If two dates contain different times of day, the difference between them will result in a non-integer number being returned. If the number is displayed as an integer, the result may not be quite as expected, depending on which of the original dates had the later time of day.

For example, the difference between 11.00 a.m. on 3-JAN-92 and 5.00 a.m. on 5-JAN-92 is 1.75 days (2 days less 6 hours). The difference between 5.00 p.m. on 3-JAN-92 and 11.00 a.m. on 5-JAN-92 is 2.25 days (two days and 6 hours). Truncated to integers, these differences would be returned as 1 and 2, respectively, even though common sense says that the difference in dates is 2 days in both cases. The problem is fixed by using the ROUND function.

Another potential problem with date arithmetic is caused by type conversion. Oracle automatically converts the datatypes of the arguments of a function to make sure they match before it evaluates an expression. In this example:

```
SELECT ROUND(SYSDATE) - '10-JAN-91'
FROM dual;
```

a character string constant containing a date is specified following a date value (SYSDATE). The ROUND function causes a type conversion on the character string date. Oracle will try to convert the string to a numeric value because ROUND operates on numbers as well as dates. The conversion will fail and result in an error message. This problem is fixed by using the TO_DATE function to convert the character string date to a proper date datatype:

```
SELECT ROUND(SYSDATE) - TO_DATE('01-JAN-91')
FROM dual;
```

## Summary: Dates

☐ Oracle has its own internal format for holding dates and times. It is possible to enter and display dates in an enormous variety of formats.

☐ It is possible to carry out arithmetic on dates to determine numbers of days between two dates and so on. But beware of errors introduced when doing arithmetic when the time of day is included; use the ROUND function to get the right answer.

☐ Beware also of adding a number of days to a date; it is always safer to use one of the date functions to increment the week, month etc.

☐ Oracle provides today's date and time as a pseudo-column.

---

**EXERCISE 4.11**

1. Select date bought for all cars in group A2, displaying the date in a form similar to 'the 10th day of January, 1992'.

2. Select the earliest booking made.

3. Select all bookings where the rental has been for longer than 2 months.

4. Select any bookings made during the last seven days.

5. If cars depreciate at 4 per cent of original cost per month, show the current written down value of all cars bought last year.

---

# 4.11 Sequences

There are a number of different types of database object, all of which are defined with the CREATE command. The important ones, such as tables, indexes and synonyms, have already been covered. There are several others which are important only to a database administrator. There is another important class of objects which is often used and which appears in the examples in later chapters: *sequences*.

### 4.11.1 Purpose of a sequence

There are many cases where a unique number is used to identify an entity. In the example database, such serial numbers are used to identify customers and bookings. When entering (for instance) new customers, a new serial number must be generated; it must not already be in use. There are a number of ways you might go about achieving this. You could, for instance, look for the highest existing customer number in the table, add one to it and use the result as the new serial. This is not a good technique for two reasons: first, it can be very inefficient if the RDBMS has to scan all the way through a large table to find the highest serial number and, secondly, you would have to take care that another user did not allocate the same serial number as you while you were processing the record for the new customer. This would involve locking other users out of the table and this also can be very inefficient.

Another possible technique would be to have a special table which is used just for the allocation of serial numbers. It holds the next serial number to be allocated for each of the number sequences used in your system. When you need to allocate a new serial number, you pick up the next value from the table, allocate the number and update the table by adding one to produce the new value of the next serial number. Only this special table needs to be locked, rather than the whole of a data table. This technique is much better and is the preferred solution if it is important that the serial numbers are to be contiguous, having no gaps.

The simplest way, however, is to let Oracle generate the numbers for you using a *sequence*. You do not have to worry about multiple users allocating the same numbers or any of the other complications. The only disadvantage is that there is no guarantee that the numbers will form an unbroken series.

### 4.11.2 Using a sequence

The CREATE command is used to name and set up the sequence. The normal naming rules apply. You have the option to specify the start number for the sequence and the increment. Both of these will default to 1 if not explicitly specified. For instance:

```
CREATE SEQUENCE cust_seq START WITH 100;
```

There are many other options: negative increments can be used to specify a sequence which counts down, the sequence can be specified to count from a minimum value to a maximum value, it can recycle after it reaches its limiting value, and so on. For instance:

```
CREATE SEQUENCE booking_seq
START WITH 9000 INCREMENT BY -1
MAXVALUE 9999 MINVALUE 1 CYCLE;
```

will create a sequence which starts counting down from 9000. When it reaches 1, it will restart at 9999 and continue cycling round, counting down from 9999 to 1.

The sequence counts from one number to another when a reference is made to the pseudo-column NEXTVAL. For example:

```
INSERT INTO customers VALUES
(cust_seq.NEXTVAL, 'Taddleton Breweries Ltd.',
NULL, NULL, NULL, NULL, NULL, NULL);
```

inserts a new (largely empty, in this case) row in the customers table, allocating the next number from the cust_seq sequence to form the customer number in the row.

The current number in the sequence (the one last allocated) is also available using the pseudo-column CURRVAL. This is useful when you want to allocate a serial number as the primary key to one table and to insert it as the foreign key in a second table. Suppose, for instance, you need to record details of a new customer and make a booking for that person at the same time. You could insert the next value from the sequence into the customers table and the current value from the same sequence into the bookings table:

```
INSERT INTO customers VALUES
(cust_seq.NEXTVAL, 'Taddleton Breweries Ltd.,
... etc ... );
INSERT INTO bookings VALUES
(booking_seq.NEXTVAL, cust_seq.CURRVAL,
SYSDATE, ... etc ...);
```

Once a sequence has started to be used, it is unlikely that it would be sensible to change any of its characteristics. The ALTER SEQUENCE command can be used to change the increment or the maximum and minimum values of the sequence. Such changes are not retrospective; they will have no effect on previously allocated numbers. The start point of the sequence cannot be changed. To achieve this, the sequence would have to be DROPped and reCREATEd.

## 4.12  Reporting with SQL*Plus

Up to now we have not concerned ourselves with how the results of queries will be displayed. So SQL*Plus's default formats would be used. SQL*Plus in fact provides several commands to control how output should appear and quite sophisticated reports can be created with these commands. Formatted output may be sent to the screen or to an operating system text file, which can then be printed.

The report formatting commands are SQL*Plus, not SQL, commands. They are, therefore, not stored on the SQL buffer as SQL statements are. They do not change the contents of the buffer, but operate to re-format the output from those statements. Once a SQL*Plus command has been executed it remains in force until it is cancelled or changed.

### 4.12.1   The COLUMN command

By default, the results returned from a SQL statement appear in a columnar format with each column headed with the column name or expression. These headings are never particularly user friendly and they can be downright cryptic and obscure. To avoid this, it is possible to assign new headings to the output by using the COLUMN command.

For example, the heading for the pay_method column could be changed like this:

    COLUMN pay_method HEADING "Account or Cash"

Notice that, because there are spaces within the heading text, it must be contained within double quotes. A column alias can also be used to change the heading of a column from within a true SQL statement. For example:

    SELECT pay_method "Account or Cash"
    FROM customers;

achieves exactly the same effect as the COLUMN command above. But the new heading will only be in effect for the one SELECT command. To avoid using too much horizontal space, headings can be split over several lines using the vertical bar, | , as a separator. For example:

    COLUMN pay_method HEADING "Account or | Cash"

Several columns can be given the same definition by using the LIKE operator. For instance,

    COLUMN pay_method HEADING "Account or Cash"
    COLUMN acct_csh LIKE pay_method

establishes the new heading for the pay_method column and then specifies the same heading for the acct_csh column.

### 4.12.2   Formatting columns

The format of the contents of a column, as well as the heading, can be redefined for display purposes. Once again, these formats can be assigned to multiple columns using the LIKE operator. Formats are specified by defining a 'format mask'. These are described in detail in Appendix B. The most important elements of a mask are shown in Table 4.12.

**Table 4.12**  Format masks.

| Mask | Effect | Example |
|---|---|---|
| 9 | Number of digits determines the display width. | 9999 |
| 0 | Display leading zeroes. | 0999 |
| $ | Prefix the value with a dollar sign. A pound sign may be used instead. | $9999 |
| B | Display zero as a space. | B999 |
| MI | Display a minus sign after a negative value. | 9999MI |
| PR | Display a negative value within angle brackets, e.g. <145>. | 999PR |
| , (comma) | Display a comma in this position. | 9,999 |
| . (full stop) | Align the decimal point in this position. | 999.99 |
| V | Multiply the value by 10 to the power of $n$, where $n$ is the number of 9s after the V. | 999V99 |
| E | Display the value in scientific notation. The format must contain four Es. | 9.999EEEE |
| An | Define a character format, $n$ characters in length. | A10 |

A pound sign may be configured by the database administrator to replace the dollar sign. There is a difficulty, though, in that this is a straight replacement. The dollar sign would then no longer be available, so you cannot mix the two currency symbols. Some examples of column format specifications:

```
COLUMN cost FORMAT $99,999
```

defines the display format of the cost column as a pound sign followed by five digits with a comma at the thousands mark; e.g. $90,000.

```
COLUMN model_name HEADING "Car model" FORMAT A9
```

defines a new heading for the model column and an output format of nine alphanumeric characters.

```
COLUMN car_group_name LIKE model_name HEADING
"Car group"
```

defines the output format of the car_group_name column to be the same as the model column but gives it a different heading.

Note that all number formats automatically round to the specified number of digits. If a numeric value is too big to fit into the format specified, the field is filled with hash marks (###...).

### 4.12.3   Page titles

Two commands are provided to put titles on each page of a report. TTITLE displays text at the top of each page, and BTITLE at the bottom. So, for example:

```
TTITLE '50K Cars Bookings Report'
BTITLE 'Company Confidential'
```

will put text at the top and at the bottom of each page.

There are two versions of the TTITLE command. If the TTITLE keyword is on its own as in the previous example and not followed by a positioning keyword, then the command will insert the date and page number in the title as well as the text. If there is a positioning keyword, such as:

```
TTITLE CENTER '50K Cars Booking Report'
```

then just the text is put in the title. BTITLE without any positioning commands will put the text in the centre of the line. The variant of TTITLE which automatically inserts date and page number is a leftover from old versions of SQL\*Plus and may not be supported in the future, so it is recommended that only the variant with positioning keywords is used. The positioning commands available with TTITLE and BTITLE can also be used in the COLUMN command. They are shown in Table 4.13. A report heading, for example, might be defined like this:

**Table 4.13**   Positioning commands

| Position | Effect |
|----------|--------|
| CENTER | Centres the text on a line (American spelling must be used) |
| LEFT | Left-justifies text |
| RIGHT | Right-justifies text |
| COL n | Specifies the column number in which to start the text |
| SKIP n | Moves to a new line. *n* specifies the number of lines to skip. This command can also be used to throw a page: SKIP PAGE. |
| TAB n | Moves forward *n* print positions; backwards if *n* is negative. |

```
TTITLE LEFT 'Heathrow Branch'
TTITLE CENTER 'Weekly Bookings'
TTITLE RIGHT 'Week 24'
TTITLE SKIP 1 COL 10 'Vehicle utilization report'
TTITLE SKIP 1 COL 10 'by vehicle group'
TTITLE TAB 20 'Utilizations in miles'
```

### 4.12.4   Printing column values in titles

It is possible to print values from columns and other variables like SYSDATE in the top and bottom title. A column value must be assigned to a variable before it is used in either the TTITLE or BTITLE commands. This assignment is done with another variant of the COLUMN command.

For example, to display the car model in the report title, assign the value of model to a variable then print the variable using the TTITLE command. Thus:

```
COLUMN model_name NEW_VALUE modelvar
TTITLE CENTER modelvar
```

displays the model centred in the top title. And:

```
COLUMN SYSDATE NEW_VALUE today
TTITLE RIGHT today
```

will display the date and time at the top right of each page. The use of the NEW_VALUE keyword in the COLUMN command ensures that the variable is re-evaluated after a page break. The keyword OLD_VALUE can also be used; see below in the section on break processing.

Both page title commands, once defined, remain in force until changed. They can be turned off and on again with the TTITLE OFF and TTITLE ON (similarly for BTITLE). Enter the TTITLE or BTITLE command without parameters to display the current title setting. To clear title settings, use the CLEAR command thus: CLEAR TTITLE.

### 4.12.5   Break processing

The BREAK command is used to specify when a control break occurs and what action should be taken.

Control breaks can be specified to occur after each row is selected from a table, on a change of column value or combination of column values, at the end of a page or at the end of a report. For example, to specify a break when the value of the model column in the cars table changes:

```
BREAK ON model_name
```

When breaking on a change of column value like this, the SELECT statement you use to extract the data must have an ORDER BY clause

(ORDER BY `model_name` in this case) to avoid breaks occurring randomly. Breaks can be specified on any number of columns in one statement. For example:

```
BREAK ON model_name ON car_group_name
```

Other variants of the `BREAK` are used to specify breaks as each row is retrieved and at the end of the complete output:

```
BREAK ON ROW
BREAK ON REPORT
```

The action to be taken at a break point is specified as part of the `BREAK` command. For example:

```
BREAK ON model_name SKIP 1
```

will ensure that there is a blank line before the next set of rows is output. Similarly, a new page could be started by using `SKIP PAGE`:

```
BREAK ON model_name SKIP PAGE
```

or just

```
BREAK ON model_name PAGE
```

Unless specified otherwise, after a break occurs on a column value, the new value of the column will only be output once and it will be blank in subsequent rows. To force the output of the value for every row, use the `DUPLICATES` qualifier. For example:

```
BREAK ON model_name SKIP 1 DUPLICATES
```

To save and print the old value of a column at a break point, use the `OLD_VALUE` qualifier in the `COLUMN` command. The variable specified in this command can then be used in a `TTITLE` or `BTITLE` command. For instance:

```
COLUMN model_name OLD_VALUE oldmodel
BTITLE RIGHT "End of data for " oldmodel
```

Only one `BREAK` command can be in effect at any time. If several breaks are required with different actions, specify them in one command. For example:

```
BREAK ON model_name SKIP 1
   ON car_group_name PAGE
```

will cause a line to be skipped on change of model, and a new page to be started on change of car group.

To examine `BREAK` settings, enter `BREAK` without any parameters. Breaks can be cleared in the same way as titles using the `CLEAR` command.

## 4.12.6 Computing totals on breaks

To calculate subtotals and totals at a break point, use the COMPUTE command. For example:

```
COMPUTE SUM OF cost ON model_name
```

will add up all the values held in the cost column for each model and display the subtotal when the value for model changes. There must be a corresponding BREAK defined for this command to operate. Multiple COMPUTEs may be defined on different break columns.

SQL\*Plus will take care of aligning the total with the correct column in the output. Subtotals and totals can be calculated on multiple columns in the same COMPUTE statement. For example:

```
COMPUTE SUM OF cost miles_to_date ON model_name
```

Mathematical functions, MIN, MAX, AVG, STD (standard deviation), VAR (variance), COUNT, can also be used in the COMPUTE command to operate on single or multiple columns. For example:

```
COMPUTE AVG OF miles_to_date ON model_name
```

These functions will ignore null values. COUNT will count duplicate values even if they are not displayed.

To check the definition of a COMPUTE enter the command without parameters. Use CLEAR to cancel a COMPUTE.

## 4.12.7 Page lengths

By default, SQL\*Plus displays the output from a query in 14-line pages. This applies whether you define your own horizontal layout or just use the defaults.

The page length can be changed by specifying a new value for the SQL\*Plus system variable PAGESIZE, using the SET command. For example:

```
SET PAGESIZE 66
```

To set the number of lines to be inserted between pages, change the value of the system variable NEWPAGE. For instance,

```
SET NEWPAGE 3
```

will insert three blank lines between pages. And:

```
SET NEWPAGE 0
```

will use a form feed to throw to the top of the new page. For output to the screen, it blanks the screen before displaying the next page of data. Note, however, that on some printers and terminals, particularly IBM equipment, this special setting of NEWPAGE does not work.

NEWPAGE is just one of a number of system variables which can be defined with the SET command. See the Oracle manuals for details.

## Summary: Reporting with SQL*Plus

☐ The results of queries can be formatted using a number of SQL*Plus commands. Once defined, they all remain in force until modified or cancelled.

☐ The COLUMN command is used to define column headings and data formats. Titles to go at the top and bottom of a page are defined with the TTITLE and BTITLE commands.

☐ Column values can be included in titles but must be assigned to a variable and the variable name then quoted in the title definition.

☐ For forward compatibility reasons, do not use the variant of the TTITLE command that automatically inserts date and time.

☐ Control breaks can be inserted at end of page, at end of report, on change of value in a column etc. They can be used to space out the report and to show totals or other arithmetic functions.

☐ When there is a break on the value of a column, the SELECT statement which retrieves the data must have a corresponding GROUP BY clause.

---

**EXERCISE 4.12**

1. Redefine the column display formats of the bookings table to (a) give each the columns the same heading as the column name but without the underscores and (b) split any column names which are longer than 10 characters over more than one line.

2. Write SQL*Plus commands to format the following report:

    (a) The registration, model, car group, maintenance interval, cost and miles to date should appear on the report. Define suitable headings for these columns. The maintenance interval and miles to date columns should be a maximum of 5 digits and 6 digits respectively. Cost should be displayed in a format like £102,050.

    (b) Each model of car should begin on a new page and subtotals for cost should be printed. Display a title at the top of each page, containing the text '50K Cars Maintenance Report' (upper and lower case characters to be observed), followed by the model. Do NOT include a page number or date.

    (c) Each page should begin at the top of a new sheet and the maximum page length should be 22 lines.

3. Write the SQL statement(s) which will supply the data for this report.

# 4.13   SQL*Plus files

## 4.13.1   Command files

So far in this book it has been assumed that SQL*Plus has been used interactively: type in a statement, get the result back. It is often useful to execute a whole series of commands in one go by building and executing a SQL*Plus command file.

To create a command file, use the system editor, such as *vi* under Unix, and enter the statements in just the same format as if they were being entered directly to SQL*Plus. Comments can be inserted anywhere in the file using the REMARK statement or /*...*/.

The command files can be executed in one of two ways. Either use the START command from within SQL*Plus or invoke the command file directly from the command line to start SQL*Plus. Note the use of the @ sign. For instance:

```
SQLPLUS @my_sql
```

When executing a command file in this way, the first line of the file may contain the username and password, separated by a solidus. Alternatively, this can be supplied in the command line. Thus:

```
SQLPLUS username/password @my_sql
```

## 4.13.2   Replaceable parameters

Replaceable parameters and substitution variables can be embedded in SQL statements contained in a SQL*Plus command file to provide runtime variables. The SQL statements in the command file can then execute against different rows and even different tables each time the command file is run.

Parameters are indicated by an ampersand, followed by a number. For example:

```
SELECT &1
FROM cars
WHERE model_name= '&2';
```

The values for the parameters are provided with the START command which executes the file:

```
START sql_commands registration 'P911 TC';
```

The parameter &1 will be given the value registration and parameter &2 will be given the value 'P911 TC'. This is just a straight textual substitution before the SQL statement is executed. So the SQL statement becomes:

```
SELECT registration
FROM cars
WHERE model_name='P911 TC';
```

Substitution variables are also preceded by an ampersand but are given a name. Values for substitution variables are not given on the command line, but are prompted for by SQL*Plus when it encounters the variable as it executes statements.

A substitution variable can start with a double ampersand (&&). This means that the value supplied for the variable will be stored and only prompted for once, when it is first encountered. For example:

```
SELECT
FROM cars
WHERE model = '&&model_name';
```

### 4.13.3   Files created during a SQL*Plus session

Several operating system files may be created during a SQL*Plus session. The SAVE command saves the contents of the SQL buffer to a file with the default filetype of .SQL. Output from SQL statements can be sent to a file, rather than appearing on the screen. To do this, use the SPOOL command. For example:

```
SPOOL mikespool
```

Such spoolfiles have a default filetype .LST. To stop spooling, use the SPOOL OFF command.

## 4.14   Adding and dropping users

### 4.14.1   The GRANT command revisited

When a user wants to access the database, a user-ID and password must be established for the user. They are created with the GRANT command. GRANT has already been used to allow access to objects owned by other users. A different form of the GRANT command is used to set up an Oracle logon.

There are three types of privilege that can be granted: CONNECT, RE-SOURCE, DBA. Granting CONNECT privilege allows a new user to access the database. It also sets up a password for the user. For example:

```
GRANT CONNECT
TO Jimbo
IDENTIFIED BY Jumbo;
```

will allow the user Jimbo, whose password has been set to Jumbo, to log on to the Oracle database. This means that Jimbo can only access existing tables and views (assuming their owners GRANT him permission to do so). He cannot create them. To be able to create new database objects, he needs RESOURCE permission as well. This can be granted separately, for example:

```
GRANT RESOURCE
TO jphilpin;
```

or it can be part of a single GRANT command:

```
GRANT CONNECT, RESOURCE
TO dtovarich
IDENTIFIED BY rubric;
```

The GRANT command is also used to change a user's password. For example:

```
GRANT CONNECT
TO <your own ID>
IDENTIFIED BY newpass;
```

sets the user's own password to newpass. A user cannot grant CONNECT privilege to anyone other than him- or herself.

DBA (database administrator) privilege allows a user to do virtually anything he or she wants with (and to) the database. In multi-user systems, it is therefore usually restricted to one or more people whose specific job it is to look after the database. The DBA then assigns privileges to the other users. Only a user with DBA privilege can grant RESOURCE and DBA privileges to other users or grant CONNECT privileges to new users.

Privileges are withdrawn with the REVOKE command. For instance:

```
REVOKE CONNECT, RESOURCE
FROM Jimbo;
```

Again, only someone with DBA privilege can revoke other users' privileges.

# 4.15 Data integrity and constraints

The original versions of SQL gave only cursory attention to how to specify rules for data integrity: such rules cover the *domain* (or range) of valid values for an item of data, whether data can appear in one table without corresponding data in another table (for instance order details without customer details) and so on. The more recent SQL standard defines the way in which such rules are specified as *constraints*.

### 4.15.1 Enforcement of constraints

The current version of Oracle (V6) allows you to specify constraints and it checks the syntax of what you specify. The only one it actually enforces, however, is the NOT NULL constraint, described earlier in this chapter. It is still worth taking the trouble to think through and specify constraints for three reasons. First, it is a very good discipline to make yourself work out in detail the rules for what constitutes valid data. Secondly, version 7 is not far off and there will then be significant benefits from the automatic enforcement of constraints. Thirdly, though the RDBMS itself does not enforce most of the constraints, SQL\*Forms (V3) can use some of the constraints to help with the automatic generation of a range of applications. This is described in Chapter 7.

### 4.15.2   Key constraints

Constraints are used to specify keys to the table (primary key) and columns in the table which are used as keys in other tables (foreign keys). The constraints are defined when the table is CREATEd or ALTERed. Constraints may be given names which are quoted after the specification of the constraint. If you do not give it a name yourself, it will be given a system-generated name. For example, set up the cars table with key specifications:

```
CREATE TABLE cars
(   registration NUMBER(7), model_name CHAR(8)
    car_group_name CHAR(2), date_bought DATE,
    ... etc ... ,
    PRIMARY KEY (registration)
        CONSTRAINT con_car_pk,
    FOREIGN KEY (model_name)
        REFERENCES models(model_name),
    FOREIGN KEY (car_group_name)
        REFERENCES car_groups(car_group_name)
);
```

This gives a name (con_car_pk) to the constraint which specifies the primary key to the table. There are two foreign keys in the table. They reference columns in the models and car groups tables. In this case the corresponding referenced column has the same name as the foreign key column, but this need not be so. The effect of these constraints will (one day) be that:

- the primary key, registration may not be null. There will be no need to include a NOT NULL constraint.

- it will not be possible to insert a row into the cars table unless the inserted values for car group name and model name already exist in their appropriate tables.

### 4.15.3   Checks

A *check* constraint limits the range of values which may appear in a column. A condition clause is specified which defines the valid values. This condition may involve only the column itself, for instance to specify that the value in a column must be less than some limit. A column check like this is specified after the column description. For instance:

```
CREATE TABLE cars
(   registration NUMBER(7)
        CHECK (registration = UPPER(registration)),
    ... etc ... ,
    status CHAR(1)
        CHECK (status IN ('A', 'H', 'X', 'S'))
);
```

will insist that the registration is always entered in upper case and that the status code has one of the valid values listed. In other cases, the condition may be more complicated and refer to the values of several columns in the table. For instance:

```
CREATE TABLE bookings
(   booking_no NUMBER(5)
    ... etc ... ,
    miles_out NUMBER(6),
    miles_in NUMBER(6),
    amount_due NUMBER(6,2),
    paid CHAR(1)
        CHECK (paid in('Y', 'N'),
    PRIMARY KEY (booking_no),
    FOREIGN KEY (cust_no) REFERENCES
customers(cust_no),
    CHECK (miles_in = miles_out) CONSTRAINT
mileage_chk
);
```

has a named check constraint which insists that the mileage of a car checked in from rental must be greater than or equal to the mileage at the start of the rental. Because this constraint involves more than column, it must be specified using the table constraint syntax, as shown. The example also has a column check constraint on the paid indicator which is specified using the column check syntax.

The condition specified in the check can be any normal SQL condition. It must evaluate *true* for the check to be satisfied. It could contain comparison operators (=, IS, etc.), membership of lists (ANY, ALL, IN, EXISTS, etc.), or even a SELECT clause to return values for the condition.

Another column constraint, the UNIQUE constraint, can be used to ensure that all values entered in a column have unique values.

*Five*
# PL/SQL

## 5.1  PL/SQL basics

### 5.1.1  Manifestation

Oracle presents PL/SQL as a technology rather than a product. The technology manifests itself in a number of products. The execution of PL/SQL is seen as a separate task from the execution of regular SQL and is carried out by a separate PL/SQL 'engine' (Figure 5.1). In a centralized database system with just one database, accessed by many applications, there is no question as to where this engine should be executed: somewhere in the database system. But in a distributed database system, perhaps with a client/server architecture, there may be performance benefits to be gained by having the engine associated with

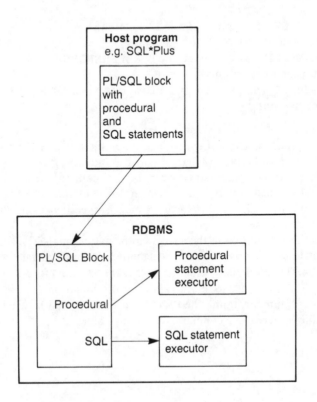

**Figure 5.1**  The PL/SQL engine within the RDBMS.

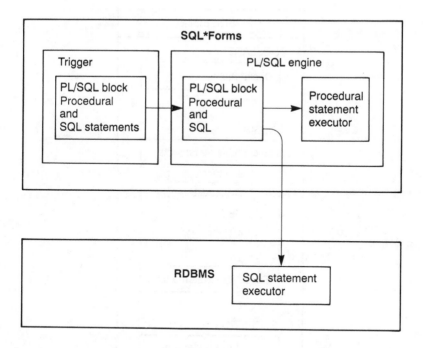

**Figure 5.2** PL/SQL engine in SQL*Forms.

the application instead of (or as well as) the database system. This way, the load on the database and network traffic can both be substantially reduced.

SQL*Plus, for instance, uses the engine embedded in the RDBMS. PL/SQL program blocks are interpreted by the engine and the SQL element of them is passed to the SQL execution part of the RDBMS.

SQL*Forms, the applications generator, which is covered in a later chapter, will often be used for production systems in a networked environment. It has its own PL/SQL engine (Figure 5.2) which looks after the execution of the procedural elements, passing true SQL to the RDBMS. This will reduce the RDBMS load when the RDBMS and SQL*Forms are located on different nodes. In some circumstances, it will also reduce network traffic.

## 5.1.2 Language structure

PL/SQL is written in *blocks*. A block can be big or small. It may contain other blocks. This structure has profound effects on the language, as will become clear. A block contains three components. **Declarations** are introduced by the keyword DECLARE and contain the definitions of variables and other elements. The **procedure** contains executable statements and is bracketed by BEGIN and END;. Within the procedure, **Exceptions** statements define what is to be done when non-routine events occur.

There are rules about how these components of a block can be put together. The

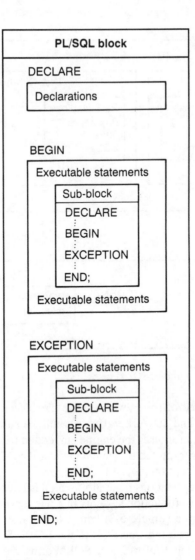

**Figure 5.3**   Nested PL/SQL blocks.

first rule is simple: a variable or other object must be declared before it is used; so the declarations always come before the procedure. Secondly, a procedure or an exception handler may contain other blocks which may be consecutive or nested (Figure 5.3). These sub-blocks may themselves be made up of other blocks. There is a limit to the levels of nesting allowed. This depends on the details of the Oracle installation but is very high and can be ignored for practical purposes.

Blocks may optionally be named. Within a block, statements are terminated by a semi-colon (; ). The examples in this chapter use the same convention as before: reserved words are in upper case and user-defined identifiers in lower case. The rules for constructing valid identifiers are the same as in SQL proper; see Chapter 4. Comments can be in the same form as SQL, starting with /* and terminated by */. Comments which fit on a single line can also be introduced with a double hyphen (--).

In contrast to SQL proper, PL/SQL has constructs for looping and for controlling program flow with GOTO and IF...THEN...ELSE.

### 5.1.3  Scoping rules

All the identifiers (or names) defined in the declarations have a *scope* in which they operate and which defines the blocks in which the identifier can be referenced. Figure 5.4 shows how these rules work. The rules are:

- Identifiers declared in a block are considered to be local to that block and global to all blocks nested within it.

- If an identifier is reused in an inner block, then for the block in which it was redefined and in all blocks nested in it, the new definition of the identifier overrides its original usage.

- An outer block may not reference an identifier declared in one of its inner blocks.

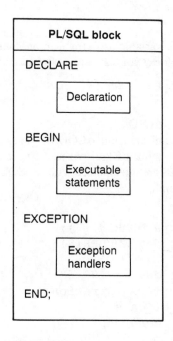

**Figure 5.4**  Components of a PL/SQL block.

The example below illustrates these scoping rules. It shows which identifiers are available to the code in the inner and outer blocks. It also shows the reuse of an identifier, v_registration, as a different variable in an inner block. While re-definition of a variable like this is quite legal, it can obviously cause confusion. Avoid it if you can.

```
/* Scope of identifiers within PL/SQL blocks */
DECLARE
    v_registration CHAR(7);
    v_miles NUMBER(6);
BEGIN
    DECLARE
        v_registration NUMBER(5);
        --(This is a new variable but same name)
        v_status CHAR(1);
    BEGIN
        /* Variables available here are:
            v_registration as NUMBER(5),
            v_miles,
        and v_status. */
    END;
    /* Variables available here are:
        v_registration as CHAR(7),
    and v_miles. */
END;
```

If you need to refer to a variable as defined in another block, rather than as defined in the current block, you can use a concatenation of the block name and the variable name.

### 5.1.4   Relationship with SQL

The PL/SQL language is an extension to SQL, not just a free-standing language of its own. It is best to think of the two as being components of a single language. SQL statements are interspersed with PL/SQL as part of declarations and procedure. For example:

```
DECLARE
    v_no_of_cars NUMBER (3);
    v_rate_per_day NUMBER(5);
BEGIN
    v_rate_per_day := 100
    SELECT COUNT(registration)
    INTO v_no_of_cars
    FROM cars, cargroup
    WHERE rate_per_day < v_rate_per_day
```

```
    AND cars.car_group_name =
           cargroup.car_group_name;
    INSERT INTO numbers_table
        VALUES(v_rate_per_day, v_no_of_cars);
END;
```

## Summary: PL/SQL basics

☐ PL/SQL is Oracle's extension to SQL to provide the procedural capabilities needed for on-line transaction processing applications. The syntax is very similar to SQL.

☐ PL/SQL statements are executed by an 'engine' which is separate from the SQL processing in the RDBMS. The engine can appear alongside the RDBMS or embedded in Oracle's application generator, SQL*Forms.

☐ Programs are written in *blocks*, each of which contains declarations of variables and other items and a procedure. The procedure can, itself, contain exception handlers.

☐ Blocks of code can be executed one after another or can be nested, one within another.

☐ The block structure defines the scope of identifiers used in a program. Identifiers may be referenced in the block in which they have been defined or in other blocks nested within it.

## 5.2 Variables

### 5.2.1 Declarations

Variables can be used to hold intermediate results, etc. They must be declared before they are referenced. The declaration includes the variable's datatype. The normal SQL datatypes can be used and PL/SQL also supports additional datatypes, for instance BOOLEAN. See Appendix B for details of SQL and PL/SQL datatypes. Some example declarations:

```
DECLARE
    v_date_bought DATE;
    v_cost NUMBER(8,2);
    v_depr_code CHAR(1);
    v_total_cost NUMBER(9,2);
    v_major_service BOOLEAN;
```

Notice that in the example all the variable names begin with 'v_'. This is not a standard insisted on by PL/SQL but it is very useful to be able instantly to distinguish between variable names and the column names in database tables. Often variables are used as temporary storage for the contents of column and so there is a constant temptation to use the same name for both. In theory this is allowable, but you are very strongly recommended not to do it; it can cause endless confusion. Prefixing variable names, as in the example, provides a simple standard which distinguishes between columns and variables and allows you to use essentially the same names.

Another useful standard when variables are used to hold column values is to pick up the datatype for the variable from the datatype of the corresponding column, rather than to specify it explicitly. This can save a lot of trouble later on if the column datatype is modified, for instance to allow more digits in a NUMBER column. This is achieved using the %TYPE attribute. The following variable declarations will pick up the datatypes of the named columns. Note that both the table and column names must be quoted.

```
DECLARE
    v_date_bought cars.date_bought%TYPE;
    v_cost cars.cost%TYPE;
    v_depr_code CHAR(1);
```

### 5.2.2  Assigning values
Initial values can also be ascribed to variables when they are first declared by following the declaration with an assignment clause. For example:

```
DECLARE
    v_monthly_depr_rate NUMBER(4,2) := 1.75;
    v_depr_code CHAR(1) := 'A';
    v_major_service BOOLEAN :=FALSE;
```

Values assigned to variables like this can be changed later on. You can define a constant whose value cannot be subsequently changed by including the keyword CONSTANT in the declaration. For example:

```
DECLARE
    v_monthly_depr_rate CONSTANT NUMBER(4,2) :=1.75;
    v_depr_code CONSTANT CHAR(1) := 'A';
```

Values assigned as part of the initial declaration of a variable are usually straightforward literals or numbers. Assignment statements can be a lot more complicated, though, particularly in the procedure part of a block. The right-hand side of the assignment can be a simple value or an expression. The expression can be built up of functions, operators, other variables and so on. Some examples:

```
v_depr := v_cost*v_monthly_depr_rate/100
        *MONTHS_BETWEEN(SYSDATE,v_date_bought);
v_short_desc := SUBSTR(v_description,1,8);
```

Another way in which values can be assigned to variables is by SELECTing data into them using the INTO clause. For example:

```
SELECT SUM(cost) INTO v_total_cost FROM cars;
```

### 5.2.3 Records

It is often convenient to define a set of variables which mirror the structure of a row from a table or of the set of columns returned by a view. This is achieved using a *record*. Records are declared and given a name. The structure of fields within the record is associated with the table or view by using the %ROWTYPE attribute. For instance:

```
DECLARE
     cars_rec cars%ROWTYPE;
     -- ...
```

will define a record containing fields which have the same structure as a row of the cars table. The fields can be accessed by quoting the record name followed by a full stop (period) then the column name from the table or view. Thus the record declared above has the following fields and datatypes:

```
     cars_rec.registration CHAR(7)
     cars_rec.model_name CHAR(8)
     cars_rec.car_group_name CHAR(2)
     cars_rec.date_bought DATE
     cars_rec.cost NUMBER(8,2)
     cars_rec.miles_to_date NUMBER(6)
     cars_rec.miles_last_service NUMBER(6)
     cars_rec.status CHAR(1)
```

Records can also be declared to mirror the structure of rows returned by a *cursor*. This is described below in the section on cursors.

## Summary: Variables

☐ Program variables must be declared before they are used. Variables can be given the same datatypes as are available in SQL. Some additional datatypes are also available in PL/SQL.

☐ Variables which are to be used to hold values from columns in a table can be defined as having the same datatype as the column by using the %TYPE attribute.

☐ Values are ascribed to variables with the := operator. This may be done when the variable is declared or in the procedure.

☐ Constants can also be declared in a similar way to variables. The value is ascribed when the constant is declared and, thereafter, may not be changed.

☐ Record structures may be defined which mirror the structure of a table or view using the %ROWTYPE attribute. The fields within the record are the same as the columns in a row of the table or the columns available in the view. They are accessed by quoting the record name followed by the column name in the table or view.

☐ Records may also be defined to mirror the columns returned by a query.

---

**EXERCISE 5.1**

1. Declare a numeric constant (with any suitable name) with a value of 981.22.

2. Declare a variable, v_cost, with the same datatype as the cost column in the cars table.

3. Use an assignment statement to change the value of the variable declared in Question 2 to equal the cost of the car whose registration is 'J232TPZ'.

4. Declare a set of variables with the same datatypes as the columns in the models table.

5. Use an assignment statement to change the value of the variable corresponding to the description column to equal just the first 20 characters of the description for Porsche 911s.

---

# 5.3 Iteration

### 5.3.1 Loops

Program loops are designated by enclosing the instructions to be iterated with the keywords LOOP ... END LOOP. The control of the iterations is handled by a FOR clause or a WHILE clause. For example, suppose you wanted to extract a table of how many cars there are which have a daily rate of less then £10, less than £20 etc., up to £100.

```
DECLARE
    v_no_of_cars NUMBER (3)
    v_rate_per_day cargroup.rate_per_day%TYPE := 10
BEGIN
    WHILE v_rate_per_day <= 100 LOOP
```

```
            SELECT COUNT(registration)
            INTO v_no_of_cars
            FROM cars, cargroup
            WHERE rate_per_day < v_rate_per_day
            AND cars.car_group_name =
                    cargroup.car_group_name;
            INSERT INTO numbers_table
                VALUES(v_rate_per_day, v_no_of_cars);
            v_rate_per_day:= v_rate_per_day + 10;
        END LOOP;
    END;
```

The same effect could be obtained with a FOR loop. Assume that the same declarations as in the previous example have been made:

```
BEGIN
    FOR i IN 1..10 LOOP
        SELECT COUNT(registration)
        INTO v_no_of_cars
        FROM cars, cargroup
        WHERE rate_per_day < v_rate_per_day
        AND cars.car_group_name =
                cargroup.car_group_name;
        INSERT INTO numbers_table
            VALUES(v_rate_per_day, v_no_of_cars);
        v_rate_per_day := v_rate_per_day + 10;
    END LOOP;
END;
```

In this case a control variable, i, is implicitly defined to control the loop. We might have used a pre-defined variable here, like v_rate_per_day. However, the increment on the control variable is always 1 so this would not have achieved the correct result. The variable name i has no special significance; any valid variable name would do and it would be implicitly declared as NUMBER. Variables are often also used in the loop counter parameter. We could, for instance, use a variable to define the upper limit of the rate per day scale like this:

```
DECLARE
    v_top_band NUMBER :=20;   -- takes us to £200
    -- other declarations, as before
BEGIN
    FOR i IN 1..v_top_band LOOP
    -- rest of the code, as before
    END LOOP;
END;
```

The EXIT statement is used to break out of a loop before it expires naturally. Suppose that we wanted to stop writing to the numbers table if the count in any one price bracket exceeds 500 (this example uses an IF statement; these are dealt with in more detail later):

```
DECLARE
    -- declarations as before
BEGIN
    WHILE v_rate_per_day <= 100 LOOP
        SELECT COUNT(registration)
        INTO v_no_of_cars
        FROM cars, cargroup
        WHERE rate_per_day < v_rate_per_day
        AND cars.car_group_name =
                cargroup.car_group_name;
        INSERT INTO numbers_table VALUES(
                v_rate_per_day, v_no_of_cars);
        IF v_no_of_cars 500 THEN
            EXIT;
        END IF;
        v_rate_per_day := v_rate_per_day + 10;
    END LOOP;
    -- exit to here
END;
```

It is quite permissible to specify a loop without a controlling FOR or WHILE clause. Such a loop will be endless unless there is an EXIT condition within it; when the condition is satisfied, control passes to the first executable statement after the END LOOP. Another way out of an endless loop is if there is a condition which RAISEs an exception condition from within the loop; in this case control passes to the exception processing code. Exception processing is covered in more detail below.

### 5.3.2 Cursors

Sometimes it will be necessary to define a query and then to process the rows it returns one by one. This is done using a *cursor*. In general, any query will return many rows and the simplest way of looking at a cursor is that it represents a pointer to the current row amongst the many returned. In fact, the cursor actually represents a whole working cell used by the RDBMS to control the processing of not just queries but other elements of PL/SQL and SQL. Many cursors are, therefore, defined implicitly as PL/SQL and SQL are executed. Amongst other things, the work area contains the pointer to the current row.

Cursors can be defined explicitly and it is these explicit cursors which are used to process rows one by one. The query associated with the cursor is defined in the declaration section of a block. This names the cursor and specifies the query with which it is associated. For instance:

```
DECLARE
    v_registration cars.registration%TYPE;
    v_cost cars.cost%TYPE;
    v_miles_to_date cars.miles_to_date%TYPE;
    CURSOR cur_cars IS
        SELECT registration, cost, miles_to_date
        FROM cars
        WHERE status = 'A';
```

Note that, although the example declares variables for registration, cost and miles to date, these are for use later in the block. The cursor's SELECT definition just quotes the column names and the selection criteria.

A cursor is OPENed before it is used. Rows are FETCHed and the cursor is CLOSEd when finished with. Continuing the same example:

```
BEGIN
    OPEN cur_cars;
    LOOP
        FETCH cur_cars INTO v_registration, v_cost,
                                v_miles_to_date;
        /* processing for each row goes in here*/
    END LOOP;
    CLOSE cur_cars;
END;
```

As written, the loop in this example does not have a tidy termination. The FETCH will return all the rows in the working set and then will cause an error. There are, however, a number of cursor attributes (see Table 5.1) which allow you to keep track of the cursor and its use. You can use one of these, %NOTFOUND, to exit tidily from the loop in the example:

```
BEGIN
    OPEN cur_cars;
    LOOP
        FETCH cur_cars INTO v_registration, v_cost,
                                v_miles_to_date;
        EXIT WHEN cur_cars%NOTFOUND;
        /* processing for each row goes in here*/
    END LOOP;
    /* Exit to here after last row of query */
    CLOSE cur_cars;
END;
```

The next example uses another cursor attribute, %ROWCOUNT, and %NOT-FOUND to pick out the ten most expensive cars:

**Table 5.1** PL/SQL cursor attributes.

| Attribute | Description |
|-----------|-------------|
| %FOUND | Evaluates to TRUE if the last FETCH succeeded in returning a row. |
| %ISOPEN | Evaluates to TRUE if the cursor is open; otherwise FALSE. |
| %NOTFOUND | The opposite to %FOUND. Evaluates to TRUE if the last FETCH found no more rows to return. |
| %ROWCOUNT | Evaluates to the number of rows FETCHed so far. |

```
DECLARE
    v_registration cars.registration%TYPE;
    v_cost cars.cost%TYPE;
    CURSOR cur_10most IS
        SELECT registration, cost
        INTO v_registration, v_cost FROM cars
        ORDER BY cost DESC;
BEGIN
    OPEN cur_10most;
    LOOP
        FETCH cur_10most INTO v_registration, v_cost;
        EXIT WHEN (cur_10most%ROWCOUNT>10)
            OR(cur_10most%NOTFOUND);
            -- (have to check for not found in case
            -- <= 10 rows in cars table)
        INSERT INTO top10cars
            VALUES(v_registration, v_cost);
    END LOOP;
    COMMIT;
    CLOSE cur_10most;
END;
```

The same effect can be achieved with a cursor FOR loop using a cursor record. The record can be explicitly defined and then used; for instance:

```
DECLARE
    CURSOR cur_cars IS
        SELECT registration, cost, miles_to_date
        FROM cars
        WHERE status = 'A';
    r_cars cur_cars%ROWTYPE
```

```
BEGIN
    FOR r_cars in cur_cars LOOP
        /* process the rows using
                r_cars.registration
                r_cars.cost
                r_cars. miles to date/*
    END LOOP;
END;
```

Alternatively, the record declaration may be omitted and the FOR statement will implicitly define a record with the structure of the cursor %ROWTYPE. In both cases the fields in the record are the same as the columns returned by the cursor's SELECT statement. Notice also that the cursor does not have to be explicitly OPENed before it is used in a FOR loop.

### 5.3.3 Cursor parameters

Cursors can have parameters which govern the effect of the cursor's query. The parameters are defined when the cursor is declared and the value of the parameter is substituted when the cursor is OPENed or used in a FOR loop. For instance, to parametrize the value of the car's status:

```
DECLARE
    v_registration cars.registration%TYPE;
    v_cost cars.cost%TYPE;
    v_miles_to_date cars.miles_to_date%TYPE;
    v_status cars.status%TYPE;
    CURSOR cur_cars (p_status CHAR) IS
        SELECT registration, cost, miles_to_date
        FROM cars
        WHERE status = p_status;
BEGIN
    /* ... probably lots of processing in here
            including assigning a value to v_status
            for instance ...*/
    v_status := 'A'
    FOR r_cars in cur_cars(v_status) LOOP
        /* process the rows using
                r_cars.registration
                r_cars.cost
                r_cars.miles_to_date/*
    END LOOP;
END;
```

More than one parameter is allowed; they are specified separated by commas both for the parameter identifiers in the cursor declaration and the values to be substituted. The example above uses a FOR loop but the OPEN...FETCH ...CLOSE construct could also be used and, in this case, the values of the parameters are supplied when the cursor is OPENed:

```
/* ... Declarations, etc. as before */
OPEN cur_cars(v_status);
LOOP
    FETCH cur_cars INTO v_registration, v_cost,
                                v_miles_to_date;
    EXIT WHEN cur_cars%NOTFOUND;
    /* processing for each row goes in here*/
END LOOP;
CLOSE cur_cars;
END;
```

The datatypes of the parameters are defined in the cursor declaration. Notice that the length is not specified, just the type. The value to be substituted can be any valid PL/SQL expression. So it could be a variable, a literal, a number or something quite complicated like UPPER(CHR(TRUNC(195/2))). The datatype of the value supplied must be the same as that defined for the parameter or must be convertible to it.

### 5.3.4 Implicit cursors

The RDBMS implicitly opens cursors as it parses each block of PL/SQL and as it parses each SQL statement within the block. The cursors associated with the block are managed entirely by the RDBMS and are not accessible to the user. But there is useful information to be found in the cursor attributes of the implicitly defined cursor associated with the processing of SQL statements, the SQL% cursor. The interpretation of the cursor attributes is the same as for explicit cursors with some special considerations for SQL%NOTFOUND and SQL%ISOPEN.

SQL%NOTFOUND is set true if an UPDATE, INSERT or DELETE did not affect any rows. It is also set true if a SELECT did not return any rows. Usually, however, this will also result in the NO_DATA_FOUND exception condition being raised, so checking SQL%NOTFOUND immediately after a query is futile because the check will never be executed. See below for an explanation of exception processing. Queries which return an aggregate function (like MAX) always return a value, even if it is null. So in this example:

```
DECLARE
    v_av_cost NUMBER(8,2);
BEGIN
    SELECT AVG(cost) INTO v_av_cost FROM cars
    WHERE status = 'A';
    IF SQL%NOTFOUND THEN -- always evaluated
```

```
    /* processing for no rows found goes here */
    END IF;
END;
```

the test for SQL%NOTFOUND **will** be executed and it would evaluate true if there were no relevant rows.

Because implicit cursors are closed immediately after executing the associated SQL statement, SQL%ISOPEN will always evaluate false. There is no point in checking it.

## Summary: Iteration

☐ The LOOP construct is used for iteration. Loops can be uncontrolled, needing an explicit exit within them; they can be controlled by WHILE and a condition; or they can be controlled by FOR...IN.

☐ Cursors are used for working through the data returned by a query. The cursor is declared and associated with its SELECT statement. Then it is OPENed, data is FETCHed and the cursor CLOSEd when finished with.

☐ When using a cursor in a FOR loop, the cursor can be implicitly opened and records corresponding to columns returned by the cursor's SELECT statement can be implicitly defined.

☐ A cursor may be given parameters to modify the effect of its associated query.

☐ Cursor attributes contain useful information on whether the cursor is open, how many rows have been returned etc.

☐ Implicit cursors are used by the system whenever SQL statements are parsed. Cursor attributes for implicit cursors can be useful, but there are limitations on their use.

---

**EXERCISE 5.2**

1. You need to insert rows into an already existing table which holds data for the maximum original cost of cars in each car group. The table is called maxcosts and has four columns, car_group, max_cost, model_name and description. Write a PL/SQL program using a cursor which analyses the cars and models tables to produce data for the new table.

## 5.4   Program flow

### 5.4.1  Labels

Program flow is controlled with conditional and unconditional branching constructs. Points in the code to which control is to be transferred are given labels. Labels can be associated with executable PL/SQL statements or with blocks. They cannot be associated with non-executable statements like END LOOP, but this is not a problem because you can always insert a NULL (do nothing) statement in front of the non-executable statement and put the label before the NULL.

Label names are enclosed in double pointed brackets and the rules for a valid label name are the same as for any other identifier. Examples are:

```
<<no_car_available>>
<<calc_rental>>
```

A label must be unique within its block but the same label name may be used in both an enclosing block and its enclosed block. This is not recommended practice, though; it is better to make all labels unique to the whole program, if you can. This may not be easy, however; for instance, there may be more than one person building the program. A branch to a label will transfer control to the label within the current block (if it is there). Otherwise, each successive level of enclosing block will be searched for the label and control will be passed to the first occurrence found.

### 5.4.2  Unconditional branching

The GOTO command can be used to branch to a label in the current block or in an enclosing block. The label could be on a statement or on the start of an enclosed block. It is not allowed to branch to a label which is out of the context of the current sequence of statements. Thus, while you may branch out of (e.g.) a loop construct, you may **not** branch into one. This example is legal:

```
BEGIN
    -- ... outer block processing
    <<enc_block_label>> -- (label on executable)
    SELECT registration, cost INTO v_reg, v_cost
    FROM cars
    WHERE status = 'X';
    -- ... more outer block processing
    BEGIN
        -- ...
        GOTO enc_block_label;
        -- ...
    END;
    -- ...
END;
```

The next example, however, is **not** legal because the branch is into a loop:

```
BEGIN
    -- ...
    GOTO inner_label;
    -- ...
    FOR v_counter IN 1..10 LOOP
        -- ...
        <<inner_label>>
        v_total := v_total + v_newval;
        -- ...
    END LOOP;
    -- ...
END;
```

### 5.4.3 Conditionals

Conditional branching is done with the IF statement. There are four components to the IF construct: IF, which specifies the condition; THEN, which specifies what to do if the condition evaluates to true; ELSIF, which tests a further condition if the original condition evaluates to false or null; and ELSE, which specifies what to do if all the preceding conditions evaluate to false or null. The construct is terminated by END IF. For example:

```
BEGIN
    v_major_service := FALSE;
    v_minor_service  := FALSE;
    v_ok_for_now := FALSE;
    /* Set one of these TRUE depending on
       the car's mileage */
    IF v_miles_to_date/v_maint_int >= 5 THEN
        v_major_service := TRUE;
    ELSIF v_miles_to_date/v_maint_int >= 1 THEN
        v_minor_service := TRUE;
    ELSE
        v_ok_for_now := TRUE;
    END IF;
END;
```

There may be more than one ELSIF clause and each will itself have a THEN clause. More IFs can be specified in the sequence of statements following the THEN and ELSE, resulting in cascaded conditionals.

The rules for specifying the condition in the IF part are similar to those for the condition in the WHERE clause of a SELECT statement. AND, OR and NOT can be used. So also can LIKE, BETWEEN and IN. Cursor attributes, %NOT-FOUND etc., may be tested in conditionals.

**Table 5.2**   Truth tables for AND, OR and NOT.

| AND | True | False | Null |
|-----|------|-------|------|
| True | T | F | N |
| False | F | F | F |
| Null | N | F | N |

| OR | True | False | Null |
|-----|------|-------|------|
| True | T | T | T |
| False | T | F | N |
| Null | T | N | N |

| NOT | |
|-----|---|
| True | F |
| False | T |
| Null | N |

It is very important to realize that a condition can evaluate to true, false **or null** and that ELSIF and ELSE clauses are activated if the main condition evaluates to null, as well as if it evaluates to false. The truth tables in Table 5.2 show under what circumstances a null result is obtained. The involvement of nulls can produce some unexpected results. For example, the two conditional statements below are **not** equivalent if either v_miles_to_date or v_maint_int is null:

```
BEGIN
    /* Version 1 */
    IF v_miles_to_date > v_maint_int THEN
        v_service_it := TRUE;
    ELSE
        v_service_it :=FALSE;
    END IF;
END;

BEGIN
    /* Version 2 */
    IF NOT(v_miles_to_date > v_maint_int) THEN
        v_service_it := FALSE;
    ELSE
        v_service_it := TRUE;
    END IF;
END;
```

If neither of the variables is null, the two versions will have exactly the same effect. But if either variable is null, both conditions will evaluate to null and the ELSE clause will be activated. Thus Version 1 will set v_service_it false while Version 2 will set it true.

## Summary: Program flow

☐ PL/SQL provides unconditional GO TO statements and conditional IF ...THEN...ELSIF...ELSE statements.

☐ Labels are enclosed in double pointed brackets, <<>>. They may only be placed before executable statements or the start of a block.

☐ There may be several ELSIF clauses in a conditional; each is evaluated if the IF and ELSIFs before it have all evaluated false or null. The ELSE is executed when all of the IF and ELSIFs evaluate false or null.

☐ The fact that a condition can evaluate null as well as true or false can cause some unexpected results.

---

**EXERCISE 5.3**

1. You need to extract details of bookings which have large value and have remained unpaid for some time. They are to be written to an already existing table called oldbills. This has four columns: customer_name, date_rent_start, amount_due and severity. Write a PL/SQL program to analyse the customers and bookings tables to extract unpaid bookings with amount due £200 or more and whose rental start date was three months or more ago. If the amount due is more than £500 or the start date is more than six months ago, set the severity code to 2. If the rental start date is 12 months or more ago, set the severity code to 3.

---

## 5.5 Unexpected events

Perhaps 'unexpected' is a poor choice of word, here. Unexpected events are routine for any program. Even the most carefully built programs have bugs and all programs have to be able to cope with unforeseen events which may be quite out of their control. They should be able to cope without crashing.

The traditional way to achieve this is to code in various checks throughout the procedure of the program. PL/SQL does it a different way by providing *exception handlers*. Each block can have an exception section in which is specified what to do if various exception conditions arise during the processing of the block. This scheme separates the exception handling from the main flow of the program. The exception condition can range from a simple event, such as no data returned from a SELECT, to a very unlikely but catastrophic event, such as an Oracle internal error. You can also define and raise your own exception conditions.

The main advantage of this approach is that it is much easier to ensure that the program can stagger on, whatever errors may occur. Foreseen exceptions can be dealt with tidily without obscuring the main flow of the program with in-line exception handling code. Unforeseen conditions can be dealt with by a general purpose exception handler.

### 5.5.1  Internal exceptions

There are a number of predefined system exception conditions which represent the most common exception events. Table 5.3 shows a list of them. The PL/SQL statements to handle the exception are specified in the EXCEPTION section of the block. For instance:

```
BEGIN
    -- ...
EXCEPTION
    WHEN NO_DATA_FOUND THEN
        v_price_per_rental := 0
        INSERT INTO temptab VALUES(v_model_name,
                     v_price_per_rental);
        COMMIT;
    WHEN VALUE_ERROR OR ZERO_DIVIDE THEN
        /* Deal with these circumstances */
    WHEN OTHERS THEN
        /* Deal with any of the other possible
            exceptions */
END;
```

There will usually be several exceptions defined, as in this example. Notice that multiple exceptions can be dealt with together by linking them with an OR and that the keyword OTHERS will catch all exceptions which have not already been explicitly catered for. The OTHERS exception must be specified on its own, not handled together with other exceptions. The range of PL/SQL statements in an exception handler and its use of variables etc. are exactly the same as in the rest of the procedure in the block.

An exception handler is activated as soon as the relevant condition is encountered, skipping any other statements in the block's procedure. When the code in the exception handler has been executed, the block is exited and control passed to the enclosing block.

### 5.5.2  User exceptions

This same structure for dealing with unusual circumstances can be used to handle application-specific events as well as system events. You can declare your own exceptions and raise exception conditions when the appropriate circumstances occur in the processing in a block. The declaration is done with all the other declarations at the start of the block, the exception is raised within the procedure section and the exception handler is specified along with the

**Table 5.3** PL/SQL standard exception handlers.

| Exception | Description |
| --- | --- |
| CURSOR_ALREADY_OPEN | Raised when an attempt is made to open a cursor which is already open. |
| DUP_VAL_ON_INDEX | Raised when an INSERT or UPDATE would result in two rows having the same value in a column constrained by a unique index. |
| INVALID_CURSOR | Raised when an attempt is made to use a non-existent or unopened cursor. |
| INVALID_NUMBER | Raised from within a SQL statement when an attempt is made to convert a non-numeric field into a number. If a similar situation occurs not within a SQL statement VALUE_ERROR will be raised instead. |
| LOGON_DENIED | Raised when the database denies an attempt to log on, for instance because of an invalid username or password. |
| NO_DATA_FOUND | Raised if a single row select statement returns no rows. |
| PROGRAM_ERROR | Raised if a PL/SQL internal error is detected. |
| STORAGE_ERROR | Raised if PL/SQL memory management fails, for instance because of insufficient memory. |
| TIMEOUT_ON_RESOURCE | Raised if Oracle is attempting to connect to a resource and times out; usually because an instance has crashed. |
| TOO_MANY_ROWS | Raised if a select statement returns more than one row. |
| VALUE_ERROR | Raised if an error is detected in string or arithmetic processing, in datatype conversions or in constraint checks while processing pure PL/SQL statements. Note that similar errors occurring when processing SQL statements embedded in the PL/SQL code will result in INVALID_NUMBER being raised. |
| ZERO_DIVIDE | Raised if an attempt is made to divide by zero. |

system exception handlers in the exception section. For example:

```
DECLARE
    -- variable declarations
    over_limit EXCEPTION;
    -- ...
BEGIN
    -- ...
    IF v_rental_cost+v_balance > v_limit THEN
```

```
            RAISE over_limit;
        ELSE
            -- ...
        END IF;
        -- ...
    EXCEPTION
        WHEN over_limit THEN
            INSERT INTO booking_log
                VALUES(v_cust_no,
                        v_date_rent_start,
                        'Refused: over limit');
            COMMIT;
        WHEN OTHERS THEN
            -- ...
    END;
```

The example shows a user-defined exception being raised explicitly. System exceptions can also be raised explicitly and the handling of user-defined and system exceptions can be combined. For example:

```
DECLARE
    -- Variables, etc.
    over_limit EXCEPTION;
BEGIN
    -- ...
    IF v_status NOT IN('A','H','S','X') THEN
        RAISE INVALID_NUMBER;
    ELSE
        -- ...
    END IF;
    -- ...
EXCEPTION
    WHEN over_limit OR INVALID_NUMBER THEN
        -- deal with exceptions
    -- ...
END;
```

### 5.5.3 Error propagation

Not every block will have exception handlers for every condition. If there is no appropriate handler in the current block and an exception is raised, either by the system or explicitly, then the block is terminated and its enclosing block is searched for the appropriate handler. This process is repeated until the appropriate handler is found or until there are no more enclosing blocks to search. When the exception has been dealt with, control is passed to the block enclosing the one which contained the handler.

In this way, you can set up the exception handlers so that some exceptions will be dealt with locally and others in the different levels of the enclosing blocks. It is good practice to make sure that the outermost block always has handlers for all possible conditions so that errors can never take you right out to the host environment without giving you the chance to fail soft. Normally, of course, in a well-debugged program, all exceptions would be handled in an inner block and never propagate out this far.

It may sometimes be necessary to do some local processing to deal with an exception and then to pass control to the same or another exception handler in a higher level block. To do this, an exception is re-raised from within an exception handler. The search for the appropriate handler is then started at the block which encloses the one re-raising the exception.

Similarly, the processing carried out by the exception handler may, itself, cause exceptions to be raised. The search for the handler to deal with these is also started in the block enclosing the one causing the second-level exception.

The identifiers used to name user-defined exceptions have the same scoping rules as other identifiers: they are local to the block in which they are defined and global to all enclosed blocks. The same name may be used for exceptions in different blocks. This is dangerous, but will work. You can see that the propagation rules will mean that the locally named exception handler will always be invoked first. One slight oddity here is that a user-defined exception may propagate out beyond its scope if not handled in the block in which it is raised. Only an OTHERS handler can then catch it.

## Summary: Unexpected events

☐ Exception conditions are dealt with by *exception handlers* within the procedure of a block. Each handler deals with one or more named exception conditions. There are a number of pre-defined system exception conditions and you can also define your own.

☐ For system exceptions, control passes automatically to the handler when the condition is detected. User-defined exceptions are RAISEd explicitly. System exceptions may also be raised explicitly.

☐ If there is no corresponding handler in the block in which an exception is detected, enclosing blocks are searched for the handler. The error propagates outwards until a handler is found. This allows you to structure the way exceptions are handled.

☐ After executing the exception handler, the block is exited and control passes to its enclosing block.

---

**EXERCISE 5.4**

1. You need to extract details of the average duration and cost of bookings for each car. These are written to an existing table called averages which has four columns: registration, model_name, ave_period and ave_amount. Write a PL/SQL program to analyse the bookings and cars tables to do this. Some cars will be new and will not have had any bookings yet; use an exception handler to set both averages to zero in this case.

---

## 5.6 Transaction control

There are many circumstances in application systems where several steps must all happen without interruption to achieve a valid outcome. For instance, when making a booking for a car, the cars table must be updated to allocate the car and the bookings table must be updated to record the booking. Either one without the other leaves the database in the inconsistent state of an allocated car without a booking or a booking without a car to fulfil it. So either both actions must be carried out or neither of them.

A unit of work like this is a *transaction*. Exactly what constitutes a transaction depends on the application. The COMMIT, ROLLBACK and SAVEPOINT statements are used to control a transaction and to make sure that it is either completed or, if an irretrievable circumstance is encountered in mid-transaction, it is undone to leave the database as it was before the transaction was started.

### 5.6.1 COMMIT and ROLLBACK

Until a COMMIT statement is issued, none of the changes to the database since the last COMMIT statement have been permanently applied to the database. Any such changes are seen only by the application (or user) who made them; other applications (or users) see the database as it was. When the COMMIT is issued, the changes are made permanent and the database rolls forward to its new, consistent state.

The ROLLBACK statement does the opposite. It wipes clean the effect of unCOMMITed changes as seen by the user who made the changes and returns the database to its original state. This could be used, for instance, to allow you to try to process failed transactions again or to log the circumstances of the failure. For obvious reasons, ROLLBACK statements are often found in exception handlers.

### 5.6.2 Savepoints

Unless qualified, the ROLLBACK statement restores the database to the state it was in after the last COMMIT. It is possible to specify intermediate points in the progress of the transaction to which you can roll back if necessary. This is achieved with the ROLLBACK TO statement.

Suppose a customer comes in and says that from now on she wants to pay on account and that she also wants to book a car for a certain date. Though there are other ways of achieving the same effect, the following code provides an example which will update the payment method even if a partial rollback is needed because no car is available.

```
DECLARE
    -- various declarations
BEGIN
    -- ...
    -- Update customer records
    UPDATE customers SET pay_method='C' WHERE ...
    -- ...
    BEGIN
        SAVEPOINT start_booking;
        OPEN available_cars;
        FOR v_counter IN 1..10 LOOP
                -- show 1st 10 cars
            FETCH available_cars INTO
                    v_registration, v_model name;
            EXIT WHEN available cars%NOTFOUND;
        -- ...
        END LOOP;
        -- ...
        UPDATE cars SET ...
        UPDATE bookings SET ...
        -- ...
    EXCEPTION
        WHEN NO_DATA_FOUND OR cancel_booking THEN
        ROLLBACK TO start_booking
        -- ... Other exception processing
    END;
    -- ... Other processing in outer block
    COMMIT -- Commit customer and booking changes
EXCEPTION -- Outer block exception handlers
    WHEN NO_DATA_FOUND THEN
    -- ... Deal with missing customer record
END;
```

It is important to realize that savepoints are not like labelled statements. The flow of execution of PL/SQL statements is not changed by a ROLLBACK or

ROLLBACK TO statement. Execution continues along its original path; it is just the content of the database which is changed.

If there are several intermediate savepoints and the transaction is rolled back to one of them, all the subsequent savepoints are erased. The one to which the rollback was taken and any before it are still retained.

## Summary: Transaction control

☐ Changes to the database are only temporary and only seen by the user who makes the changes until they are COMMITed.

☐ It is often necessary to ensure that several changes to the database are either all completed or none of them are. This unit of work is a transaction. Any errors or exceptions in the middle of processing must not leave the database in an intermediate state.

☐ This is achieved by committing the changes only at the end of the transaction and by rolling back the database if exceptions or errors occur.

☐ Savepoints can be marked and a partial rollback done to reinstate the database as it was when last at the savepoint.

☐ A rollback clears all savepoints more recent than the one to which the rollback is taken.

# Part 3

*Interactive applications*

# Six

# SQL*Forms applications generator

Any application system has components of three main types. There are interactive, screen-based programs which usually form the major part of the system; reports to extract data (which are non-interactive except for specifying a few parameters); and, finally, there are batch jobs used to tidy up old data, to carry out system administration tasks and so on. SQL*Forms is the main Oracle development tool to produce interactive, screen-based programs. It is often used in conjunction with SQL*Menu. Reports and batch jobs are covered by SQL*ReportWriter, SQL*Report and SQL*Plus.

## 6.1   Introduction to SQL*Forms

SQL*Forms is going through a period of rapid change. Version 2.3, which is still widely used, has recently been superseded by version 3.0. Oracle are talking about version 4 and even version 5. Version 3 is significantly different from version 2 and version 4 is expected to be significantly different again. One can only speculate about what version 5 will look like.

In this Part of the book we cover versions 2.3 and 3.0, with the emphasis on version 3. The differences between the two versions centre around the user interface and the way in which forms are built. The concepts behind both versions are the same. The two versions of SQL*Forms also work with different versions of SQL*Menu. Version 5 of SQL*Menu is closely integrated with version 3 of SQL*Forms. Version 2 of SQL*Forms works with earlier versions of SQL*Menu and there is not such a close integration of their facilities.

### 6.1.1 Concepts

SQL*Forms is an **applications generator**. There is no universally accepted definition of exactly what that term means; you will see as this section unfolds. The important things are that, firstly, it is not a traditional 4GL in that, for the most part, you do not write statements to tell it what you want to do. Instead you select options from menus to specify the details. Secondly, it is default-driven, in that it

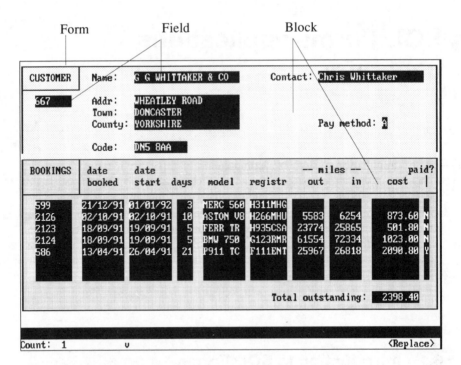

**Figure 6.1** Components of a form.

has all the logic built in to produce working applications of a range of types, and you specify how your particular application differs from its default model.

Programmers familiar with procedural languages or development environments often have trouble shaking off their old habits and getting the most from SQL\*Forms. It is important to understand some of the special Oracle terminology associated with forms-based applications (Figure 6.1):

- **Form**: A form is a structure of screen layouts and associated logic and processing. It allows a user to interrogate an Oracle database and to insert and update the data in the database. A form can consist of many pages (or screens). In the context of the way in which real applications are built, a form is analogous to a program module. It is the smallest unit that does something useful and forms are usually strung together in a hierarchical structure in the same way as program modules.

- **Page**: An element of the form which usually corresponds to a screen and which contains one or more blocks. In version 3, pages can be defined as being 'pop-up', overlaying part of the previously displayed page.

- **Block**: A block usually corresponds to an area of a screen. The fields in a block all relate to columns in a single database table or view.

- **Field**: A field is an area on the screen that can display a value. The value is usually one derived from a column in a database table but can be used to hold a non-database value, for instance a total.

- **Trigger**: A trigger is a collection of statements which are executed (triggered) when an event takes place. The event can be the operator initiating a query, updating a field or even just moving the cursor from one field to another. Triggers have a defined *scope* and can operate over the whole form, over a block or just for a field. Triggers usually represent the biggest proportion of development effort for a form. The way in which they are specified differs between version 2 and version 3.

### 6.1.2  Use of function keys

Oracle works on a wide range of hardware with different types of terminals and keyboard layouts. As a consequence, the mapping of the physical key or key sequence to the function it carries out varies depending on the type of terminal in use. To start with, you will find that it takes quite a time to learn the keys. If you regularly use different types of hardware, you will find that it is a constant annoyance; you never seem to know which key does what. To make matters worse, the mapping is different between version 2 and 3 for the same hardware. After a while, however, you will get used to it and find that it does provide a powerful and concise way of driving the system. The important thing is to know which key shows you what all the keys do.

Therefore, throughout this section, keys are not referred to by the label on the key but by the function carried out. For instance, [*Show Function Keys*] is the key which displays a mapping of functions to keys. On many terminals PFK8 is the physical key which achieves this. SQL\*Forms also has a very useful facility to redefine the effect of the function keys whilst running a form, and this can be used to provide a consistent set of key actions, even if a form is to be run on several different types of hardware.

SQL\*Forms makes extensive use of nested levels of menus. To select an option on a menu, position the cursor anywhere within the option using the [*Next Field*], [*Previous Field*] and cursor keys and then press the [*Select*] key. To leave a menu, having made a selection, and return to a previous menu, press the [*Accept*] key. Press the [*Exit/Cancel*] key to discard a selection and return to the previous menu.

Version 2 is rather rigorous in the way it uses the return key, assigning a fixed meaning to it, [*Next field*], whatever the context. Version 3 is more intuitive and the return key usually means what you expect it to: [*Select*], [*Accept*], [*Next field*] or [*Next line*], depending on the context.

## 6.2   SQL*Forms basics

### 6.2.1   Components

The whole package of software known as SQL*Forms is made up of a number of components (Figure 6.2). The breakdown is the same for versions 2 and 3 but the terminology is slightly different.

- SQL*Forms (**Design**) was previously known as the Interactive Applications Designer (IAD). It creates and modifies form definitions stored in the database. It also provides the framework from which the other components can be invoked.

- SQL*Forms (**Convert**) was previously known as the Interactive Applications Converter (IAC). It converts the format of the form definition from the database format to a text file format and vice versa. This allows forms to be moved from one Oracle database to another.

- SQL*Forms (**Generate**) was previously known as the Interactive Applica-

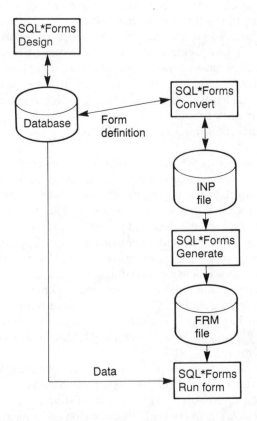

**Figure 6.2**   SQL*Forms components.

tions Generator (IAG). This generates a runtime version of the form in a file with .INP filetype.

- SQL*Forms (**Run Form**) was previously known as the Interactive Applications Processor (IAP) or RUNFORM. This component reads and executes the form .INP file compiled by SQL*Forms (Generate).

SQL*Forms (Design) is the main component which is used to design, build and test forms. The other components are usually invoked from within it, except when running a production version of a form when RUNFORM would be run separately.

### 6.2.2 Loading SQL*Forms

From the operating system command line type SQLFORMS (or sqlforms if, like Unix, the operating system command processor is case-sensitive). SQL*Forms displays an identification screen asking for the user's username and password. In SQL*Forms version 2 you must press [*Accept*] after filling in the username and password; version 3 interprets the return key as [*Accept*] in this context. The username and password can also be provided as part of the command line. For instance:

```
SQLFORMS mike/carborundum
```

To get out of SQL*Forms, version 3 has a *Quit* option on the *Action* submenu on the main menu bar. For version 2, press the [*Exit/Cancel*] or [*Accept*] key from the CHOOSE FORM window.

## 6.3 The next three chapters

The next chapters cover SQL*Forms (version 3, then version 2) and SQL*Menu version 5.

For most people, there will be little point in learning about both versions of SQL*Forms. Read one or other of the next two chapters, depending on which version is installed at your site. If in doubt, learn version 3.

SQL*Forms makes extensive use of pop-up menus and point-and-select. Very little of it is command driven. So, in order to explain how to use SQL*Forms and to navigate through the menus, the next chapters illustrate the product by working through an example application. There are diagrams to show what appears on the screen, but you will find that it is useful to have SQL*Forms running in front of you.

By the end of whichever chapter you choose, you should have a good understanding of the ideas behind SQL*Forms and of how it works. Work through the examples and exercises to build simple applications yourself and tailor and enhance them to create realistic systems.

## Summary: SQL*Forms overview

☐ SQL*Forms is Oracle's application generator for interactive, screen-based programs.

☐ There are two versions in use. They differ in important ways and are described in separate chapters.

☐ Both versions use menus and point-and-select, operating on default models, to define the characteristics of the program.

☐ Keyboard handling in SQL*Forms is not consistent across all the types of hardware on which it can run. The two versions also have different schemes. Keys are referred to by their function, not by their label.

☐ SQL*Forms is made up of a number of software components. During development of a form, they are usually invoked from the single umbrella environment. Finished forms are usually run separately.

# Seven

# SQL*Forms version 3

## 7.1 The user interface

### 7.1.1 The main menu bar

When you start up SQL*Forms, the main menu appears with the first option, *Action*, highlighted (Figure 7.1). At the bottom of the screen is a message line which is used to display messages from SQL*Forms to you, the form designer. At this point, it shows a short explanatory message corresponding to the option currently picked out on the menu bar. Beneath the message line is a status line which shows which form, which block, which field and which trigger you are currently working on. At this point, they are all blank. When you are using the screen painter, the status line also shows you the page number within the form and the coordinates of the cursor. Finally, there is an indicator to show whether you are in replace (overtype) or insert mode for keyboard entry.

Options on the menu bar can be selected by moving the cursor to the option

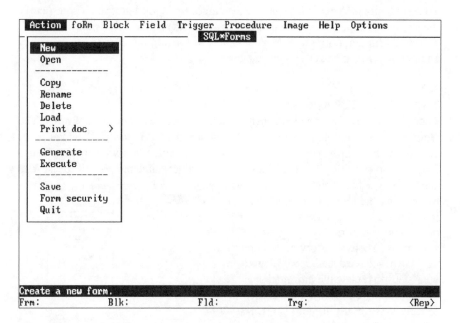

**Figure 7.1** The main menu bar and *Action* submenu.

and pressing [*Select*] or by typing a single letter for each option. This letter is usually the first letter of the option but is *R* for the *foRm* option. Not all the menu options are available at all times. When you first invoke SQL\*Forms and before you load or build a form, only *Action, Help* and *Options* are available. You cannot invoke the other options by either of the methods. Note that the explanatory text on the message line changes as you go from option to option.

Many of the options on the menu bar lead on to subsidiary menus. For instance, selecting *Action* drops down a menu for acting on forms – opening, generating, etc. Not all of the options are always available on these subsidiary menus, either. Available options are highlighted. To escape from a subsidiary menu and get back to the main menu bar, press [*Cancel/Escape*].

### 7.1.2  List of values

The [*List of values*] key can be used at many of the prompts to show you the alternatives from which the system expects you to pick. When the list is available, the right-hand end of the status line has a List indicator. To make a choice, move the cursor to the one you want and press [*Select*]. This closes the list of values window and inserts the value into the original prompt.

Occasionally there may be so many alternatives in the list that it is tedious to move the cursor to find the correct one. You can use a skeleton of the value or range of values you might want and let SQL\*Forms find the values for you. To do this, press [*Next field*] to move the cursor to the find prompt. Then specify the skeleton in the form of the leading character(s) of the value or by using the wildcards (underscore matches against any single character, per cent matches against any string of zero or more characters).

### 7.1.3  The HELP system

There is an extensive, context-sensitive help service built into SQL\*Forms. The *Help* option on the main menu has a subsidiary menu (Figure 7.2) which gives access to the help service, taking you in at an introductory screen (Figure 7.3). It also provides lists of values for form names, table names and so on. You can always get directly into the help service by pressing the [*Help*] key. This takes you in at the appropriate place to provide help on what you are currently trying to do. The system also keeps a history of the screens you have accessed and lets you retrace your steps to review the information.

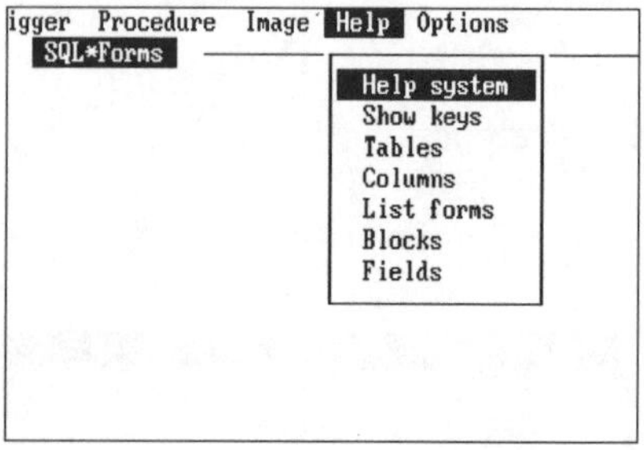

There is often more than a screenful of help text on any topic. Use [*Cursor up*] and [*Cursor down*] to move between the pages. The scroll bar on the

**Figure 7.2**  The *Help* submenu.

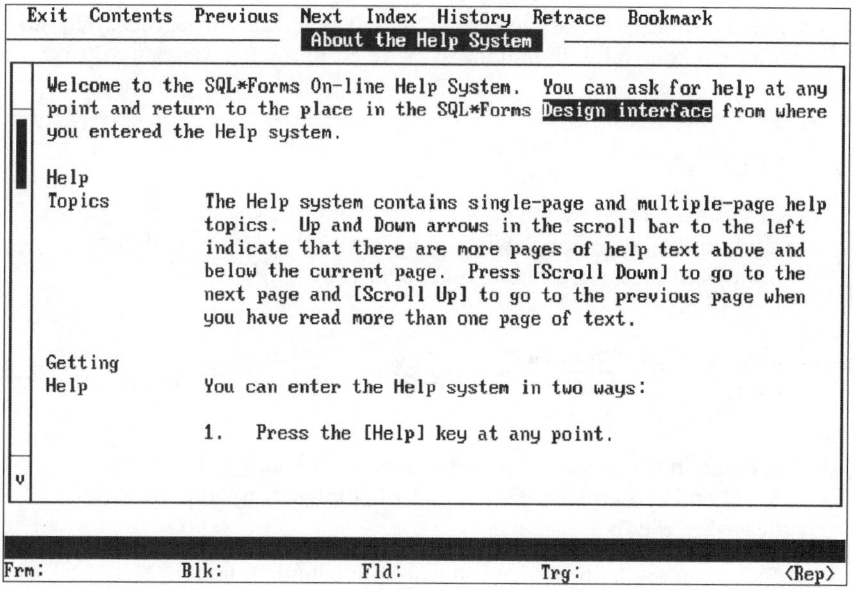

```
 Exit  Contents  Previous  Next  Index  History  Retrace  Bookmark
                          About the Help System
┌──┬──────────────────────────────────────────────────────────────────
│  │ Welcome to the SQL*Forms On-line Help System.  You can ask for help at any
│▌ │ point and return to the place in the SQL*Forms Design interface from where
│  │ you entered the Help system.
│  │
│  │ Help
│  │ Topics       The Help system contains single-page and multiple-page help
│  │              topics.  Up and Down arrows in the scroll bar to the left
│  │              indicate that there are more pages of help text above and
│  │              below the current page.  Press [Scroll Down] to go to the
│  │              next page and [Scroll Up] to go to the previous page when
│  │              you have read more than one page of text.
│  │
│  │ Getting
│  │ Help         You can enter the Help system in two ways:
│  │
│  │              1.   Press the [Help] key at any point.
│  │
│v │
├──┴──────────────────────────────────────────────────────────────────
│                                                                      ▓
├─────────┬─────────┬─────────┬─────────────────────┬─────────────────
│Frm:     │   Blk:  │   Fld:  │        Trg:         │             <Rep>
```

**Figure 7.3**   The *Help* introductory screen.

left shows where you are within the total amount of information for the topic. At the top of the screen, above the help information, there is a menu bar to let you navigate around the help service, to mark important places etc. Use the [*Menu*] key to get to this menu bar.

Certain words or phrases in the help text are highlighted. These are buttons to allow you to move on to related topics. Move the cursor to the button you want to activate by using [*Next field*] and [*Previous field*] and activate the button by pressing [*Select*].

## Summary: Forms 3 user interface

☐ Overall control of SQL*Forms V3 is with a menu bar at the top of the screen. The options on this bar lead to further menus.

☐ There are indicators at the bottom of the screen which show the name of the form components currently being handled, cursor coordinates and other status information.

☐ At many of the points where you are prompted for input there is available a list of possible values to be entered. The one you want can be selected off the list. An indicator shows at the bottom of the screen when such a list is available.

☐ There is a context-sensitive help system. Navigation through the help text is with a menu and with buttons to move on to related topics.

---

**EXERCISE 7.1**

1. Select the *Action* option on the main menu bar. Use the [*Help*] key to get into the help service with the cursor on the various different options in the *Action* menu. Notice how the help is context-sensitive.

2. Use the *Help* option on the main menu bar to display the intro-ductory page of the help service. Follow the buttons until you get to the index.

3. Use the index to get to the screen describing bookmarks. Read how to set and call up a bookmark. Set a bookmark on the page which describes the block menu.

4. Exit from the help service and call up the marked help page again.

---

## 7.2   Creating a default form

This section describes how to build a simple form to maintain the `cars` table. The object is to show how a basic form can be built very quickly by allowing SQL\*Forms to use its defaults. Most of the more complicated aspects of building a form are skipped over to be dealt with in subsequent chapters. Having generated the default form, it is then tailored to improve its screen layout.

### 7.2.1   Routes to the finished form

Building a complete working form of realistic complexity can involve quite a lot of detailed work. There are three routes to get to the finished form. You can cut much of the effort by getting SQL\*Forms to do the work for you by generating a default form. Such default forms have an extensive set of capabilities built in. They can query, update and so on. But they lack any of the specific functionality needed by an application and the detailed cosmetic features which make forms easier to use. Things like the positioning of items on the screen and captions are crude and there are no niceties like boxes around data.

Such forms are quite adequate for quick one-off jobs but serious applications will usually require a customized form. The second route is to use SQL\*Forms' screen painter to build the form from scratch. The process is intricate but not difficult and is certainly a lot quicker than traditional methods of program development.

The third way, which is probably the most commonly used, is a combination of the other two: first let SQL*Forms generate the default screen, then tailor it to your exact requirements. This is the route taken in this chapter.

### 7.2.2 Defining a new form

Select *New* on the *Action* menu. You are prompted for the name of the new form (Figure 7.4). Form names follow the usual naming rules: up to 30 characters, starting with an alphabetical character, and with only alphanumeric and underscore characters allowed. We will call this form `car_tab_maint`. The [*List of values*] key can be used to show which forms are already defined and, therefore, the names which may not be used.

Next, select the *foRm* option and *Modify* to get to the form definition screen. There are two items of information we need to specify on thij screen. First, we need to specify at what point data input will be validated when running the finished form. Use [*Next field*] to get to the `Validation Unit` and press [*List of values*]. Validation can be carried out when the whole form is processed, when the block has been entered etc.

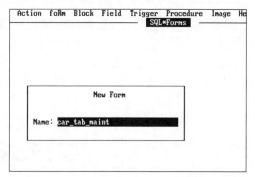

**Figure 7.4** The form name prompt.

Validation at field level (when each field has been entered) is the most commonly used and it is the one we want here. Select `Field`.

The second thing we need to put in here is a short description of the form. Use [*Next field*] to skip to the comment field. Enter a description such as that in Figure 7.5 and press [*Accept*].

### 7.2.3 Block definition

Select the *Block* menu and then the *Default* option. This will set up a default layout and definition of the block which will contain details from the `cars` table. Give the block a name as in Figure 7.6. The block is associated with the `cars` table; enter `cars` as the base table. All the rest of the default block screen can be left to SQL*Forms' defaults. Nothing more needs to be done to define the form; all that is left is to generate the form and execute it. Press [*Accept*].

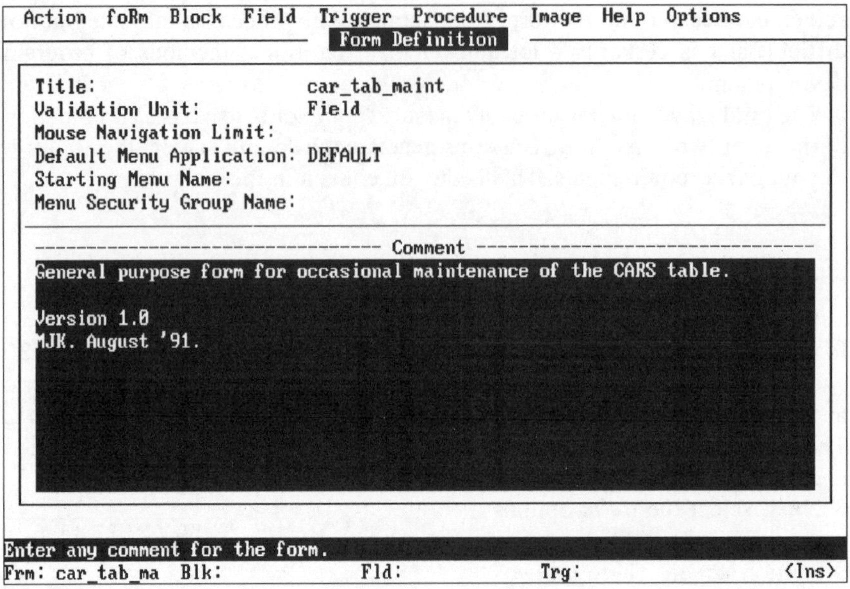

```
 Action  foRm  Block  Field  Trigger  Procedure  Image  Help  Options
 ─────────────────────────────── Form Definition ──────────────────────
   Title:               car_tab_maint
   Validation Unit:     Field
   Mouse Navigation Limit:
   Default Menu Application: DEFAULT
   Starting Menu Name:
   Menu Security Group Name:
 ───────────────────────────────── Comment ─────────────────────────────
   General purpose form for occasional maintenance of the CARS table.

   Version 1.0
   MJK. August '91.




 Enter any comment for the form.
 Frm: car_tab_ma  Blk:            Fld:             Trg:             <Ins>
```

**Figure 7.5** The form definition screen.

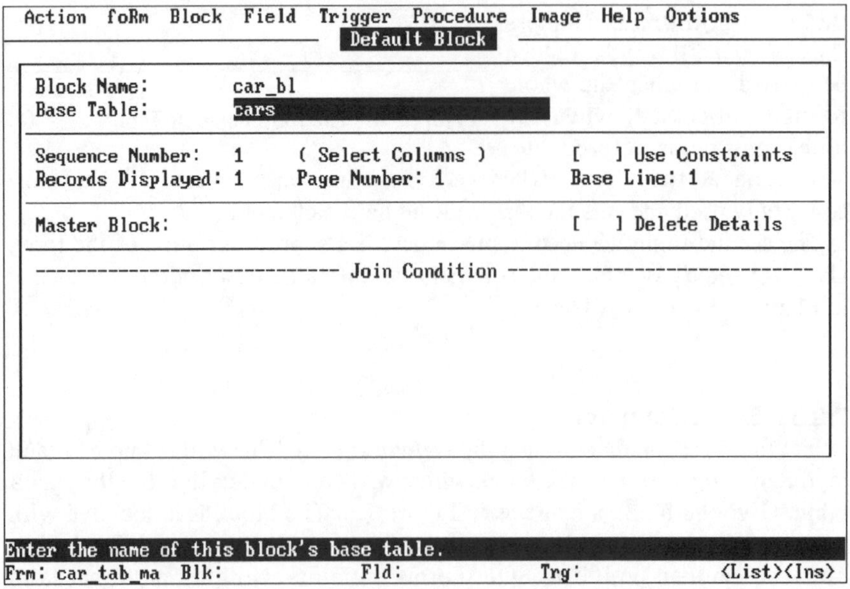

```
 Action  foRm  Block  Field  Trigger  Procedure  Image  Help  Options
 ─────────────────────────────── Default Block ────────────────────────
   Block Name:        car_bl
   Base Table:        cars

   Sequence Number:  1     ( Select Columns )      [   ] Use Constraints
   Records Displayed: 1     Page Number: 1          Base Line: 1

   Master Block:                                   [   ] Delete Details
 ───────────────────────────── Join Condition ──────────────────────────






 Enter the name of this block's base table.
 Frm: car_tab_ma  Blk:            Fld:             Trg:        <List><Ins>
```

**Figure 7.6** The default block form.

### 7.2.4 Generate and run

To generate the form select *Generate* on the *Action* menu (Figure 7.7). The form name has already been inserted (so has the name of the file to hold the generated form), but notice that the system may have to truncate the form name here in order to make a valid filename.

To run the form, select the *Ex-ecute* option on the *Action* menu and the generated form will be run. The form displays the details of each car in the table, one per screen. All the columns in the table are displayed and column names are used for captions. The layout is a bit basic, but it suffices.

A default form like this has all the logic to query, insert, update and delete rows built in. The run-time operation of a form is dealt with in a later section. For the mo-ment, though, retrieve all the rows in the table by executing a blank query. Leave all the fields on the form blank and press [*Execute query*]. Flip through the rows

**Figure 7.7**   The form generation prompt.

using [*Next record*] and [*Previous record*]. Press [*Exit/Cancel*] when finished.

As well as the rough layout, you will notice a couple of things about the way in which the data is displayed. Firstly, the rows are not presented in any obvious sequence and, secondly, the format of the cost field does not always have the two digits of pence. We will now tailor the form to fix all these points.

## 7.3   Tailoring the default form

Select *Image* and *Painter* to get into the screen painter. The system prompts for which page you want to see; there is only one page in this case. The screen layout generated by using the default block option is displayed (Figure 7.8). This layout looks just like the running form, but is not executable. It is ready to be redesigned by 'painting' the changes on to the screen.

### 7.3.1   Captions, boxes, moving fields

The captions used for the fields have been taken from the column names. They can easily be changed by just typing over the text. To draw a box, move the

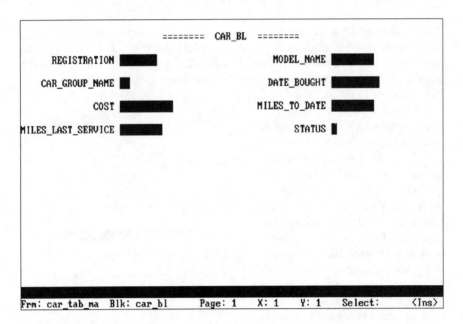

**Figure 7.8**   The generated default form.

cursor to one corner of where you want the box to be and press [*Select*]. Then move the cursor to the opposite corner and press [*Select*] again. Press [*Draw box/line*]. Horizontal and vertical lines are drawn in exactly the same way, selecting either end of the line. The point where a line joins another line is automatically given the correct T-shaped graphic. Because boxes and lines often get overwritten as you arrange the other elements of the form, always draw them last.

This process of selecting an item and then operating on it is how most of the screen painter's functions work. You will notice that the number of selections made is indicated on the status line, as are the coordinates of the cursor.

The default layout has all the data crammed at the top of the screen. Individual items or whole areas of the screen are moved by selecting them, cutting them out and pasting them back in the new position. To move a whole area, select opposite corners in the same way as to draw a box. For the sake of the example, suppose you selected the top left corner of the area first. Move the cursor to the place where you want the top left of the area to appear after the move. Press [*Cut*] and then [*Paste*]. You can move the cursor to the new position after cutting and before pasting, but it is usually much easier to get things into the right place if you move the cursor before cutting. If you were to select the bottom left corner of the area first, then you would put the cursor to the place where you want the bottom left corner to appear after the move, then cut and paste.

Words on the screen can be selected by putting the cursor anywhere within the word and pressing [*Select*]. They can then be cut and pasted, as before. Note that you must position the cursor to where you want the first letter of the word to go, even if you pressed [*Select*] on, say, the third letter of the word. Data fields are implicitly selected by putting the cursor within the field. There is no need to press [*Select*].

The form will be modified as part of the next set of exercises. When you have finished using the screen painter, press [*Accept*] to get back to the main menu.

## 7.3.2  Sequence of rows

When the default block was generated, there was no specification of the sequence in which the rows for the block were to be retrieved. The result is that they come out in what is effectively an indeterminate sequence. To specify the sequence, you need to write an ORDER BY clause for the block.

Select the *Block* option on the main menu and then *Modify*. This displays the block definitions 'spread table'. (See Figures 7.9 and 7.10.) The spread table has one line for each block of the form, though in this case there is only one block. It extends horizontally across several screens. Use [*Next field*] and [*Previous field*] to move across the spread table. There are scroll bars on the left and at the bottom to show where you are within the whole spread table. (There is more information on spread tables in the next section.)

The ORDER BY is specified in a small window on the far right screen of the block definition spread table. Enter ORDER BY model_name. The window scrolls as you enter the clause. Press [*Accept*] to get back to the main menu.

| Action   foRm   Block   Field   Trigger   Procedure   Image   Help   Options |
|---|
| Block Definition |

| Block Name | Base Table | Seq Num | Records Disp | Records Buff | Records Lines | A |
|---|---|---|---|---|---|---|
| car_bl | cars | 1 | 1 | | | |

Enter the name of the block.

Frm: CAR_TAB_MA   Blk: car_bl        Fld:              Trg:                    ⟨Rep⟩

**Figure 7.9**  Block definitions spread table.

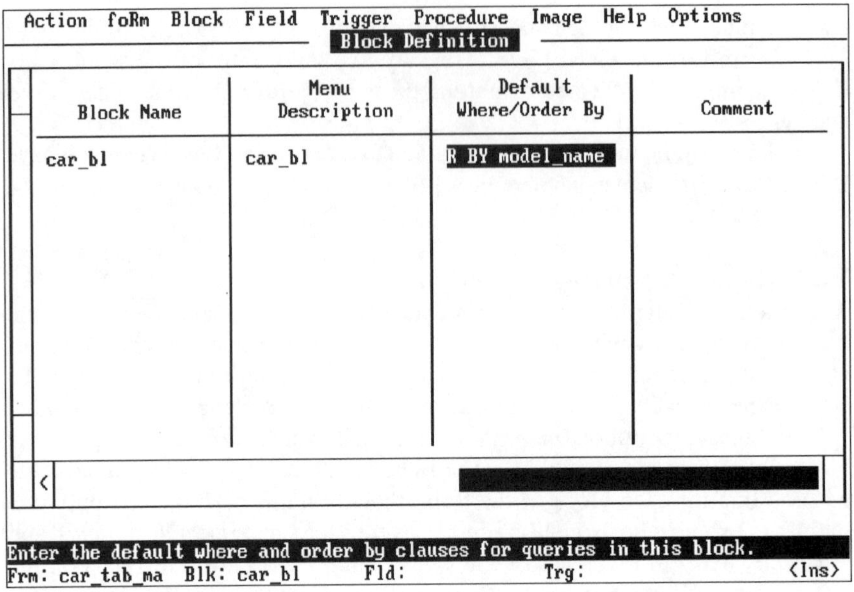

```
Action  foRm  Block  Field  Trigger  Procedure  Image  Help  Options
                            Block Definition
```

| Block Name | Menu Description | Default Where/Order By | Comment |
|---|---|---|---|
| car_bl | car_bl | R BY model_name | |

```
Enter the default where and order by clauses for queries in this block.
Frm: car_tab_ma  Blk: car_bl     Fld:          Trg:              <Ins>
```

**Figure 7.10**   The block default sequence.

### 7.3.3  Display formats

The display format of the cost field on the generated screen is taken from the column definition of NUMBER (8,2). This gives a left-justified display with a variable number of decimals, depending on the value of the cost. This is not the way to display a money value; what is needed is a right-justified display which always has two decimals. There are two ways of achieving this: either use one of SQL\*Forms' MONEY datatypes or specify a format mask. The datatypes are covered later; this time, use a format mask.

Select *Field* and *Modify*. This displays the field definitions spread table. (See Figures 7.11 and 7.12). All the fields in the block are listed vertically and the details of each field are spread horizontally. The scroll bar at the bottom of the table shows where you are horizontally among the screens. The display format mask definition is on the next screen to the right. Enter the format specification shown in Figure 7.12. Press [*Accept*] to get back to the main menu.

## 7.4   Navigating around the options

So far, the main menu has been used to get around between the various functions in SQL\*Forms; there are, however, short cuts. And we have used

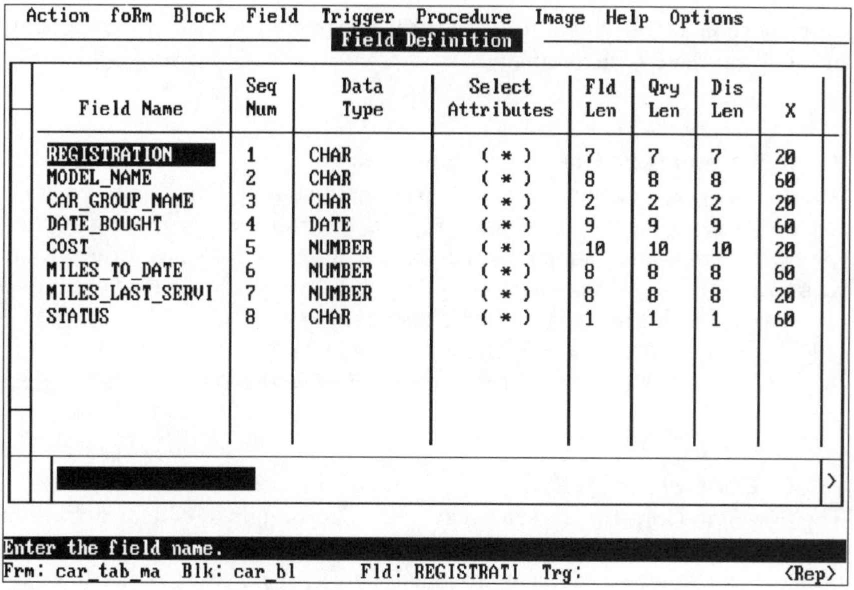

```
 Action  foRm  Block  Field  Trigger  Procedure  Image  Help  Options
├───────────────────────────┤ Field Definition ├───────────────────────────
```

| Field Name | Seq Num | Data Type | Select Attributes | Fld Len | Qry Len | Dis Len | X |
|---|---|---|---|---|---|---|---|
| REGISTRATION | 1 | CHAR | ( * ) | 7 | 7 | 7 | 20 |
| MODEL_NAME | 2 | CHAR | ( * ) | 8 | 8 | 8 | 60 |
| CAR_GROUP_NAME | 3 | CHAR | ( * ) | 2 | 2 | 2 | 20 |
| DATE_BOUGHT | 4 | DATE | ( * ) | 9 | 9 | 9 | 60 |
| COST | 5 | NUMBER | ( * ) | 10 | 10 | 10 | 20 |
| MILES_TO_DATE | 6 | NUMBER | ( * ) | 8 | 8 | 8 | 60 |
| MILES_LAST_SERVI | 7 | NUMBER | ( * ) | 8 | 8 | 8 | 20 |
| STATUS | 8 | CHAR | ( * ) | 1 | 1 | 1 | 60 |

```
Enter the field name.
Frm: car_tab_ma  Blk: car_b1      Fld: REGISTRATI  Trg:                <Rep>
```

**Figure 7.11** Fields spread table, left screen.

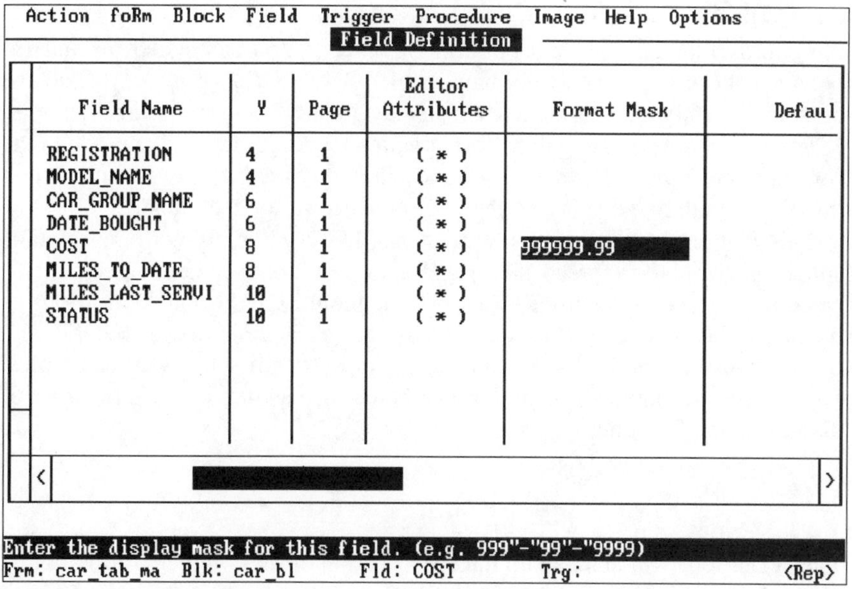

```
 Action  foRm  Block  Field  Trigger  Procedure  Image  Help  Options
├───────────────────────────┤ Field Definition ├───────────────────────────
```

| Field Name | Y | Page | Editor Attributes | Format Mask | Defaul |
|---|---|---|---|---|---|
| REGISTRATION | 4 | 1 | ( * ) | | |
| MODEL_NAME | 4 | 1 | ( * ) | | |
| CAR_GROUP_NAME | 6 | 1 | ( * ) | | |
| DATE_BOUGHT | 6 | 1 | ( * ) | | |
| COST | 8 | 1 | ( * ) | 999999.99 | |
| MILES_TO_DATE | 8 | 1 | ( * ) | | |
| MILES_LAST_SERVI | 10 | 1 | ( * ) | | |
| STATUS | 10 | 1 | ( * ) | | |

```
Enter the display mask for this field. (e.g. 999"-"99"-"9999)
Frm: car_tab_ma  Blk: car_b1      Fld: COST        Trg:                <Rep>
```

**Figure 7.12** Fields spread table, centre screen.

only the spread table layout for defining the characteristics of the components of the form; there is an alternative.

### 7.4.1   To and from the screen painter

You can always get into the screen painter (assuming that there is a form loaded) by using the *[Screen painter]* key. In doing so, there is often an implied *[Accept]*. For instance, suppose you have just defined the display format of the cost field and press *[Screen painter]*. The changes made to the field definition are accepted and the screen painter is displayed.

From the screen painter, you can get straight to a field definition by moving the cursor to the relevant field and pressing *[Define field]*.

### 7.4.2   General navigation

The *[Navigate]* key can be used at any time to go straight to edit the definition of any of the form objects. A pop-up window appears for you to enter the name of the object you want to deal with. (See Figure 7.13.) Lists of valid names are available with the *[List of values]* key. Fill in the names and press *[Accept]*; the corresponding definition screen is displayed.

### 7.4.3   Spread tables and forms

The spread table layout can be awkward to use when you want to specify all the details for just one item. An alternative layout is available which shows all the details for just one item on a single screen. You can switch to and fro between these two display formats using *[Change display type]*. Move the cursor vertically in a spread table display to the item you want and press *[Change display type]* to get the form display layout for that item. When in the form display layout, *[Next record]* and *[Previous record]* move you through the items available, displaying the full-screen form for each item.

This method of displaying several items, listed vertically with their details spread horizontally (spread table) and also providing separate screens dedicated to just one item (forms) is used throughout SQL\*Forms. Definitions of blocks, fields, triggers, procedures and pages all have both spread table and form layouts available. By default, SQL\*Forms will first show spread tables, but *Options* on the main menu bar can be used to switch to the form style of display as the first one shown.

### 7.4.4   Zoom

The definitions which make up the specification of the complete form are in a hierarchical structure. The form definition is at the top, then come block definitions, then field definitions (triggers also fit into this hierarchy, but are

```
┌────────────────────────────────────────────────────────────────────────┐
│ ▐Action▌ foRm  Block  Field  Trigger  Procedure  Image  Help  Options    │
│ ───────────────────────── ▐SQL*Forms▌ ─────────────────────────          │
│                                                                          │
│                                            ┌───────────────────────────┐ │
│                                            │          Field Name       │ │
│                                            │  Find:                    │ │
│   ┌────────────────────────────────┐       │  ┌──────────────────────┐ │ │
│   │          Edit Object           │       │  │▐REGISTRATION▌         │ │ │
│   │                                │       │  │ MODEL_NAME           │ │ │
│   │  Block:      car_bl            │       │  │ CAR_GROUP_NAME       │ │ │
│   │  Field:                        │       │  │ DATE_BOUGHT          │ │ │
│   │  Trigger:                      │       │  │ COST                 │ │ │
│   │  Procedure:                    │       │  │ MILES_TO_DATE        │ │ │
│   │  Page:                         │       │  │ MILES_LAST_SERVICED  │ │ │
│   │                                │       │  │ STATUS               │ │ │
│   └────────────────────────────────┘       │  │                      │ │ │
│                                            │  │                      │ │ │
│                                            └──┴──────────────────────┘ │ │
│ ───────────────────────────────────────────────────────────────────── │
│ Frm: car_tab_ma  Blk: car_bl      Fld: COST      Trg:        <List><Rep>│
└────────────────────────────────────────────────────────────────────────┘
```

**Figure 7.13** Navigate prompt with list of values.

dealt with in a later section). You can move from one level to another in this structure using [*Zoom in*] to go to more detailed levels and [*Zoom out*] to go the other way. For instance, if you have a block definition form displayed and press [*Zoom in*], you will get the field definition form for the first field of the block. Other fields in the same block can be then displayed using [*Next record*] and [*Previous record*]. Similarly, [*Zoom out*] would now take you back to the block definition form.

## Summary: Generating and tailoring a default form

☐ Forms can be built up entirely from scratch but they are more usually built by generating a default form and then modifying it.

☐ The default block option will produce a working form very quickly, but the cosmetic appearance of the form is not very good.

☐ The screen painter is used to rearrange the layout of the form. It moves elements of the form around using *cut* and *paste*. Boxes can be drawn.

☐ The block definition spread table is used to specify the details of the blocks in the form, including the default sequence in which rows are retrieved into the block by the generated form.

☐ The field definition spread table is used to specify the details of the fields in the form, including the display format of the fields.

□ Spread tables show details of all the form's components of a particular type. Another layout is available which shows the details of just one component in a single screenful.

□ SQL\*Forms provides several routes to navigate around the various options used to specify the form.

---

**EXERCISE 7.2**

1. Use the screen painter to modify the form just built so that it corresponds to Figure 7.14. The layout needs to be changed and boxes drawn. The format of the date bought field needs to be changed. Generate and test the form.

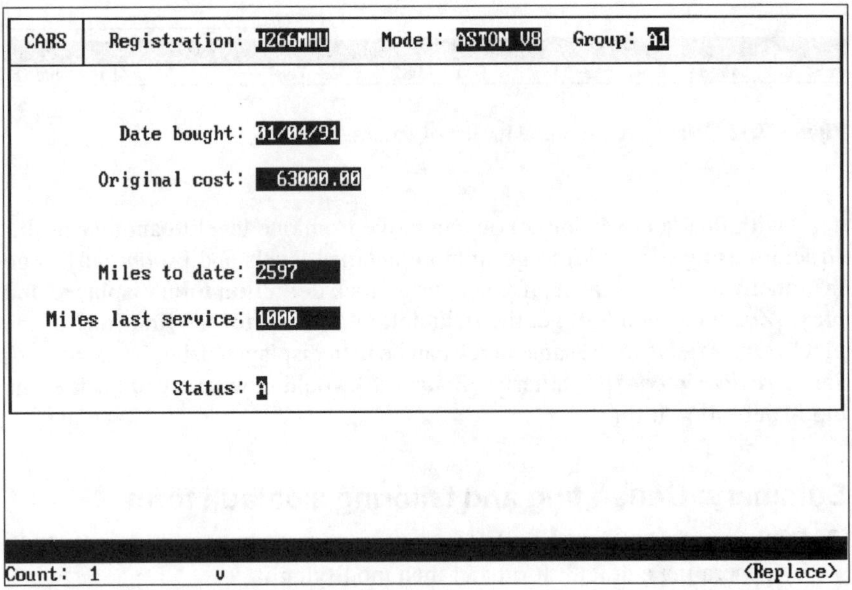

---

| CARS | Registration: H266MHU | Model: ASTON V8 | Group: A1 |

Date bought: 01/04/91

Original cost:   63000.00

Miles to date: 2597

Miles last service: 1000

Status: A

Count: 1         υ                                    ⟨Replace⟩

**Figure 7.14**  The tailored cars form.

## 7.5  A master–detail form

The techniques used to produce more complicated forms are just the same as the ones used in the previous section with a few extensions. The next worked example is a master–detail form, showing customers' details and the bookings they have made. The form will be built using the default options and

| CUSTOMER | Name: | G G WHITTAKER & CO | | | | Contact: | Chris Whittaker | |
|---|---|---|---|---|---|---|---|---|

```
 CUSTOMER    Name:   G G WHITTAKER & CO        Contact: Chris Whittaker

  567        Addr:   WHEATLEY ROAD
             Town:   DONCASTER
             County: YORKSHIRE                  Pay method: A

             Code:   DN5 8AA

 BOOKINGS    date    date                              -- miles --         paid?
             booked  start  days  model   registr    out    in     cost     |

  599       21/12/91 01/01/92   3  MERC 560 H311MHG
  2126      02/10/91 02/10/91  10  ASTON V8 H266MHU  5583   6254    873.60  N
  2123      18/09/91 19/09/91   5  FERR TR  H935CSA 23774  25865    501.80  N
  2124      18/09/91 19/09/91   5  BMW 750  G123RMR 61554  72334   1023.00  N
  586       13/04/91 26/04/91  21  P911 TC  F111ENT 25967  26818   2090.80  Y



                                              Total outstanding:   2398.40


 Count: 1         v                                              <Replace>
```

**Figure 7.15**    The finished example form.

then modifying the result to get the layout needed. In later sections, the form will be further developed to provide additional functionality.

### 7.5.1    Description of the form

This form has two blocks, one showing the details of a customer, the other showing the details of the bookings the customer has made in the past; see Figure 7.15. The blocks are synchronized so that they both deal with the same customer. The form deals with just one customer at a time in the customers block but can show several of the customer's bookings.

The form can be used to display and modify customer or booking details, to insert new bookings for existing customers or to insert new customers. The layout is quite carefully designed and the formats of the data fields are generally not the default formats used in the previous example.

### 7.5.2    The default blocks

Open a new form which will become the customer and bookings form. Give it an appropriate name; on the example screens it is called cust_bookings. Use the form definition screen to define the validation unit as FIELD and to write a short description of the form. (See Figure 7.16.)

Define a default block based on the customers table; call the block cust. Next, define another default block based on the bookings table; call it book.

```
 Action  foRm  Block  Field  Trigger  Procedure  Image  Help  Options
 ─────────────────────────── Form Definition ───────────────────────
  ┌─────────────────────────────────────────────────────────────────┐
  │ Title:                   cust_bookings                           │
  │ Validation Unit:         Field                                   │
  │ Mouse Navigation Limit:                                          │
  │ Default Menu Application: DEFAULT                                │
  │ Starting Menu Name:                                              │
  │ Menu Security Group Name:                                        │
  │                                                                  │
  │ ─────────────────────────── Comment ───────────────────────────│
  │ An example master/detail form showing details of each customer and the │
  │ bookings he may have made.                                       │
  │                                                                  │
  │ Version 1.0                                                      │
  │ MJK. Sept '91                                                    │
  │                                                                  │
  │                                                                  │
  │                                                                  │
  │                                                                  │
  │                                                                  │
  └─────────────────────────────────────────────────────────────────┘
 Enter any comment for the form.
 Frm: cust_booki  Blk:            Fld:            Trg:            <Rep>
```

**Figure 7.16**  Form definition: master–detail form.

This is a subsidiary block; the data shown in it depends on the data in the cust block. So define the master block and the join condition, which links the two blocks, as shown in Figure 7.17. If the foreign key constraints have been defined in the data dictionary (as they have in the example database), you can save yourself the trouble of writing the WHERE clause. Select the Use Constraints option and press [*List of values*] when in the Master Block field. This uses the foreign key relationships to display all the possible master blocks for this block. Select the one required (the customers block, in this case) and the join condition is automatically inserted for you.

Leave the rest of the default block definition for the moment. Although this block is going to have several rows displayed, the default block layout does not give enough room for more than one and the system will not allow more to be specified.

Get into the screen painter (via the main menu or via [*Screen painter*]) and rearrange the layout of the cust block. This is just a matter of selecting the fields in turn and moving them with [*Cut*] and [*Paste*]. Notice that there is no caption for the customer number or booking number on the final screen.

It is often useful first of all to move the default caption together with the field to its final position as a single block by selecting the left end of the caption and the right end of the field. Then correct the captions. This means that you do not lose track of which field is which. If you do lose track, just put the cursor on the field and press [*Define field*] and this displays all the field details, including the name.

```
Action  foRm  Block  Field  Trigger  Procedure   Image  Help  Options
                               Default Block

 Block Name:         book
 Base Table:         bookings

 Sequence Number:   2     ( Select Columns )        [   ] Use Constraints
 Records Displayed: 1     Page Number: 1            Base Line: 13

 Master Block:       cust                           [   ] Delete Details

 --------------------------- Join Condition ---------------------------
 cust.cust_no = book.cust_no




Enter join condition WHERE clause if block has a Master Block.
Frm: cust_booki  Blk: cust        Fld:            Trg:              <Rep>
```

**Figure 7.17**  The default block definition.

It is also a good idea to leave the drawing of boxes until you have finished manipulating the fields and captions. Boxes often go to the right edge of the screen and you cannot push anything off the right side of the screen; insert mode just stops working if you try. So, as you move the fields and captions around, you almost always have to mess up any boxes which are already there and then redraw them.

When you have finished rearranging the customer block (Figure 7.18), press [*Next block*] to move on to the bookings block.

### 7.5.3  Rearranging the bookings block

The bookings block currently has only one row displayed. Most of it is on page 1 of the form, but a couple of fields have been put on page 2. Use [*Next page*] and [*Previous page*] to see the pages. The whole lot is to be rearranged to fit on a single line. The block definition will then be changed to show several rows at a time.

A useful trick when laying out a line of fields like this, especially when the field length may need to be changed, is to arrange the captions first and then to fill in the size of the various fields beneath them: see Figure 7.19. Fields which are not required in the modified version of the form can be removed either by getting to the appropriate record in the field definition spread table and pressing [*Delete record*] or by using the screen painter to cut the field without later pasting it.

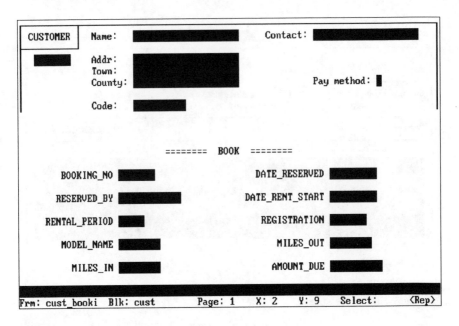

**Figure 7.18**   The rearranged customer block.

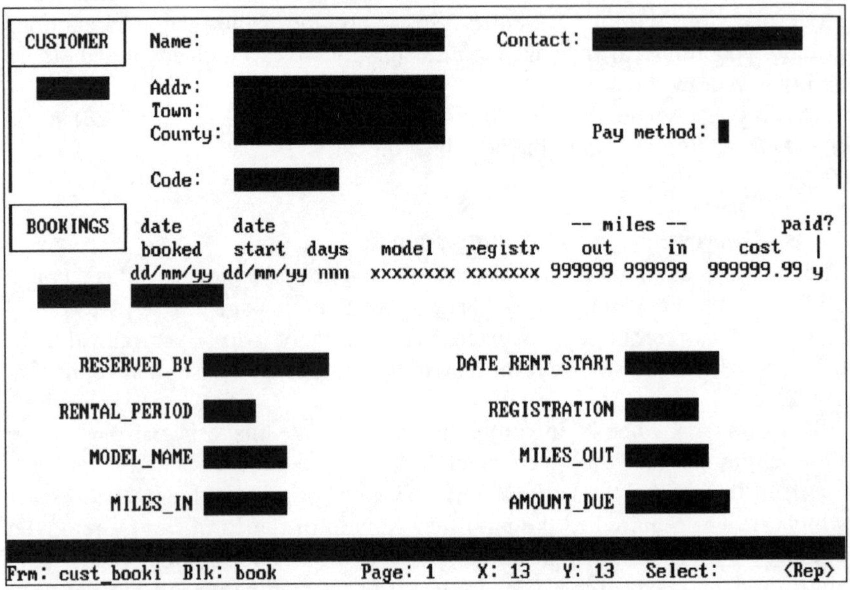

**Figure 7.19**   Dummy data to lay out the line.

Some of the field lengths need to be adjusted to fit the available space. For instance, the default date format of DD-Mon-YY is too long. Move the cursor to the date reserved field and press [*Define field*]. Change the field length, display length and query length to 8 and put in the format mask as shown in Figure 7.20.

By default, all the number fields will be left-justified and the cost (amount due) will not have a fixed two digits of pence. These will all need to be changed as well. Bring up the field definition screen for, for example, the cost field, move to the datatype prompt and get the list of values. There are a number of extra datatypes in SQL*Forms, in addition to the database datatypes, including MONEY, both left- and right- justified. (See Figure 7.21.) Pick RMONEY for the cost field and RINT (right-justified integer) for the other numeric fields. Adjust the lengths as well so that the fields will fit on the line.

The paid indicator is on page 2 of the form and can be moved into the line with the same cut and paste method. Note, though, that in this case you cannot position the cursor to the destination of the field before cutting. The field is de-selected when you move from page to page.

The other field on page 2 is the customer number. Because it is already displayed in the other block and because it is the subject of the join between the blocks, the default block definition has automatically put it at the end of all the other fields without a caption and defined it as not being displayed. It has not, however, minimized its size. Get into the field definition for the customer

```
 Action  foRm  Block  Field  Trigger  Procedure  Image  Help  Options
                             Field Definition

  Field Name:          DATE_RESERVED
  Sequence Number:     2     Data Type:     DATE      ( Select Attributes )
  Field Length:        8     Query Length: 8          Display Length: 8
  Screen Position: X: 13    Y: 13    Page: 1          ( Editor Attributes )
  Format Mask:         DD/MM/YY
  Default Value:
  Hint: Enter value for : DATE_RESERVED
  Valid Range: Low:                       High:
  Enforce Key:
  List of Values: Title:                            Pos: X:      Y:

  ---------------------- List of Values SQL Text ----------------------


  ---------------------------- Comment ----------------------------



 Enter the field name.
 Frm: CUST_BOOKI   Blk: book        Fld: DATE_RESER   Trg:              <Rep>
```

**Figure 7.20** Redefining the date format.

```
 Action  foRm  Block  Field  Trigger  Procedure  Image  Help  Options
                              Field Definition

   Field Name:            AMOUNT_
   Sequence Number:    9    Da       Data Type            ( Select Attributes )
   Field Length:       9    Qu                            Display Length: 9
   Screen Position: X: 68    Y:                           ( Editor Attributes )
   Format Mask:                     CHAR
   Default Value:                   NUMBER
   Hint: Enter value for  : AMO     RNUMBER
   Valid Range: Low:                DATE            gh:
   Enforce Key:                     JDATE
   List of Values: Title:           EDATE                     Pos: X:    Y:
                                     TIME
   --------------------- Li          ALPHA          t  ----------------------
                                     INT
                                     RINT
   _____         MONEY          _____
   --------------------------       RMONEY         ----------------------------
                                 v  DATETIME



 Frm: CUST_BOOKI  Blk: book         Fld: AMOUNT_DUE   Trg:        <List><Rep>
```

**Figure 7.21**  SQL*Forms' field datatypes.

```
 Action  foRm  Block  Field  Trigger  Procedure  Image  Help  Options
                              Field Definition

   Field Name:          CUST_NO
   Sequence Number:     11                               ( Select Attributes )
   Field Length:        1       [ X ] Base Table         Display Length: 1
   Screen Position: X: 79       [   ] Primary Key        ( Editor Attributes )
   Format Mask:                 [   ] Displayed
   Default Value:               [   ] Required
   Hint:                        [   ] Input Allowed
   Valid Range: Low:            [   ] Update Allowed    :
   Enforce Key:        cust.    [   ] Update if Null
   List of Values: Title:       [   ] Query Allowed          Pos: X:    Y:
                                [   ] Uppercase
   ---------------------        [   ] Echo Input         ----------------------
                                [   ] Fixed Length
   _____     [   ] Automatic Skip     _____
   ---------------------------  [   ] Automatic Hint     ----------------------------



 Is the field based on a column in the base table?
 Frm: CUST_BOOKI  Blk: book         Fld: CUST_NO   Trg:              <Rep>
```

**Figure 7.22**  Field attributes for customer number.

```
Action  foRm  Block  Field  Trigger  Procedure  Image  Help  Options
                          Block Definition

Block: book                      -- Records --    Array Size:
Table: bookings                  Displayed: 5     [  ] Prim Key
Sequence Number: 2               Buffered:        [ X ] In Menu
                                 Lines per: 1     [  ] Column Sec

Description: book

-------------------------- Default Where/Order By --------------------
ORDER BY date_rent_start DESC, booking_no



--------------------------------- Comment ----------------------------





Enter the default where and order by clauses for queries in this block.
Frm: CUST_BOOKI   Blk: book        Fld:           Trg:               <Ins>
```

**Figure 7.23**  Row sequence for bookings block.

number and move the cursor to *Select Attributes* (Figure 7.22); note that the field has not been marked as being displayed. Move on and set the display length to 1. Go back to the screen painter and move the field to column 79 of the bookings line. Delete the caption at the top of page 2. The customer number field still shows up in the screen painter as a one character field, but it will not show on the form when it is generated and run.

Get to the block definition screen for the bookings block and change the number of records to 5 and the lines per record to 1. Next define the sequence in which the rows will be returned by entering the ORDER BY clause in Figure 7.23. This is reverse chronological order. Move back to the customers block and bring up the block definition form. Enter an ORDER BY clause to display customers in ascending sequence of customer number.

### 7.5.4  Field sequence

When the original version of the block layout was generated with the default block option, the sequence in which the cursor would go through the fields in the generated form was set up to be the same as the sequence of the columns in the bookings table. Rearranging the physical position of the fields on the form does affect this sequence: every time you move a field, it is put last in the sequence. This does not generally result in the sequence you want and we now need to change it.

Get to the field definition spread table for the bookings block and change the sequence numbers. As you change a sequence number and move on to the next field in the table, the one you just resequenced is automatically moved to its new position on the spread table.

### 7.5.5   Field attributes

No special care has been taken so far to ensure that the characteristics of the fields are set up correctly. It is sensible, for instance, that the customer name and address should always be in upper case so that queries have a consistent format to work on. The key fields of customer number and booking number should not be updateable. Finally, it should not be possible to insert duplicate values for customer number and booking number.

Get to the field definition spread table for the customers block. Move the cursor to the attributes column for the customer number and press [*Select*]. This lists the available attributes. (See Figure 7.24.) The 'X' shows that the corresponding attribute has been selected for this field. Move the cursor to the relevant line and use the [*Select*] key to toggle the attribute on and off. SQL\*Forms has already defined some of the attributes; most of them are self-explanatory, but use the help service to explain any that are not. In this case (customer number) make sure that update is not allowed and that it is a primary key. For the customer name and address fields, make sure that uppercase is set.

Move on to the field definitions for the bookings block. Define booking number as a primary key and not updateable.

```
 Action  foRm  Block  Field  Trigger  Procedure  Image  Help  Options
 ─────────────────────────── Field Definition ──────────────────────

   Field Name:          CUST_NO
   Sequence Number:     11                              ( Select Attributes )
   Field Length:        5      [ X ] Base Table         Display Length: 1
   Screen Position: X: 79      [   ] Primary Key        ( Editor Attributes )
   Format Mask:                [   ] Displayed
   Default Value:              [ X ] Required
   Hint:                       [   ] Input Allowed
   Valid Range: Low:           [   ] Update Allowed    :
   Enforce Key:        cust.   [   ] Update if Null
   List of Values: Title:      [   ] Query Allowed         Pos: X:     Y:
                               [   ] Uppercase
   ─────────────────────────  [   ] Echo Input        ─────────────────────
                               [   ] Fixed Length
                               [   ] Automatic Skip
   ─────────────────────────  [   ] Automatic Hint    ─────────────────────



 Is the field based on a column in the base table?
 Frm: CUST_BOOKI  Blk: book          Fld: CUST_NO       Trg:          <Rep>
```

**Figure 7.24**   cust_no attributes, customers block.

You might be tempted to enforce unique values for the primary keys for a block by checking the primary key attribute on the field and also setting the primary key characteristic in the block definition. This does, indeed, work, but is inefficient and not recommended. It is much better to define a unique index on the primary key column and let the index enforce unique values.

### 7.5.6   List of values

You will have seen the list of values in operation as you have used SQL*Forms. The same facilities are available in the finished form. For the example, a list of values will be provided for the `model_name` field in the bookings block so that, when a new booking is being inserted, the operator may look at the possible values in order to select the relevant one.

Go to the field definition form for the model name. The list of values section in the lower part of the form defines the pop-up window which is used to display the values. Enter the title for the window and its position on the screen as shown in Figure 7.25.

The SQL text for the list of values is a SELECT statement which retrieves the values. In this case it should be

```
SELECT model_name, registration
INTO :book.model_name, :book.registration
```

```
Action  foRm  Block  Field  Trigger  Procedure  Image  Help  Options
┌──────────────────────── Field Definition ────────────────────────┐
│                                                                    │
│  Field Name:         MODEL_NAME                                    │
│  Sequence Number:   6     Data Type:   CHAR    ( Select Attributes )│
│  Field Length:      8     Query Length: 8      Display Length: 8   │
│  Screen Position: X: 36   Y: 13   Page: 1      ( Editor Attributes )│
│  Format Mask:                                                       │
│  Default Value:                                                     │
│  Hint: Enter value for : MODEL_NAME                                │
│  Valid Range: Low:                       High:                     │
│  Enforce Key:                                                      │
│  List of Values: Title: Models available are:     Pos: X: 50  Y: 8│
│                                                                    │
│  -------------------- List of Values SQL Text ------------------- │
│  FROM cars                                                         │
│  ORDER BY model_name                                              │
│                                                                    │
│  ------------------------ Comment ------------------------------- │
│                                                                    │
│                                                                    │
└────────────────────────────────────────────────────────────────┘
Enter the query criteria for the list of values.
Frm: CUST_BOOKI   Blk: book          Fld: MODEL_NAME   Trg:              <Ins>
```

**Figure 7.25**   List of values for car model.

```
FROM cars
ORDER BY model_name
```

The space on the form to enter this is only two lines deep, but it scrolls vertically.

## Summary: A master–detail form

☐ SQL*Forms version 3 can automatically generate master–detail forms, where the rows retrieved into one block (the detail block) of the form depend on the values in another block (the master block).

☐ The best route to get to a tailored master–detail form is usually to generate default blocks and then to use the screen painter to rearrange them.

☐ The detail block often has several rows, but the default block layout tends to waste space and you often cannot specify more than one row when generating a default block layout.

☐ Field formats can be specified with format masks. SQL*Forms also provides a range of field datatypes, in addition to the column datatypes of the database, with their own display formats. The money datatypes are particularly useful.

☐ Field attributes are specified to define how SQL*Forms handles a field. It can enforce unique values and upper case. It can define whether the operator is allowed to query or update the field, and so on.

☐ Lists of values can be associated with a field. The user of the form can then use the [*List of values*] key to have the list displayed.

---

**EXERCISE 7.3**

1. In the customers block of the example form, force the pay method field into upper case. Make sure that queries cannot be made on the customer contact field.

2. In the bookings block, make the rental start date display as DD/MM/YY. Force the registration and model name to upper case.

3. Increase the number of rows displayed in the bookings block to 7.

4. Ensure that the customers block displays rows in sequence of customer number.

5. Generate and run the form.

# 7.6   Forms runtime

The forms built in the previous sections all have quite an extensive default functionality as well as the specific features you have built in. You can query the data in several ways and you can update, insert and delete. To show how these work, generate and then run the form built in the previous sections.

Function keys are used to navigate around the form. The blocks of the form are given a sequence when they are defined and the cursor moves through the blocks of the generated form in that sequence. You can move from block to block with the [*Previous block*] and [*Next block*] keys. [*Next record*] and [*Previous record*] move from row to row in a multi-row block and [*Next field*] and [*Previous field*] move the cursor from field to field within a row.

## 7.6.1   Query

Retrieval criteria can be specified on any of the fields of the form. The simplest method is to specify a single value in one or more fields. Press [*Enter query*], move the cursor to the appropriate fields and type in the values to retrieve on. Press [*Execute query*] and all the matching rows are retrieved. [*Next record*] and [*Previous record*] take you through the retrieved rows.

For character fields, you can also match against a pattern of characters using wildcards. Press [*Enter query*], move to the appropriate field and type in the pattern to be matched against. A per cent sign in the pattern matches against any string of zero or more characters; an underscore matches against any single character. Thus a pattern specification of _W% in the postcode field would retrieve rows with postcodes starting SW, NW, etc.

As well as specifying equality, for numeric fields, you can specify minimum and maximum values by typing in greater-than, less-than, greater-than-or-equal-to, etc. and a value. You can also use equal-to and not-equal-to for both numeric and character fields. For character fields, though, the value must be quoted as a literal. For example, the query shown in Figure 7.26 selects customers with a customer number of less than 1000 and whose address is not in London.

Still more sophisticated queries can be built by specifying the retrieval criteria as a SQL clause. When entering the query, you enter a variable name, starting with a colon, in each field which you want to involve in the query. When you press [*Execute query*], you are prompted to enter a WHERE clause which defines the retrieval criteria. This clause uses the variable names you have entered in the fields rather than the column names in the database. The example in Figure 7.27 will pick out customers in the counties of Avon and Wiltshire (which might have been originally entered as WILTS or WILT-SHIRE.

Having specified a query like this, you may find that the results were not quite as you expected and you want to refine it. Pressing [*Enter query*] twice brings back the last query entered for you to modify and re-execute.

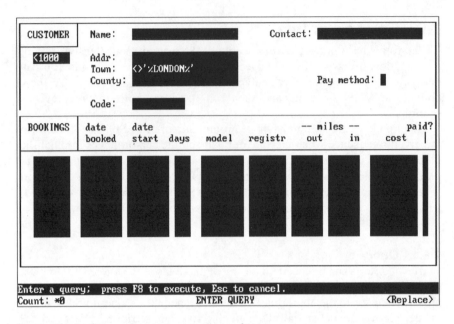

**Figure 7.26** Query of customer number and town.

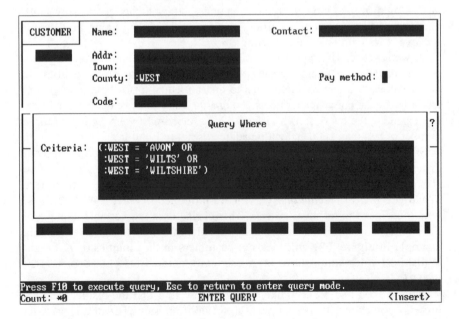

**Figure 7.27** The query specification window.

### 7.6.2   Modifying existing data

Having found the data you want to modify using a query, the data can be modified by just changing the values of the fields. Use [*Next block*] and [*Previous block*] to move between blocks and [*Next field*] and [*Previous field*] to get to the appropriate data, then type over or insert new values.

In the example, all the fields can be updated except customer number. Fields are marked as not available for update as one of the field attributes when the field is defined. An attempt to change a non-updateable field is immediately blocked.

Changes are not made permanent until you commit them. This may be done explicitly with the [*Commit*] key or it may be prompted by the system when you move on to carry out another function.

### 7.6.3   Inserting rows

To insert data, move to the requisite block and press [*Insert record*]. This clears a record ready for you to enter the data. Type in the values for the fields. If there is already a blank record in the block, as there often will be in multi-record blocks, you can enter the data in it without first pressing [*Insert record*]. The [*Help*] key brings up a line of help text on the message line. The default help available in the example is rather basic, but can be tailored on the field definition form. Fields can be defined with lists of values, accessed by the [*List of values*] key. The value for the field can then be picked from this list.

Note that if you make a mistake and want to abandon the insertion of the row, you must use [*Delete record*] to delete the partially inserted record rather than just [*Exit/cancel*].

Insertions are not permanent and need to be committed, just like updates.

### 7.6.4   Deleting rows

To delete a row, move to the appropriate block and record (if a multi-record block) and press [*Delete record*]. By default, the generated form will not allow the deletion of a master record for which subsidiary records exist. For instance in the example form, you cannot delete a customer for whom there are bookings records in the booking table. Deletions also need to be committed.

### 7.6.5   The default menu

Normally the operator of the form uses the various function keys to work the form. SQL*Forms also provides a default menu which allows the operator to use menu selections to carry out the functions, rather than keys. The default menu appears at the top of the screen when [*Menu*] is pressed. It has drop-down submenus which cover all the major functions.

## Summary: Forms runtime

☐ All forms generated by SQL*Forms have built-in functions to query, insert, update and delete rows in the database.

☐ The simplest form of query finds rows with values equal to those entered in the fields of the form.

☐ You can enter simple arithmetic and logical expressions in fields. This will find rows where the values in the corresponding columns satisfy the expressions.

☐ Complex queries can be specified in SQL.

☐ New rows are inserted by using [*Insert record*] to put in a blank record and then filling in the values.

☐ Rows are updated by just entering the new values.

☐ Rows are deleted with the [*Delete record*] key. By default, SQL*Forms will not let you delete a master record for which there are detail records.

☐ All changes must be committed before they become permanent.

---

**EXERCISE 7.4**

1. Execute the form and find the details of customer 1086. How many bookings has he made recently?

2. Enter a new booking record. What happens if you skip the booking number field? Why? Use the list of values to find out which cars can be booked.

3. Find a customer whose postcode starts with 'KT'. Delete this customer record. What happens? Why?

---

## 7.7  Triggers

Up to now, the example forms have had only fairly simple, generic functions: the sort of functions which are needed in every form. Much of the real power of SQL*Forms, though, comes from its ability to use SQL (and other) statements to control the behaviour of a form and to tailor it to specific applications. This is achieved with triggers. A word of caution on terminology, here: although the word has similar meanings whoever's products are being discussed, there are differences. In particular, some other database systems use the word trigger to mean a sequence of actions stored in the database and executed by the database itself when certain events occur (like when a database field is updated). In SQL*Forms, triggers are associated with the operation of the form, not the database.

In SQL*Forms, there are three types of trigger: key triggers, navigational triggers and transaction triggers. Key triggers are actioned when the operator presses the corresponding function key or when the processing of the form results in the same effect being automatically generated. Navigational triggers are actioned as the operator of the form moves the cursor around the form: when the cursor moves from one block to another, when the cursor enters a field etc. Transaction triggers are actioned when data is changed; inserting a record, changing the value of a field, committing changes to the database and many other events can all have triggers associated with them.

Each of these triggers has a standard name. The trigger processing is specified by writing the PL/SQL and SQL statements to be executed by the named trigger. A complete list of trigger types is given in Appendix C.

### 7.7.1   Trigger definition and scope
The same trigger can be defined at Form, Block and Field level. Field level triggers are the most common as they are particularly suitable for field level validation. A trigger has a defined scope within which it will operate. Field-level triggers have narrow scope and act only on the field for which they are defined. Block-level triggers act only within the block for which they are defined. Form-level triggers have widest scope and act for the whole form.

Triggers defined at a lower level take precedence over those defined at a higher level. So, for instance, a key trigger defined at field level will override the definition for the same trigger defined at block level just while that field is being processed. When the next field is being processed, the block level definition will operate again (assuming the trigger is not also redefined for the next field).

### 7.7.2   Trigger syntax
Version 3 of SQL*Forms allows you to define triggers using two different syntaxes. They can be written in the same way as for version 2, or they can be written using the full range of PL/SQL. Unless there are very compelling reasons to use the version 2 syntax, you are strongly recommended to stick to the version 3, PL/SQL, syntax, which is less clumsy and much more powerful. The version 2 syntax is described in the next chapter. This chapter deals exclusively with version 3 syntax.

Actions to be carried out in a trigger can be specified as a series of statements in the trigger or they can be defined as a global procedure and then invoked as a single statement. The latter is obviously useful where several triggers all have to carry out the same or similar functions. Procedures must be written with the full PL/SQL syntax, starting with a PROCEDURE statement and bracketed by BEGIN ... END;. PL/SQL as trigger steps can be written as *anonymous* blocks without the BEGIN ... END;.

The example built in the previous sections will be developed to illustrate the syntax. First, the form will be made easier to use when inserting new customers or bookings by providing the automatic generation of customer and booking numbers. Then a running total of unpaid bookings will be generated.

## 7.8  A simple key trigger

As developed so far, the form is quite adequate for general-purpose use, but its ergonomics could be improved. The system expects the operator to enter the ID number for a customer in order to retrieve the customer's details. This is all right for existing customers, but it means that the operator has to allocate and enter the number for a new customer. The system should do it for the operator.

To achieve this, the system needs to generate an unique serial number for each new customer. This example assumes that a *sequence* has been set up for this purpose, as described in Chapter 4. This sequence is used to generate the number whenever a new record is created in the customers block, i.e. when the operator presses [*Insert record*] or when SQL\*Forms creates a record of its own accord. What is needed is a key trigger associated with the [*Insert record*] key. This definition of the [*Insert record*] key should only apply for the customers block of the form, so it should be a block level trigger for the customers block.

Select the *Trigger* option on the main menu. This shows the spread table of all the triggers defined (Figure 7.28). The trigger needed in this case is KEY-CREREC. It already exists, having been set up by the default block option used earlier. This default trigger will be modified.

Move to the definition form for the trigger with [*Change display*]. The trigger is already correctly defined as a block-level trigger for the customers block (had a field name been entered, it would have been defined as a field-level trigger). The *Show keys* and *Descrip* fields of this form apply only if you wish the new version of the key's actions to be included in the display produced by pressing [*Show keys*], which is not relevant in this case.

The default trigger makes use of predefined procedures, clear_cust_ details and create_record, to carry out standard functions; what they do is obvious from their names. There is also a standard exception handler in the default trigger, but its action is null. The procedure create_cust_de- tails was created when the *Default block* option was used and is specific to this application. The procedure create_record is one of a range of stand- ard *packaged procedures* which are available in all forms. A list of them is

```
Action  foRm  Block  Field  Trigger  Procedure  Image  Help  Options
                              Trigger Definition
```

| Trigger Name | Block Name | Field Name | Trigger Style | Show Keys |
|---|---|---|---|---|
| KEY-CLRBLK | cust | | V3 | [ X ] |
| KEY-CLRREC | cust | | V3 | [ X ] |
| KEY-CREREC | cust | | V3 | [ X ] |
| KEY-DELREC | cust | | V3 | [ X ] |
| KEY-DOWN | cust | | V3 | [ X ] |
| KEY-ENTQRY | cust | | V3 | [ X ] |
| KEY-EXEQRY | cust | | V3 | [ X ] |
| KEY-NXTREC | cust | | V3 | [ X ] |
| KEY-NXTSET | cust | | V3 | [ X ] |
| KEY-PRVREC | cust | | V3 | [ X ] |
| KEY-SCRDOWN | cust | | V3 | [ X ] |
| KEY-SCRUP | cust | | V3 | [ X ] |
| KEY-UP | cust | | V3 | [ X ] |

```
Enter the name of the trigger.
Frm: CUST_BOOKI  Blk: cust      Fld:        Trg:          <List><Rep>
```

**Figure 7.28**   The trigger definition spread table.

given in Appendix C. Many of them mimic the effect of pressing the various control keys; the `next_field` procedure, for instance, has the same effect as the [*Next field*] key. It has been inserted to move the cursor on from the customer number field when its value has been generated. The most common use of the packaged procedures is, in fact, to control the navigation around the form.

Insert the trigger steps as shown in Figure 7.29. Then put the next value in the sequence in the customer number field and move the cursor on.

Press [*Accept*] when you have finished. The trigger is parsed and checked. If an error is found, an explanation is displayed in the comment field and the cursor is positioned in the trigger text field, ready for you to make corrections. You will find that not all possible errors are always detected at this stage. Sometimes they are also found when you generate the form or when you execute it. Generate and execute the form to check it out. Press [*Insert record*]. The new customer number is correctly inserted on the form. Note that this technique does not give a sequence of contiguous numbers; there may be gaps in the sequence. There may be apparent gaps where other users of the system have also allocated numbers from the sequence; there may also be real gaps where numbers have been allocated but not used because the record was never committed.

One of the exercises at the end of this section will be to set up a similar trigger for the bookings block.

```
 Action  foRm  Block  Field  Trigger  Procedure  Image  Help  Options
                             Trigger Definition
 ┌──────────────────────────────────────┬──────────────────────────────┐
 │ Trigger: KEY-CREREC                   │ ---- For Key Triggers Only ----│
 │ Block:   cust                         │ [ X ] Show Keys               │
 │ Field:                                │ Descrip:                      │
 │ Trigger Style:  V3                    │                               │
 ├──────────────────────── Trigger Text ─┴──────────────────────────────┤
 │ clear_cust_details(TRUE, ASK_COMMIT);                                 │
 │ create_record;                                                        │
 │ SELECT cust_seq.NEXTVAL INTO :cust.cust_no                            │
 │ FROM dual;                                                            │
 │ NEXT_FIELD;                                                           │
 │ exception when form_trigger_failure then null;                       │
 │                                                                       │
 ├──────────────────────────── Comment ──────────────────────────────────┤
 │                                                                       │
 │                                                                       │
 │                                                                       │
 └───────────────────────────────────────────────────────────────────────┘
 Enter the name of the trigger.
 Frm: CUST_BOOKI  Blk: cust        Fld:           Trg:         <List><Rep>
```

**Figure 7.29**   Row sequence for bookings block.

## 7.9   Keeping a running total

One of the most common requirements in a form is to keep a running total of one or more fields in a multi-record block. It is surprisingly difficult to achieve this while allowing for all the possible actions of the operator of the form. The next example extends the previously developed form by showing how to keep a running total of the amount outstanding on each customer's account.

### 7.9.1   The logic

It is easy enough to derive a total of the amount outstanding when the bookings rows are retrieved into the bookings block. The problem is to keep the total correct as the data is updated, inserted, deleted and so on. The steps needed are:

- Create a field on the form to hold the total. It should be part of the customers block. This is just a simple job with the screen painter.

- Get the total unpaid amount due from the bookings table when the bookings block is queried. This involves writing a *pre-query* trigger for the bookings block to select the total.

- Adjust the total if the `amount_due` field or the `paid` indicator of any of the displayed rows is updated. This is where it begins to get tricky. Whenever the amount due or the paid indicator are changed, it may be necessary to subtract the old value from the total and add in the new value. Whether it is necessary or not depends on whether the row is marked as having been paid or not. This implies saving the old value of the amount due before update.

- Adjust the total if the operator deletes a row. This involves decrementing the total.

- Re-calculate the total if the operator clears the bookings block or a row within it. If the block is cleared, then the total can be recalculated from the bookings table. If a row is cleared, the action needed depends on whether the row was a new one, just inserted, was an updated one or an unchanged row from the table.

This is not the only way to keep a running total, but, using this technique, the steps are roughly the same for any running total. This example is slightly more complicated than some because only unpaid amounts are added in to the total.

### 7.9.2 Definition of the field

First, a field must be defined to hold the total. Refer back to the illustration of the finished form in Figure 7.15 to see where it goes, at the bottom of the column of cost figures. Note that, although the field is geographically in the area of the screen occupied primarily by the bookings block, the field is part of the customers block. Use the screen painter to set up the field. The field's datatype is RMONEY and the field attributes should be set so that it is not a database field, just displayed (see Figure 7.30).

### 7.9.3 Procedures

There are a number of common procedures which need to be invoked at several different places. The same code could be written out in full in each place, but this gets tedious and it is quicker to use a procedure which can be invoked from anywhere in the form. In this case, the procedures are to calculate the total from the bookings table, to update the total when values are changed, to decrement the total when an item is deleted and to save the old value of the amount due.

Select *Procedure* on the main menu bar. The system displays a spread table of all the procedures currently defined (Figure 7.31). There are some already there; these have been automatically generated by SQL*Forms' default processing. Some of them use parameters, listed in the first line of the procedure.

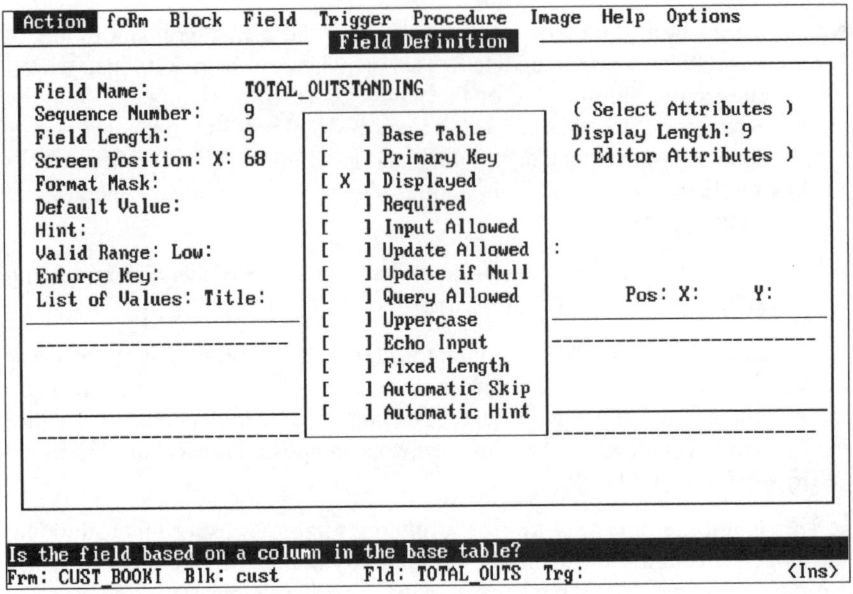

**Figure 7.30**   Total definition field form.

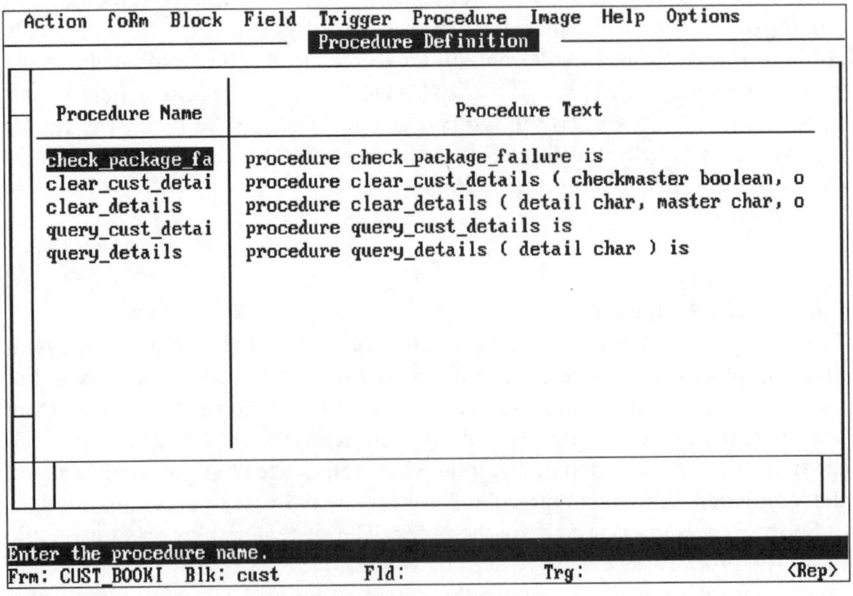

**Figure 7.31**   The procedure definition spread table.

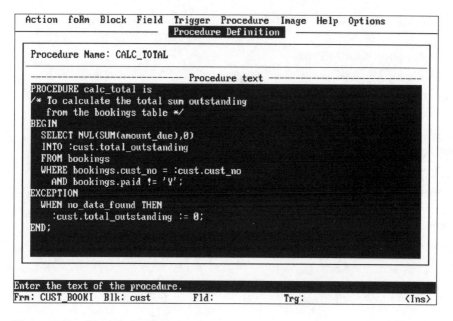

**Figure 7.32**   Procedure to calculate the total.

Press [*Insert record*] to create a new procedure and [*Change display*] to get a more convenient window to insert the text of the procedure. Procedures are always specified in the same format. The first line gives the procedure its name and specifies the parameters (if any). What follows is a normal PL/SQL program of one or more blocks, starting with BEGIN and finishing with END;. All the default-generated procedures are given names in lower case. It is a useful standard to specify the names of your own procedures in upper case so that they are instantly recognizable. First the procedure to calculate the total from the bookings table: enter the procedure shown in Figure 7.32. It is not a complicated procedure; notice the use of the NVL function to avoid the possibility of a null total and the exception handler to cope with the possibility of there not being any relevant rows in the table.

The update process for the total involves saving the old value of the amount due. This requires a global variable, available to all the procedures and triggers, into which to save it. Such a global variable is implicitly defined just by referencing it. Its name must start with :GLOBAL.. All global variables are character strings so it is necessary to convert datatypes when storing a numeric field. Figure 7.33 shows the procedure for saving the old value of the amount due.

The procedure to carry out the update of the total (Figure 7.34) will be invoked whenever the amount due field or the paid indicator is changed. Its basic function is to subtract the old value from the total and to add in the new value. The conditional statement is necessary to cope with the fact that the paid indicator may be changed as well as the value of the amount due. Notice, again,

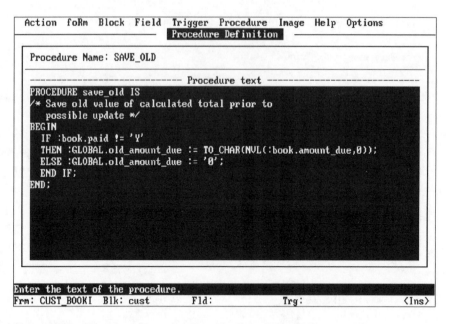

**Figure 7.33**   Procedure for saving the old value of the total.

```
 Action  foRm  Block  Field  Trigger  Procedure  Image  Help  Options
 ────────────────────────── Procedure Definition ─────────────────

   Procedure Name: UPDATE_TOTAL
   ─────────────────────────────────────────────────────────────────
   ─────────────────────────── Procedure text ──────────────────────
   PROCEDURE update_total IS
   /* Update the total with values from the form */
   BEGIN
     IF :book.paid != 'Y'
     THEN :cust.total_outstanding := :cust.total_outstanding
                                     + NVL(:book.amount_due,0)
                                     - TO_NUMBER(:GLOBAL.old_amount_due);
     ELSE :cust.total_outstanding := :cust.total_outstanding
                                     - TO_NUMBER(:GLOBAL.old_amount_due);
     END IF;
   END;



 Enter the text of the procedure.
 Frm: CUST_BOOKI  Blk: cust        Fld:          Trg:              <Ins>
```

**Figure 7.34**   Procedure to update the total.

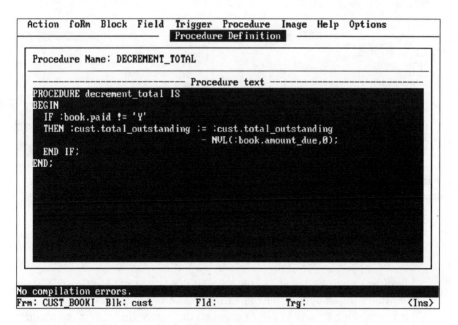

**Figure 7.35** Procedure to decrement the total.

that the old amount due has to be converted back to a number datatype. The final procedure is to decrement the total whenever a row is deleted (Figure 7.35).

### 7.9.4 Invoking the procedures

These procedures now have to be woven into the triggers to provide the total. The points of the form when the total needs maintenance are:

- When the bookings block is queried the total needs to be calculated from the bookings table. For this use a block-level PRE-QUERY trigger on the bookings block. This fires once just before SQL*Forms retrieves the data rows for the block. This trigger should invoke the procedure CALC_TOTAL (Figure 7.36).

**Figure 7.36** The pre-query trigger.

- When the cursor enters a booking record on the form, potentially for an update, the old value of the amount due should be saved. For this use a

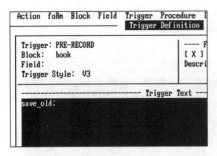

```
Action  foRm  Block  Field  Trigger  Procedure  I
                              Trigger Definition
  Trigger: PRE-RECORD                    ---- F
  Block:    book                         [ X ]
  Field:                                 Descri
  Trigger Style:  V3

  ----------------------------- Trigger Text ---
 save_old;
```

```
Action  foRm  Block  Field  Trigger  Procedure  I
                              Trigger Definition
  Trigger: PRE-FIELD                     ---- F
  Block:    book                         [ X ]
  Field:    AMOUNT_DUE                   Descri
  Trigger Style:  V3

  ----------------------------- Trigger Text ---
 save_old;
```

**Figure 7.37** The pre-record trigger.

**Figure 7.38** The pre-field trigger.

block-level PRE-RECORD trigger for the bookings block. This trigger should invoke the SAVE_OLD procedure (Figure 7.37).

- When the cursor enters either the amount due or the paid indicator fields, potentially for an update, the old value of the amount due should be saved. It is not enough to just do this once when the cursor first enters the record, because the field may be updated more than once without going out of the record. For this, use field-level PRE-FIELD triggers on the amount due and the paid indicator. This trigger fires whenever the cursor enters the field. The triggers should invoke the SAVE_OLD procedure (Figure 7.38).

- When either the amount due or the paid indicator is changed, the total should be adjusted to reflect the new value. To achieve this, use field-level ON-VALIDATE-FIELD triggers on the amount due and the paid indicator. This trigger fires when the field has been changed and the cursor has been moved on to another field. The triggers should invoke the UPDATE_TOTAL procedure (Figure 7.39).

```
Action  foRm  Block  Field  Trigger  Procedure  I
                              Trigger Definition
  Trigger: ON-VALIDATE-FIELD             ---- F
  Block:    book                         [ X ]
  Field:    AMOUNT_DUE                   Descri
  Trigger Style:  V3

  ----------------------------- Trigger Text ---
 update_total;
```

**Figure 7.39** The ON_VALIDATE_ FIELD trigger.

- When a booking record is deleted, the total should be decremented. Use a block-level KEY-DELREC trigger on the bookings block. This trigger redefines the action of the [*Delete record*] key. The trigger should invoke the DECREMENT_TOTAL procedure and then delete the record with the DELETE_RECORD packaged procedure (Figure 7.40).

- If the whole of the bookings block is cleared, the total should be re-calculated from the bookings table. For this, use a block-level ON-CLEAR-

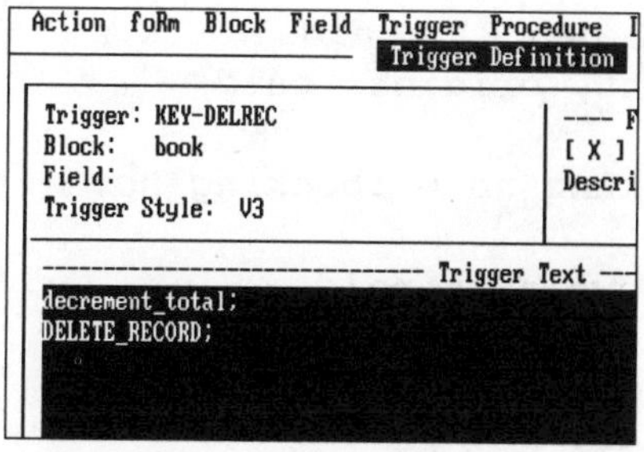

```
Action  foRm  Block  Field  Trigger  Procedure  I
                            Trigger Definition
  ------------------------------------------
  Trigger: KEY-DELREC                    ---- F
  Block:   book                          [ X ]
  Field:                                 Descri
  Trigger Style:  V3
  ------------------------------ Trigger Text ---
  decrement_total;
  DELETE_RECORD;
```

```
Action  foRm  Block  Field  Trigger  Procedure  I
                            Trigger Definition
  ------------------------------------------
  Trigger: ON-CLEAR-BLOCK                ---- F
  Block:   book                          [ X ]
  Field:                                 Descri
  Trigger Style:  V3
  ------------------------------ Trigger Text ---
  calc_total;            o
```

**Figure 7.40**   The KEY_DELREC
trigger.

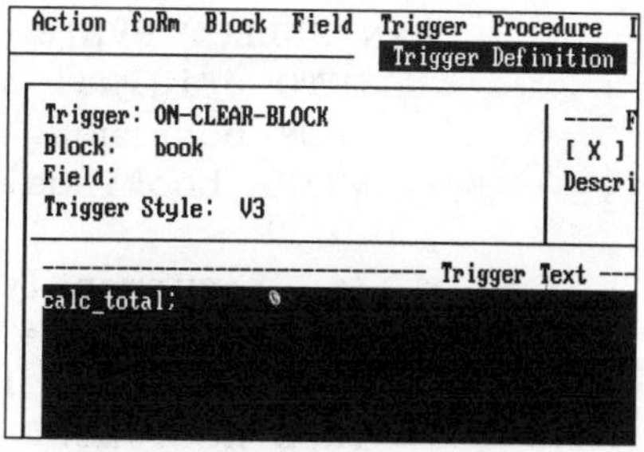

**Figure 7.41**   The
ON_CLEAR_BLOCK trigger.

BLOCK trigger on the bookings block. This trigger fires just before the block is flushed clear. It should invoke the CALC_TOTAL procedure (Figure 7.41).

## 7.9.5  Clear record trigger

These triggers deal with all the processing for the total bar one: what should be done when the operator clears a record? It could be a record that has just been updated and which may therefore have caused an adjustment to the total. It could be a new record which would also potentially have caused an adjustment of the total. Or it could be an unchanged record which would have contributed to the original total but would not have caused any adjustment of the total. Different actions are needed in each case.

SQL*Forms provides a system variable, :SYSTEM.RECORD_STATUS which allows you to determine whether a record is an insert or has been updated. This can be used so that, if the record has been updated, the original value can be retrieved from the table and the total adjusted by subtracting the current value and adding in the original value. If the record is an insert, it is only necessary to subtract the current value. If the record is unchanged, no action is necessary.

The program to achieve this is:

```
DECLARE
    /* Variables to hold original values from
       table */
    original_amount NUMBER;
    original_paid CHAR;

BEGIN
    /* Adjust total for changed records */
    IF :SYSTEM.RECORD_STATUS = 'CHANGED'
    /* Retrieve original value from table */
```

```
    THEN SELECT NVL(amount_due,0), paid
        INTO original_amount, original_paid
        FROM bookings
        WHERE bookings.booking_no = :booking_no;

        /* If currently shown as unpaid,
            decrement */
        IF :book.paid != 'Y'
        THEN decrement_total;
        END IF;

        /* If originally shown as unpaid,
            increment */
        IF original_paid != 'Y'
        THEN :cust.total_outstanding :=
                :cust.total_outstanding +
                original_amount;
        END IF;
    END IF;

    /* If an insert, decrement the total */
    IF :SYSTEM.RECORD_STATUS = 'INSERT'
    THEN decrement_total
    END IF;

    /* Clear the record whatever its status */
    CLEAR_RECORD;
END;
```

Enter this code as a block-level KEY–DELREC trigger. The record status is just one of a number of useful system variables which can be used in triggers. A list of them is in Appendix C. When you have entered all the procedures and triggers, the form should be able to keep the running total of the amount due. Generate and test the form.

## Summary: Triggers

☐ Triggers provide much of the flexibility and power of SQL\*Forms. They are elements of logic and processing which are invoked (triggered) when certain events occur during the running of a form.

☐ There are three principle types of trigger: *key triggers* which are actioned when the operator presses one of the function keys, *navigational triggers* which are actioned as the cursor moves around the running form, and *transactional triggers* which are actioned when field values are changed, inserted or deleted and when changes are committed.

☐ Triggers have a defined scope. They may be defined to operate throughout the form, over a block or just for a field. When a trigger is redefined at several levels, the lower level definition takes precedence.

☐ Triggers in version 3 of SQL*Forms are normally written in PL/SQL. For compatibility reasons, they can also be written in the style used by version 2 of SQL*Forms. This is clumsy in comparison and you are recommended to stick to the PL/SQL style.

☐ There are a number of standard actions which can be invoked in a trigger using *packaged procedures*. They deal with moving the cursor around the form, inserting and deleting records and so on.

☐ A set of actions needed in several triggers can be written as a form-level procedure and then invoked from the triggers.

☐ Variables declared in the PL/SQL of a trigger are local to that trigger. Global variables, available in any trigger or procedure can also be defined. They are always of character datatype.

☐ There are a number of system variables which can be accessed by the trigger code and which have useful information on the state of the form and its processing.

---

**EXERCISE 7.5**

1. Use a trigger to modify the form built up in the examples so that, if anything other than 'Y' is entered in the paid indicator, the field value becomes 'N'.

2. Use a trigger to modify the form so that a booking number is automatically generated for new bookings.

---

## 7.10  User exits

User exits are a way of integrating procedural code, written in a traditional third-generation programming language, into a SQL*Forms application. They were quite widely used with old versions of SQL*Forms which did not have available the procedural capabilities of PL/SQL. There is less need for them in version 3. The sorts of things you might need them for are check-digit or other complex validation, complex computations and so on where SQL and PL/SQL cannot do what you need or where they are excessively inefficient.

Sometimes user exits are written just to increase the performance of a form. They are called from any level and type of triggers. Any detailed treatment of user exits is really beyond the scope of this book. In outline, though, once you have written and compiled your code, it can be called from a trigger by using the packaged procedure USER EXIT. The procedure has two parameters: the user exit string containing the name of the user exit and any parameters to be passed to it and, second, an optional error message used if the user exit should fail. For example

```
USER EXIT validate 10 25 var1
```

calls the user procedure validate, passing as parameters the numbers 10 and 25 and the variable called var1. Parameters may be literals or variables.

## 7.11   Testing and debugging

SQL\*Forms has several features to help with testing and debugging forms. Firstly, a form can be executed from within the SQL\*Forms designer environment thereby avoiding the need to exit from the designer to do a separate run. This is the way all the examples and exercises have been done. This facility is useful to show up and correct simple errors very quickly.

If an Oracle error message is displayed on the status line, the [*Display error*] key will give more information by displaying the statement which caused the error and an indication as to its cause.

The next level of testing is provided by running the form in debug mode. This mode can be activated using *Options* on the main menu bar or by using the –d switch when invoking RUNFORM. Normally all run options selected from within SQL\*Forms remain in force only for the duration of that run of SQL\*Forms, but it is possible to set up a file of preferences which will be acted on whenever you log on to SQL\*Forms.

Debug mode provides two useful features. Firstly, every trigger is identified and explained as it fires, so you can see exactly which triggers are firing in what order and what is causing them to fire. Secondly, you can use the BREAK packaged procedure in triggers to stop normal processing to get diagnostic information. BREAK is ignored when not in debug mode.

It is possible to get SQL\*Forms to echo all the user's keystrokes to a file. This file can then be replayed to operate the system. This is useful for building reference tests for regression testing. It is also useful when you are worried that your base system may be likely to crash during a SQL\*Forms session. You could replay the keystrokes file to get back to the point where the crash occurred. This option is invoked by an option on the command line.

## 7.12   Multi-user considerations

When designing and building a form, it is necessary to take into account how it will behave when used by several users at the same time. This brief section considers COMMIT processing, table locking and runtime options that control how the form will work on a multi-user system.

### 7.12.1   COMMIT processing

When changes are made to the fields on a form or when records are inserted or deleted, the modifications only take place on the copy of the data held in memory. The database is not modified until the user presses the [*Commit*] key or until a trigger executes the COMMIT function.

The processing gone through when a COMMIT is actioned is:

```
For each block
    for each record
        for each field
            If field has been changed then
                validate field
For each block
    for each deleted record
        execute pre-delete trigger
        delete row from database
        execute post-delete trigger
    for each inserted record
        execute pre-insert trigger
        insert row in database
        execute post-insert trigger
        if record updated then
            execute pre-update trigger
            update row in database
            execute post-update trigger
COMMIT transaction
```

This sequence is followed for every block of the form each time a commit is requested. Should any of the operations fail, the commit for the whole form fails and the database remains unchanged. This strategy is rather drastic, but is the simplest to implement and control.

### 7.12.2   Locking

Before any changes can be applied to the database, SQL*Forms has to take out locks on the tables or rows it is going to update. This is to prevent several users trying to update the same rows at the same time and overwriting one another's changes. For the most part, SQL*Forms automatically handles the locking and you do not have to worry about its details. It is, however, important to understand the principles of how locking is handled so that you can design forms which fit with the way the locking is done and which, therefore, make efficient use of system resources in a multi-user environment.

First and most important, querying the data does not require any locks on the data. Oracle automatically makes sure that all users see the same version of the data even while other users are in the process of updating it. Locks are required, however, when data is updated; there are differences in the detail of the locking between those systems with the Transaction Processing Option and those without it:

- With the Transaction Processing Option: when a row is updated on the screen, a lock is taken on the row which prevents other users from updating it. They can still query that row and can query and update other rows in the same table. When the updates are committed, the lock remains just on the row and is released when the commit cycle has completed.

- Without the Transaction Processing Option: when a row is updated on the screen, a lock is taken out on the row, as before. Again, users can query the row and can query or update other rows in the same table. When the changes are committed, however, the lock is escalated to apply to the whole table. During the commit process, other users can continue to modify the rows on their form but their commits are queued up.

When several users are accessing and updating the same rows at the same time, they can change the values on the screen without having to worry about what other users are doing. When one user (*A*) commits, however, it is possible that the changes made by another user (*B*) have got in first and that the original values in the row, as seen by *A* when she first queried the data, have been changed. In this case, user *A* is warned of the change and is invited to re-query the data. Because he committed first, user *B* is unaware of user *A*'s involvement.

This locking process applies to the base tables of all the blocks in a form and is handled entirely automatically by SQL\*Forms. If you update other tables in trigger processing and you are using Oracle without the Transaction Processing Option, you should explicitly specify the type of locking to be used with the SQL LOCK TABLE statement in the trigger code:

```
LOCK TABLE tablename IN ROW SHARE MODE;
```

## 7.13   Portability

Oracle and SQL\*Forms run on many different types of hardware and version 3 of SQL\*Forms works on all three main classes of screen: bit-mapped screens, character screens and block-mode screens. Within each of these classes, the forms you generate are virtually device independent. You can design and build a form on one make of terminal and run it quite happily on another. In most cases, though, the form will need to be regenerated when you move it to new hardware.

If you know your form is to be portable across different styles of screen, you will need to design such portability in from the start.

### 7.13.1 Bit-mapped screens

There are a number of cosmetic differences in the way in which forms are designed and run on bit-mapped screens. Some of these are dependent on the windowing environment being used. None of them will surprise you if you are used to bit-mapped environments. There are drop-down menus, lists of values and pages defined as pop-ups are presented in separate windows and so on.

You do, however, have to think carefully about how the form will be used. On bit-mapped screens, the operator can use the mouse to navigate to any part of the screen in any sequence, unless you establish restrictions. This can have unexpected effects on the firing of triggers. The KEY-NXTFLD trigger, for instance, will not fire if you navigate directly from one field to another with the mouse. If you know that your form will be used on bit-mapped screens, you can avoid possible trouble by not using the navigational triggers. Also avoid pre- and post-field triggers and use on-new-field-instance and on-validate-field instead.

By default the operator of the finished form can move to any field in the form. This can be restricted by defining the mouse navigation unit in the form definition option on the main menu bar. Form level navigation is the default and allows unrestricted navigation. Block level navigation allows navigation anywhere within the current block; function keys must be used to navigate between blocks. Record level navigation allows navigation anywhere within the current record; function keys must be used to navigate between records and between blocks. Field level navigation means you can only use the mouse to select the current field, which means you cannot use the mouse for anything useful at all.

### 7.13.2 Block-mode screens

Apart from bit-mapped screens, there are two different strategies used to handle terminal screens: asynchronous and block-mode. Async (or character) screens handle data a character at a time, while block-mode screens transmit and receive whole screensful of data at a time. Terminals like the IBM 3270 and its derivatives use block mode transmission, while the terminals on Unix machines, DEC VAX and so on are almost always asynchronous.

With async connections, the machine has complete control over what is going on at the terminal. The software knows every time a key is pressed. This gives SQL*Forms much more control over what is displayed and much more awareness of what the operator is doing.

Block mode is intended to minimize the transmission of data to and from the terminal. The mainframe usually knows very little of what is going on on the screen. It does not know where the cursor is, for instance. This means that field-level triggers do not normally fire. It is sometimes possible to force the terminal to behave asynchronously and, in this case, triggers will fire; there is a performance penalty, however, because you are creating more traffic on the network between the terminal and the computer.

Therefore, when designing a form to run on block-mode terminals, you should use block-level triggers to perform all of the field-level processing of the block together. You should also set the validation unit of the forms to be a block. If you are developing in a block-mode environment, this will be the default. But, if you are developing in a character-mode environment for later use in block mode, you should use SQL*Forms' runtime option to set block-level validation.

Because SQL*Forms cannot keep track of where the cursor is on block-mode terminals, fields cannot automatically scroll horizontally when the space on the screen is full, so always leave enough space for the full size of the fields. Vertical scrolling in multi-row blocks will scroll up the captions as well as the variable data on block-mode terminals, so avoid scrolling multi-row blocks.

Finally, always make sure that there is at least one space between the caption and the field and between the field and the edge of the screen. Block-mode terminals need this space for field attributes, such as reverse video or blink attributes.

*Eight*
# SQL*Forms version 2

In this chapter, we deal with an older version of SQL*Forms, version 2.3. Although this version has been superseded, many application systems have been built using it. These systems have to be maintained; it is therefore described in detail. As with the previous chapter, an example application is built as the chapter progresses. The whole of this section is written as if you had SQL*Forms on a terminal in front of you.

## 8.1 Building a default form

To start with, we go through how to generate a default form, letting SQL*Forms do all the work. Later, we will show how to build forms from scratch and to modify forms. The simplest form that can be built has a single block and is created by using the DEFAULT BLOCK option. The form which will be built (Figure 8.1) will allow a user to query customer billing details.

### 8.1.1 Routes to the finished form

Building a complete working form of realistic complexity can involve quite a lot of detailed work. There are three routes to get to the finished form. You can cut out much of the effort by getting SQL*Forms to do the work for you by generating a default form. Such default forms have an extensive set of capabilities built-in. They can query, update and so on. But they lack any of the specific functionality needed by an application and the detailed cosmetic features which make forms easier to use. Things like the positioning of items on the screen and captions are crude; there are no niceties like boxes around data.

Such forms are quite adequate for quick one-off jobs but serious applications will usually require a customized form. The second route is to use SQL*Forms' screen painter to build the form from scratch. The process is intricate but not difficult, and is certainly a lot quicker than traditional methods of program development.

The third way, which is probably the most commonly used, is a combination of the other two: first let SQL*Forms generate the default screen, then tailor it to your exact requirements.

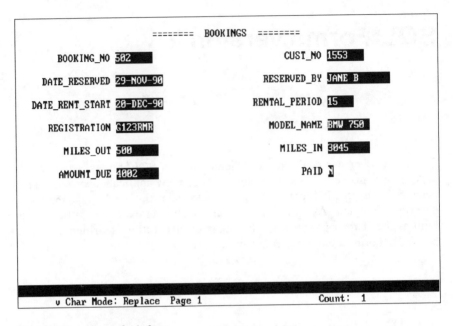

======== BOOKINGS ========

BOOKING_NO 502                     CUST_NO 1553

DATE_RESERVED 29-NOV-90           RESERVED_BY JANE B

DATE_RENT_START 20-DEC-90         RENTAL_PERIOD 15

REGISTRATION G123RMR              MODEL_NAME BMW 750

MILES_OUT 500                     MILES_IN 3045

AMOUNT_DUE 4002                   PAID N

v Char Mode: Replace  Page 1                    Count: 1

**Figure 8.1**   The default form.

## 8.1.2  The CHOOSE FORM window.

On entry to SQL\*Forms the CHOOSE FORM window is displayed (Figure 8.2). The whole system is controlled by a series of such windows in a hierarchical structure. A window can provide a menu of actions and a prompt for a name, as this one does; it may contain a list of items for you to select from or it may contain switches which can be toggled on and off. This top level window covers the actions you might want to carry out on a form. Selecting one of the actions in the window would take you to the next level, perhaps to specify what you want to do with a block.

Use [*Previous field*] and [*Next field*] to move around the window, [*Select*] to choose an action and [*Exit/cancel*] to abandon a selection. In this case, a new form called BILLINGS is going to be created. Enter the name, move the cursor to the CREATE action and press [*Select*]. If the form already existed, then the MODIFY option would be used to load it ready for changes or for running.

The message Working... appears momentarily at the bottom of the screen. The CHOOSE BLOCK window will be displayed, partially overlaying the CHOOSE FORM window on the screen (Figure 8.3).

The status line, displayed at the bottom of the screen, shows useful information about the current activity. **Form** specifies the name of the form currently being worked on; **Block** specifies the name of the current block; **Page** shows the page number within the form where the current block will appear; **Select**

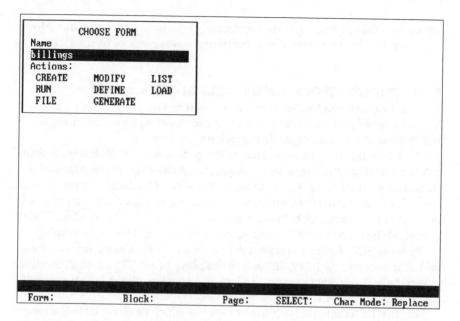

**Figure 8.2** The CHOOSE FORM window.

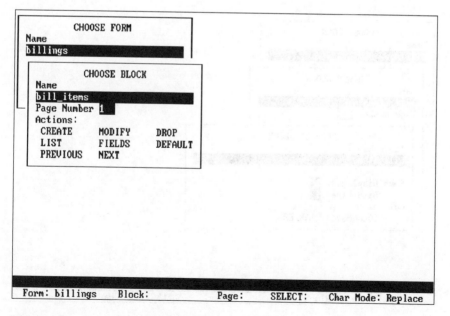

**Figure 8.3** The CHOOSE BLOCK window.

shows how many objects (fields, blocks etc.) have been selected. **Char Mode** indicates whether text entered will overwrite existing text or be inserted.

### 8.1.3   CHOOSE BLOCK and DEFAULT BLOCK windows

There are no existing blocks in this form, as it has only just been created, so the block name prompt is blank. For an already existing form, the block name will default to the name of the first block for the form.

The `Page Number` prompt refers to the page you want to display. A form can consist of several pages and a block can spread over all the pages of the form. It is more usual, however, to have the whole of the block within a single page. Pages are numbered starting at 1. There is also a special page number 0 associated with each block, but this is reserved for use by 'hidden fields' and is beyond the scope of this chapter. Look in the manuals for more details.

We want SQL\*Forms to create a default block. Enter a name for the block, move the cursor to the DEFAULT action and press [*Select*]. The CREATE action is used only if you want to create a blank block and do all the layout yourself. The DEFAULT BLOCK window appears next (Figure 8.4).

The `Table Name` prompt is used to specify which database table the block is to be based upon. It defaults to be the same as the name of the block entered previously, but can be overwritten if this is not correct. The block is, in fact, based on the bookings table, so the name should be changed. You can just type

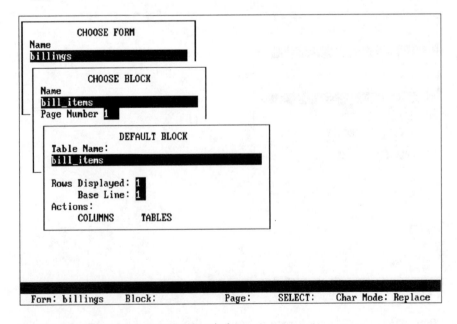

**Figure 8.4**   The DEFAULT BLOCK window.

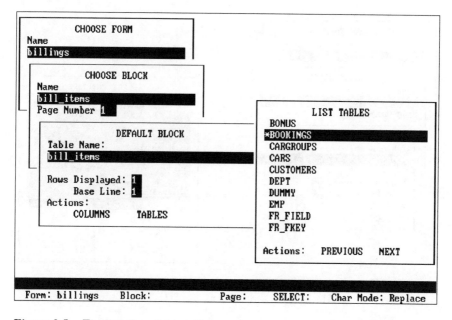

**Figure 8.5**   The list of available tables.

in the correct name or leave the name as it is and select the TABLES action. This displays a list of available tables (Figure 8.5). Use [*Next field*] and [*Previous field*] to get to the one you want and press [*Select*]. [*Accept*] then closes the tables window and inserts the selected table name at the prompt in the default block window.

The Rows Displayed prompt allows the user to specify the number of rows of data to be displayed on the screen at one time. For simple single row forms this will be left at 1. The Base Line prompt indicates where the first row of this block will be placed on the screen. Line 1 is the top of the screen. Again, for simple forms this will be left at 1.

## 8.1.4   The COLUMNS window

By default, all the columns of the table will be used in the generated form. Use the COLUMNS option to limit the range of columns to be displayed on the form (Figure 8.6).

The window shows the available columns; the ones to be included are highlighted. Initially all of them are highlighted to show that they have all been automatically selected.

To de-select a column, move to the column using [*Next Field*]) and then press [*Select*]. Highlighting will be switched off for that column. The [*Select*] key

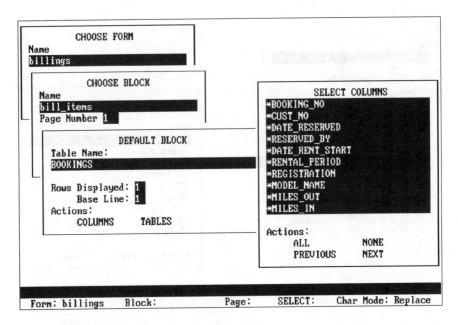

**Figure 8.6**   The list of available columns.

acts as a toggle that will select and de-select columns. The option ALL will
cause all columns to be selected (the default), while option NONE will de-select
all columns, following which individual columns can then be re-selected.
PREVIOUS and NEXT are used to move through this list of columns if there
are more of them than can be displayed on the screen at one time. Once you
have selected/de-selected the required columns, press [*Accept*] to return to the
DEFAULT BLOCK window.

Once the columns to be displayed have been selected, the system can work
out how much space each row will take up on the screen. This is shown in the
DEFAULT BLOCK panel as Maximum Rows. It is shown for information only
– it cannot be directly altered by
the user. It indicates the maximum number of rows of data
that can actually be displayed on
the screen at one time if the user
is creating a multi-row block
(indicated by entering a value
other than 1 at the Rows Displayed prompt). (See Figure
8.7.)

All the information needed by
SQL\*Forms to create a default
form has now been entered.

**Figure 8.7**   The number of rows is calculated.

Press [*Accept*] to return to the CHOOSE BLOCK window. To see the default screen layout choose the MODIFY option. The screen layout can be altered by using the screen painting facilities described later.

Press [*Accept*] to return to the CHOOSE BLOCK window. [*Accept*] again will return to the CHOOSE FORM window.

### 8.1.5 Save and generate the form

To save the form for later use, move to the FILE option and press [*Select*]. The FILE window will appear (Figure 8.8). Select the SAVE option and the message Working... will appear at the bottom of the screen again. When

the form has been saved you will be returned automatically to the CHOOSE FORM window. From here, [*Exit/cancel*] will take you out of SQL*Forms and back to the operating system prompt. If changes to a form have not been saved, SQL*Forms will prompt to check whether to save them before exiting.

The other options on the FILE window cause all changes made to a form to be lost (DIS-

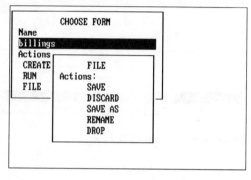

**Figure 8.8** The FILE action window.

CARD), to be saved under another name, the original form remaining unaltered (SAVE AS), to be renamed (RENAME) or to be removed from the database altogether (DROP).

Note that the form cannot yet be run. All SAVE does is to save the form definition in the database for later modification. Before you can run a form, it has to be converted from the format handled by the screen painter to a semi-compiled format. This process is known as 'generation'.

### 8.1.6 Simple tailoring of a default form

There is nothing special about the default screens just produced; you can use the screen painter to tailor them to whatever level of customization you want, just as if they were custom built from the start. This is, in fact, how screens are usually built in real life: produce a default screen and then rearrange the layout and enhance the logic to make it do exactly the right job.

To modify the form, enter the form name on the main window (BILLINGS in this case) and select the MODIFY option. This displays the CHOOSE BLOCK window. Enter the block name and select MODIFY again. This displays the form in screen painter mode.

Captions can be modified by typing over existing text. Boxes can be drawn using function keys: move the cursor to one corner of the where the box is to

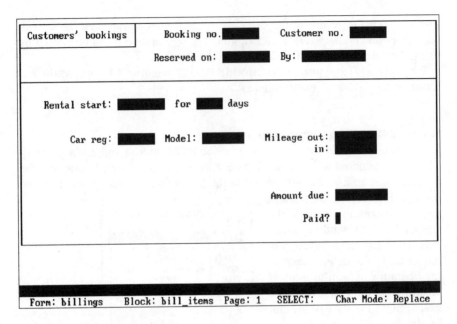

**Figure 8.9**   The modified form.

go; press [*Select*]. Move the cursor to the diagonally opposite corner of the box, press [*Select*] again and then press [*Draw box/line*]. Lines can be drawn as a one-dimensional box. Both of the points selected have the same horizontal or vertical position.

A field or area of the screen may be cut from the screen by selecting it (in the case of a field) or by selecting diagonally opposite corners (in the case of an area) and then pressing [*Cut*]. The cut field or area is held in memory and may be reinstated by pressing [*Undo*]. It can be moved to another part of the screen by moving the cursor and pressing [*Paste*]. To save the modified form layout, press [*Accept*]. Figure 8.9 shows a modified version of the form. The captions have been changed, fields moved and boxes and lines drawn. All this is to improve the appearance of the form; the functionality of the form, which is explored in the next section, is all provided automatically by SQL\*Forms' defaults.

## 8.2   Using the form

### 8.2.1   Invoking the form

The form can be invoked from within SQL\*Forms by selecting the RUN action on the CHOOSE FORM window or with a separate run of RUNFORM. If the latter, you can supply the username and password on the command line, for instance

```
runform billings jtaylor/carborundum
```

or RUNFORM will prompt for them before running the form.

The form displayed looks just as it was painted with screen painter. There is a help line and a status line at the bottom of the screen, though there is no text on the help line at first. The status line shows whether input from the keyboard overwrites or is inserted, the page number within the form and the number of the row currently displayed on the form. The row number is a serial number within the group of rows retrieved by a query. When you first get into the form, the help line is blank and, because no query has yet been executed, the count is zero. The form is driven using function keys in the same way as when the form was being built.

In spite of being very easy to generate, this form has a lot of functionality built in. You can insert, update, delete and query the data in flexible ways.

### 8.2.2 Query

First, enter the criteria for the query, then press [*Execute query*] to retrieve the data. The simplest form of query is to retrieve records which match values which you have entered into the fields on the form. If you do not specify any values (an open query), all the rows of the table are returned. In the example form, the booking number provides a unique key to the bookings records. So to retrieve details of a specific booking, press [*Enter query*], type in the booking number and press [*Execute query*]. You can fill in several fields on the form to retrieve all records that match these values in the fields. Any fields which have no values entered are interpreted as 'don't care what is in this column' so executing a query with no values in any of the fields will retrieve all the rows in the table.

A query like this, where no key value has been specified, will generally result in several records being retrieved and you can look through them using [*Next record*] and [*Previous record*]. As you do this, you will notice that two indicators appear on the left of the status line to show whether there are any records in front of and after the one currently displayed on the screen. A caret (^) indicates that there are records in front and the letter V indicates that there are records after the current one.

As well as exact values, expressions can be entered in the fields to define the query. For instance, Figure 8.10 shows a query to retrieve bookings made on 4 September 1991 for a rental of more than 5 days. Note that dates and character strings are entered in the fields without quotes if they are being specified for a match, as in this example. If, however, there are logical operators in front of dates and character strings, they must be enclosed in single quotes. Again, to set up a query like this, press [*Enter query*], fill in the fields and press [*Execute query*].

The fields on the form are of fixed size and do not scroll horizontally. There is not usually room to specify anything other than simple logical conditions

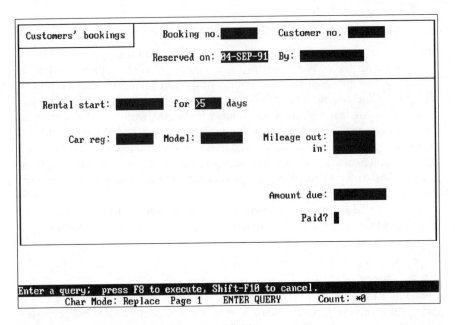

**Figure 8.10**   Query on a combination of fields.

within the field. In any case this method of specifying the logic always has an implicit 'AND' relationship between fields; it is not possible to specify a query like 'booking number greater than 500 OR booking date before 1 July 1991'. To deal with these problems, it is possible to enter what is in effect a SQL WHERE clause for the query.

This is done by entering a variable name in one or more fields when you define the query. Variable names start with a colon (:) or ampersand (&); to provide forwards compatibility, you are recommended to use a colon. When the query is executed, a prompt appears at the bottom of the screen for the WHERE clause to be entered. Figure 8.11 shows an example to retrieve all bookings made before 4 September 1991 or which are for more than 10 days. When you press [*Next field*] to move the cursor off the definition, the WHERE clause is analysed and the query executed.

If you need to modify the query after you have executed it, pressing [*Enter query*] twice will redisplay the last query defined.

### 8.2.3   Modifying the database

Records can be updated simply by finding the right record with a query and then changing the values in the fields. The changes will not be permanent until [*Commit*] is pressed. You can do this after changing a single record or after changing several. The system displays how many rows you have updated. If you fail to commit the changes before moving on to some other action, like

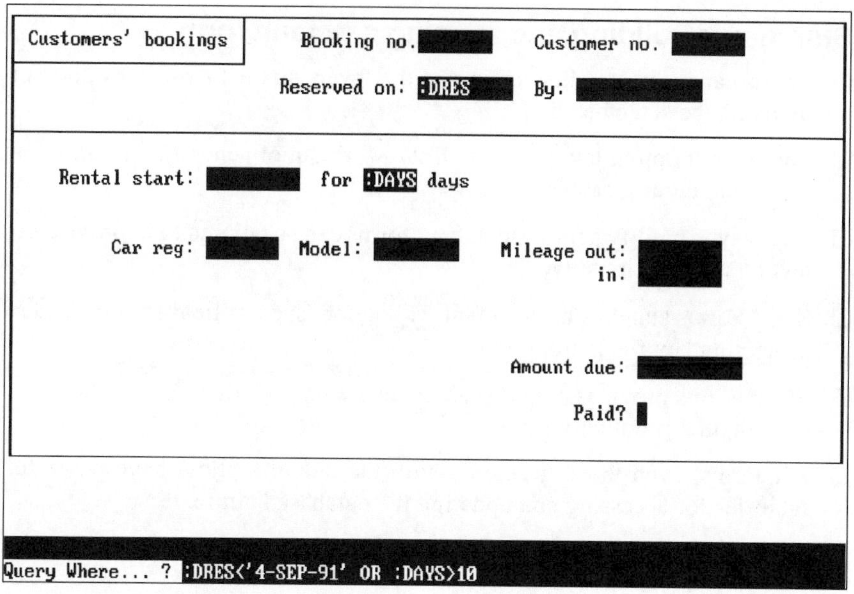

**Figure 8.11**   Specifying a more complex query.

quitting the form, you will be prompted whether you want to commit or abandon the changes. Similarly, to delete a record find the appropriate record and press [*Delete record*].

To insert a record, press [*Create record*] and type in the field values. You can also add records by moving to the end of the records retrieved, where there is always a blank record. Type in the values. A blank record will still be there, after the one you have just entered. So you can enter a whole series by repeatedly pressing [*Next record*] and filling in the values.

To protect the integrity of the data in the database, a certain amount of validation and consistency checking must take place when data is entered or modified. When a form is created using SQL*Forms default options, the built-in validation and consistency checks are derived from the definition of the data items, held in the on-line dictionary.

The field type of fields on the form are set to the same datatype as the column in the database. When the form is run, the data entered must be valid for the datatype (so no alphabetical characters in a numeric field etc.). The field lengths for the display are set to the same length as the relevant column in the table. This way, only values up to the maximum length are allowed. Any column defined as NOT NULL will be marked as mandatory by SQL*Forms. This is the only type of constraint which is enforced.

SQL*Forms also provides one line of help text for each field. The default help text is not very informative without a bit of tailoring. It is displayed by pressing [*Help*].

## Summary: Building and running a default form

☐ Forms can be created in two ways, either by using the DEFAULT option or by using the screen painter.

☐ The default option takes almost all the work out of generating a form, but the form layout is rather clumsy.

☐ It is easy to modify a form, so default forms can be tailored to improve their layout and functionality.

☐ SQL\*Forms supplies basic default validation, such as field length checks, protecting key fields from update etc.

☐ SQL\*Forms provides help text associated with each field. Unless tailored, though, this is not very useful.

☐ All forms, even those generated with the default option, have powerful facilities for accessing and updating the database built in.

---

**EXERCISE 8.1**

1. Use the SQL\*Forms default options to build a screen to display the customers table showing customer name and address. Discard this form when you have finished with it.

2. Build a similar screen for the cars table, this time showing registration, model, car group, rate per mile, rate per day and original cost. Save this form as cars_exercise.

3. Generate and run the form cars_exercise.

4. Query the cars table to show all the rows.

5. Find the car with registration H286 MHU. What model is it?

---

## 8.3   Building a more complex form

The previous section concentrated on a form consisting of a single screen with a single block, created using the DEFAULT option. The next step is to develop a more ambitious form (Figure 8.12), and this section explains the steps required to do this entirely by hand, using the screen painter. This is quite a long and tedious process and, in practice, you may find that you seldom have to do as much of the work by hand. Nevertheless, it is still worth going through

```
┌─────────────────────────────────────────────────────────────────────┐
│ CUSTOMER                                                              │
│                                                                       │
│  No. 567      Name: G G WHITTAKER & CO    Contact: Chris Whittaker    │
│               Addr: WHEATLEY ROAD                                     │
│               Town: DONCASTER                                         │
│             County: YORKSHIRE                     Pay method: 9       │
│                                                                       │
│               Code: DN5 8AA            Amount due: 2398.40            │
├─────────────────────────────────────────────────────────────────────┤
│ BOOKINGS                                                              │
│                date      date                        -- miles --     │
│  cust  book  reserved   start   days   reg.   model   out    in  cost │
│                                                                       │
│  667   586  13-APR-91 26-APR-91  21  F111ENT P911 TC 25967 26818 2090.80│
│  667   599  21-DEC-91 01-JAN-92   3  H311MHG MERC 560                 │
│  667  2123  18-SEP-91 19-SEP-91   5  H935CSA FERR TR  23774 25865  501.80│
│  667  2124  18-SEP-91 19-SEP-91   5  G123RMR BMW  750 61554 72334 1023.00│
│  667  2126  02-OCT-91 02-OCT-91  10  H266MHU ASTON V8  5583  6254  873.60│
│                                                                       │
│                                          Total bookings:  4489.20     │
├─────────────────────────────────────────────────────────────────────┤
│                                                                       │
│        v Char Mode: Replace   Page 1              Count:  1           │
└─────────────────────────────────────────────────────────────────────┘
```

**Figure 8.12**   The finished form.

it all because, in doing so, you will understand the scope for customization which can be applied to pre-built skeletons of forms or to default forms.

The form is a customers and bookings enquiry and input screen. It allows you to select a customer or number of customers, automatically to display their associated car bookings and to enter new bookings. The form has two blocks: the first displays details of a single customer and the second displays details of the customer's multiple bookings. The form is built with the following steps:

• Define the customer block, specifying the sequence the rows will be displayed and number of rows per block.

• Use the screen painter to lay out the customer block. This will define the fields in the block and their attributes, captions to the fields and other text.

• Define the bookings block, specifying the sequence of the rows and the number of rows displayed.

• Lay out the bookings block, defining the fields and text in the same way as for the customers block.

### 8.3.1   Creating the first block

At the CHOOSE FORM window enter the form name, cust_book, and select the CREATE action from the window.

Enter the block name, customers (as in Figure 8.13), and
select CREATE from the window.
The screen painter will now be displayed to define the properties of
the block. First select it by pressing
the [*Select block*] key, then press
[*Define*]. The DEFINE BLOCK
window appears (Figure 8.14).

The window shows the name
of the block, an optional description and the name of the base
table for the block. The name of

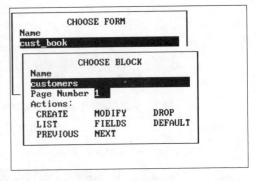

**Figure 8.13** The CHOOSE BLOCK window.

the base table defaults to the block name (correctly, in this case).

Customers details are to be retrieved and displayed in ascending order of
customer number, so select the ORDERING option from the window and enter
ORDER BY cust_no (Figure 8.15). Press [*Accept*] to save these changes.

Next, define the remaining properties of the block. Select OPTIONS. Make
the selections on the OPTIONS window as follows and then press [*Accept*]
(Figure 8.16).

When the UNIQUE KEY option is selected, SQL\*Forms will check for a
unique value when entering data in any column defined as a primary key. This
technique is not recommended, however, because it is inefficient and applies

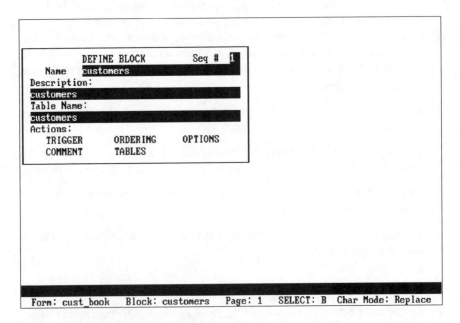

**Figure 8.14** The DEFINE BLOCK window.

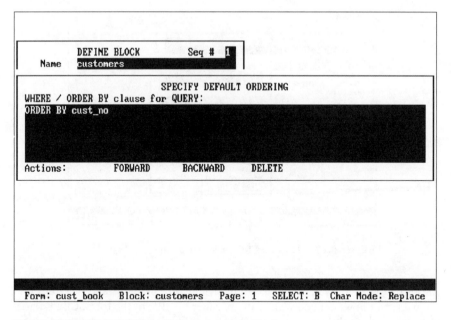

**Figure 8.15** ORDER BY for the customers block.

only to data entered using the form, rather than to the database as a whole. It is better to enforce uniqueness by defining a unique index for the columns. The BLOCK MENU option determines whether the block name should appear in the block menu, displayed when a form is running (by pressing [*Block menu*]). This runtime block menu can be used to navigate between blocks, but is not often used. De-select this

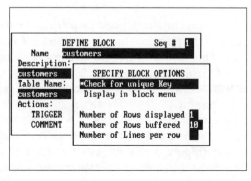

**Figure 8.16** The OPTIONS window.

one. The ROWS DISPLAYED option defines the number of rows to be displayed in the block. Set it to 1 for a single row block. The ROWS BUFFERED option tells SQL*Forms how many rows to hold buffered in store ready for display. Set this to 10. The NUMBER OF LINES option specifies the number of lines each row covers. This is only for multi-row blocks and we have specified a single-row block (ROWS DISPLAYED set to 1), so leave it alone.

### 8.3.2 Filling in the customers block

Now that the basic block properties have been defined, the screen text is laid out (or 'painted') and the block fields defined. Press [*Accept*] and you are

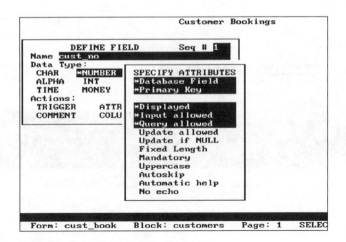

**Figure 8.17**   Attributes for customer number.

presented with a blank screen to fill in. The text of captions and headings etc. is just typed in where you want it to go. Enter the title of the form, `Customer Bookings`, on the top line, centred. Leave a blank line and enter `Customer Number` followed by a space. This is the prompt for the first field in the block.

To create the field, press [*Select*], move the cursor 4 places to the right and press [*Select*] again. This gives room for a 5 digit field. Press the [*Create Field*] key. The `DEFINE FIELD` window appears. Enter the name of the field, `cust_no`. The datatype of the field, again the same as the database field, is `NUMBER`. This is selected in the same way as before, by positioning the cursor and pressing [*Select*]. Datatypes for all the columns in the example database tables are shown in Appendix A. Now specify the attributes of the field by selecting the `ATTRIBUTES` option. The window shows the attributes you can define (Figure 8.17). As with the other panels, the [*Select*] key selects and de-selects the choices; selected choices are highlighted. For this field, select:

- `DATABASE FIELD`, to indicate the source of the field.

- `PRIMARY KEY`, to indicate that the field is a primary key.

- `DISPLAY`, `INPUT` and `QUERY`, to show how the field may be used.

- Customer number is a key field and, once entered, should not be changed, so de-select `UPDATE ALLOWED`.

It is possible to define non-database fields by de-selecting the `DATABASE FIELD` option. This type of field is used to display information derived from other fields. Press [*Accept*] to save the choices.

Next, select the `VALIDATION` option from the window to specify the validation requirements for the field (Figure 8.18). The `FIELD LENGTH` and

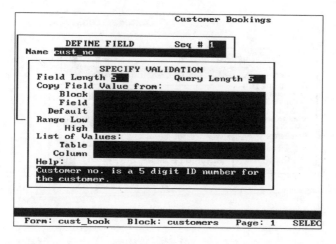

**Figure 8.18**   The VALIDATION window.

QUERY LENGTH prompts are to specify the length of the field when stored by SQL*Forms and the length allowed to be entered for a query. These have both already been set by SQL*Forms. For the moment, ignore the COPY FIELD, DEFAULT, RANGE and LIST OF VALUES options.

The final field in the window is to specify the help message to be displayed when the user of the finished form presses the [*Help*] key. This text can also be displayed each time the user puts the cursor in the field by selecting AUTOMATIC HELP from the SPECIFY ATTRIBUTES window. Put in a useful message.

The definition of the first field is now complete. Press [*Accept*] to get back to the screen painter. The other fields in the block are defined in exactly the same way, but rather than go through it all in detail now, the building of the rest of the block is part of the next set of exercises.

### 8.3.3   Adding a second block
Now define the second block of the form. This block will display all the bookings, old ones and current ones, for a customer. Therefore, make it a multi-record block.

In the CHOOSE BLOCK window, enter the block name, BOOKINGS. Select the CREATE option from the window to get into the screen painter. To define the new block, press [*Select block*] followed by [*Define*] to display the DEFINE BLOCK window.

Once again, a default block name has been entered. Write a description of the block in the description field. The table name is the same as the block name, so there is no need to change that. Notice the sequence number field, set as 2. This defines the order in which the blocks are entered as the cursor moves down the screen of the finished form. So this block will come after the customer

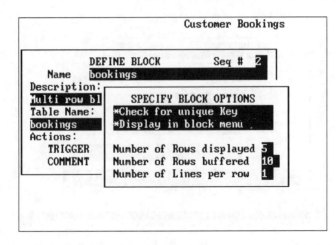

**Figure 8.19**   Block options window.

block, which is correct. This sequencing can be overridden by changing the sequence numbers of the blocks.

Select OPTIONS (Figure 8.19). Define the number of rows to be displayed as 5. Set the number of rows held in memory once again to 10. Each of the rows will only take up a single line so set lines per row to 1. Press [*Accept*] to save and again to leave the DEFINE BLOCK window and return to the screen painter.

Now start painting the block. When laying out a block, it is often useful to sketch in all the fields which are going to appear with a line of dummy data to show how big the fields are (Figure 8.20). These dummies are then deleted as you define the fields properly. This time, the fields are defined below the caption, as several rows are to be displayed at a time.

To define the customer number field move the cursor to the start of the field and press [*Select*] then [*Create field*]. Enter the field name, cust_no, and datatype, and then select the ATTRIBUTES option (Figure 8.21). Define the attributes as PRIMARY KEY, DISPLAYED, and INPUT ALLOWED. De-select all the others except MANDATORY and press [*Accept*].

Now go into the VALIDATION window to define the validation requirements for the field (Figure 8.22). The DEFAULT option is used to specify a default value for the field when the form is executed. In some applications (not this one) you might want to use today's date as a default in a date field, for example. RANGE allows us to specify a range of values and SQL\*Forms will only allow values within that range to be entered. The LIST OF VALUES option means that the data entered must be one of a list of valid values. The list is specified as the values of a particular column in a table. This could be set up in advance and be static or could be constantly updated, perhaps by another application. The actual list is available when using the form and filling

```
┌──────────────────────Customer—Bookings─────────────────────────┐
│┌─────────┐                                                      │
││CUSTOMER │                                                      │
│└─────────┘                                                      │
│  No. ▐███  Name: xxxxxxxxxxxxxxxxxxxxx  Contact: xxxxxxxxxxxxxxxxxxxxx│
│            Addr: xxxxxxxxxxxxxxxxxxxxx                          │
│            Town: xxxxxxxxxxxxxxxxxxxxx                          │
│          County: xxxxxxxxxxxxxxxxxxxxx          Pay method: c   │
│                                                                 │
│            Code: xxxxxxxxx                                      │
│┌─────────┐                                                      │
││BOOKINGS │                                                      │
│└─────────┘      date    date                      -- miles --  │
│ cust  book   reserved   start  days   reg.   model    out   in    cost│
│                                                                 │
│ 99999 99999 dd-mon-yy dd-mon-yy 999 xxxxxxx xxxxxxxxxxxxx 999999 999999 9999.99│
│                                                                 │
│                                                                 │
│                                                                 │
│                                                                 │
│                                                                 │
├─────────────────────────────────────────────────────────────────┤
│ Form: cust_book    Block: bookings    Page: 1   SELECT:    Char Mode: Replace│
└─────────────────────────────────────────────────────────────────┘
```

**Figure 8.20**    Dummy fields to help paint the block.

```
┌──────────────────────Customer—Bookings─────────────────────────┐
│┌─────────┐                                                      │
││CUSTOMER │                                                      │
│└─────────┘                                                      │
│┌────────────────────────────────┐                              │
││    DEFINE FIELD      Seq # ▐1  │ x  Contact: xxxxxxxxxxxxxxxxxxxxx│
││ Name cust_no                   │ x                             │
││ Data Type:                     │                              │
││  CHAR   ▐NUMBER ┌──────────────────────────┐                  │
││  ALPHA  INT    │ SPECIFY ATTRIBUTES         │  Pay method: c   │
││  TIME   MONEY  │ Database Field             │                  │
││ Actions:       │ Primary Key                │                  │
││  TRIGGER  ATTR │▐Displayed                  │      -- miles -- │
││  COMMENT  COLU │▐Input allowed              │eg.   model   out   in   cost│
││                │ Query allowed              │                  │
││                │ Update allowed             │                  │
││     99999 dd-mo│ Update if NULL             │xxxx xxxxxxxxxxxxx 999999 999999 9999.99│
││                │ Fixed Length               │                  │
││                │▐Mandatory                  │                  │
││                │ Uppercase                  │                  │
│└────────────────│ Autoskip                   │                  │
│                 │ Automatic help             │                  │
│                 │ No echo                    │                  │
│                 └──────────────────────────┘                  │
├─────────────────────────────────────────────────────────────────┤
│ Form: cust_book    Block: bookings    Page: 1   SELECT: 2  Char Mode: Replace│
└─────────────────────────────────────────────────────────────────┘
```

**Figure 8.21**    Attributes of customer number field.

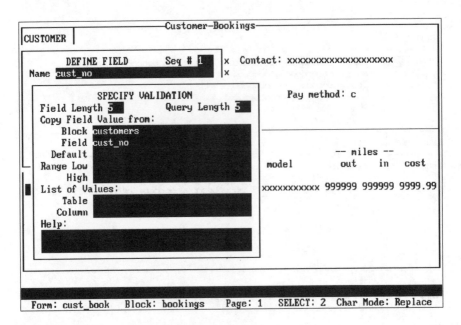

**Figure 8.22** Validation window joining the blocks.

in the field by using the [*List of values*] key. The user can then select one of the values displayed and copy it into the field.

SQL\*Forms has to be instructed to join the two blocks together on the customer number field so that when the user of the form queries a record in this block, it will automatically only retrieve records for the customer whose details are shown in the first block. The join is specified by telling SQL\*Forms to copy the value of customer number from the first block into this field in the second block. This will be done each time a record is retrieved or input in the customer block. This is just the start; there is a lot more to joining the blocks together and making them easy to use. This is explored in the next section on triggers.

Fill in the block name and the field name where the data is to be found. In this case it is the CUSTOMERS block and the cust_no field. This has now specified the join. You can do this for as many fields as you need. Put in some sensible help text as well.

## Summary: Building a more complex form

☐ This section dealt with building a customer bookings and enquiry screen, by hand, using the screen painter.

☐ First, define a block and its properties using the DEFINE BLOCK window. This specifies the underlying table (or view), the sequence in which to retrieve data, number of rows to be displayed etc.

☐ Next, define the fields in the block with the DEFINE FIELD, AT-TRIBUTES and VALIDATION windows.

☐ Repeat the process for all the blocks in the form.

☐ Blocks are joined (synchronized) by specifying that a field in the subsidiary block is copied out of the equivalent field in the controlling block. This is specified in the VALIDATION for the field in the subsidiary block.

---

**EXERCISE 8.2**

1. Modify the form just developed to set up the rest of the customers block. The layout should be as in Figure 8.12. The attributes for all the fields should be DATABASE FIELD, DISPLAYED, QUERY ALLOWED, INPUT ALLOWED, UPDATE ALLOWED.

2. Define the fields for the bookings block with the names and captions below. Lay the fields out as in Figure 8.12. All should be DATABASE FIELD, DISPLAYED, INPUT ALLOWED, UPDATE ALLOWED. The car group and date reserved should also be MANDATORY. Specify your own help text for the fields.

---

# 8.4 Triggers

U p to now, the example forms have only had fairly simple functions. Much of the real power of SQL*Forms, though, comes from its ability to use SQL (and other) statements to control the behaviour of a form, to provide validation facilities and to impose security restrictions. This is achieved with **triggers**. A word of caution on terminology, here: some other database systems use the word trigger to mean a sequence of actions stored in the database and executed by the database itself when certain events occur (such as when a database field is updated). This is rather different from the SQL*Forms meaning of the word, as will become apparent.

In SQL*Forms, there are two types of trigger: **Event** and **Key** triggers. Event triggers are so named because they are actioned (triggered) when a particular event on the form occurs. Different events result in different triggers being activated. An event can be the updating of a field, when the cursor enters or leaves a field, before or after a query has been executed, before a deletion takes place and so on. Key triggers are assigned to function keys and actioned when the key is pressed.

Triggers can be defined at form, block and field level. Field-level triggers are the most common as they are particularly suitable for field-level validation. Triggers may consist of several trigger steps, a trigger step simply being an executable statement. These steps may contain SQL statements, SQL\*Forms commands and macro functions.

### 8.4.1   Trigger definition and scope

A trigger has a defined scope within which it will operate. Field-level triggers have narrow scope and act only on the field for which they are defined. Block-level triggers act only within the block for which they are defined. Form-level triggers have widest scope and act for the whole form.

Key triggers redefine the action of the function key. They, too, have a scope, depending on how they are defined. They may act for the whole of a form, just within a block or only when a field is active.

Triggers defined at a lower level take precedence over those defined at a higher level. So, for instance, a key trigger defined at field level will override one defined at block level just while that field is being processed.

### 8.4.2   A block-level trigger

A block-level trigger on the bookings form, created earlier, will be used to illustrate the use of triggers. The trigger will automatically display a total of the customer's unpaid bookings when a user queries the database using the customer number. The block-level trigger is set up as part of the block definition. Load the form and get into the screen painter to modify the customers block. Get into the DEFINE BLOCK window and select the TRIG-GER option. There are several different types of trigger each named after the type of event that activates them. To have a look at the types, select the TYPES option (Figure 8.23). A PRE-QUERY trigger, for instance, is activated when the user hits the [*Execute query*] key but before the query is actually executed.

The one wanted in this case is the POST-QUERY trigger. It will be activated each time a record is retrieved from the database. So select the POST-QUERY trigger from the list and press [*Accept*]. Now select the CREATE option. The trigger step window is displayed and we enter the SQL to be executed each time the post-query event occurs:

```
SELECT SUM(amount_due)
INTO :customers.total_due
WHERE cust_no = :customers.cust_no
AND paid  'Y'
```

This just fits into the panel for entering a trigger step. Had there not been enough room, you would type in as much as will fit and then move to select the FORWARD action. This gives more blank space to enter the rest of the

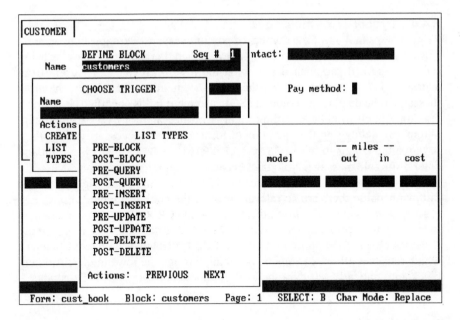

**Figure 8.23** Types of event trigger.

trigger. This trigger has only one step, the SELECT statement, but there can be several steps. Each step is defined in a separate panel and you move between the steps by selecting the NEXT STEP and PREVIOUS STEP options.

### 8.4.3 SQL syntax in triggers

There are two differences between the syntax of the SQL entered for this trigger and that of the SQL used with SQL*Plus. The first is minor: the SQL statement does not have to be terminated by a semicolon. The second change is the introduction of the INTO clause. This clause is only valid in SQL statements in triggers in SQL*Forms; it cannot be used in SQL*Plus interactive statements.

The purpose of the clause is to specify the fields on the form into which the column values retrieved from the database are to be put. The example referenced the fields on the form by using the construct of colon followed by blockname followed by a full stop (period) and then the field name. The colon indicates that we are talking about a field on the form, not in a table in the database. An ampersand can be used instead of the colon for compatibility with previous releases of SQL*Forms. The colon is the preferred form, however.

There are also some restrictions on the SQL statements you can put in triggers. Data manipulation statements, like INSERT, UPDATE and DELETE, can only be used in pre- and post-insert, update and delete triggers.

### 8.4.4   Trigger error messages

Trigger steps may fail for a number of possible reasons. Perhaps there were no rows to retrieve or the table could not be accessed. Perhaps someone else using the database had established a lock on the row to prevent other users from accessing it. So, having entered the SQL statement for the trigger, the error message to be displayed should the SQL statement fail is specified. It is worth making a habit of always putting in an error message for every trigger step. Without it, debugging the operation of forms can be unnecessarily difficult.

Move the cursor to the MESSAGE IF TRIGGER STEP FAILS option and enter a suitable message. Note that, because an aggregate function, as used in this trigger, always returns a value even if it is only null, this trigger will not fail just because there are no relevant rows in the bookings table.

Keep on pressing [*accept*] until you get to the CHOOSE FORM window and then save the form. Generate the BOOKINGS form and run it using the GENERATE and RUN options on the CHOOSE FORM window. Execute a query which retrieves all the customers. Scrolling through the rows in the customers block automatically retrieves the total of unpaid bookings for that customer.

### 8.4.5   Key triggers

Key triggers, as their name implies, redefine the programmable keys, such as the function keys, on a keyboard. There is a key trigger for each programmable key. For example the KEY-EXEQRY trigger redefines the [*Execute query*] key, KEY-DELREC redefines the [*Delete record*] key and so on.

There are two exceptions to this one-to-one mapping. The KEY-OTHERS trigger applies to all programmable keys that are not specifically defined by another key trigger. This allows you to specify actions based on the press of any key on the keyboard. The KEY-STARTUP trigger allows you to specify actions which are triggered when a form is first entered.

### 8.4.6   User-named triggers

Up to now, the trigger names used have been those defined by SQL\*Forms. It is quite possible to define your own trigger names. These can then be invoked from the SQL\*Forms triggers. This allows you to define a function just once and then to invoke it from several different places in a form. A piece of validation logic which is needed in several places on a form is a typical application. You can use any SQL statement and SQL\*Forms macro functions in a user-named trigger. The syntax is exactly the same as that used in a normal trigger.

User-named triggers are not triggered by a particular event; instead, they are called from other triggers. They can be defined at any level and then called at that level or a lower one. Generally, therefore, it is better to define them at form level and then use them throughout the form.

To create a user-named trigger, you just create a trigger at the appropriate level and give it a name that is not one of the standard SQL*Forms trigger names. You can use any valid name, following the normal Oracle rules for naming objects.

As an example, imagine it was necessary to prevent a form from being able to operate between 17.30 and 09.30. You would need to check the time of day when the form was first run by checking the time (held in SYSDATE) in the KEY-STARTUP trigger or in the PRE-FORM trigger. But you would also need to check it at other places in the form so that, if it was already running, it would close down at 17.30. The sensible way to achieve this would be to create a user-named trigger to check the time and then to invoke it from the PRE-FORM or KEY-STARTUP trigger and from other triggers in the form.

### 8.4.7 Trigger control

When a trigger is executed, there are three possible outcomes: it may succeed, it may fail or it may cause a fatal error. A trigger statement succeeds if it does not contain a syntax error and is able to act on at least one row in the database or is able to execute a SQL*Forms command properly.

A trigger statement will fail if it is unable to retrieve a row or cannot execute a SQL*Forms command for some reason. If a trigger contains a syntax error or the database table referred to does not exist then a fatal error occurs.

It is important to bear in mind that SQL*Forms does not check the trigger statements for syntactical errors until execution time. It does, however, carry out a check to ensure that the type of SQL statement is valid for the type of trigger.

It is possible to specify that SQL*Forms should branch to another trigger step for exception processing should a trigger step fail. Otherwise the entire trigger will be aborted. Note that this means that if a trigger does not return any rows from a table, this is considered a failure and the trigger is aborted.

It is possible to avoid termination of a trigger by reversing its success or failure. This is achieved by selecting a combination of the REVERSE RETURN CODE, RETURN SUCCESS WHEN ABORTING TRIGGER and ABORT TRIGGER WHEN STEP FAILS options on the TRIGGER STEP attributes window (Figure 8.24).

When the REVERSE RETURN CODE switch is set and a trigger step succeeds, SQL*Forms will assume it has failed. This condition is useful if you wish to prevent a user deleting, say, a customer record if an order is outstanding for that customer. This would be implemented by getting the trigger to fail if it retrieved any rows from the database. Conversely, you can avoid a trigger step failing if it fails to return any rows (quite a likely situation to arise) by setting the RETURN SUCCESS WHEN ABORTING TRIGGER switch. This will ensure any additional steps following the failed one will still be executed.

The consequences on processing of a trigger failure depends upon which trigger type it is and from which level it is invoked. In the majority of cases, if

```
┌─────────────────────────────────────────────────────────────────────┐
│ CUSTOMER │                                                            │
│  ┌──────────────────────────────────────────────────────────────────┐│
│  │       DEFINE BLOCK           Seq #  ▋  │ntact: ████████████████    ││
│  │  Name  customers                                                   ││
│  │  ┌────────────────────────────────────┐   Pay method: █           ││
│  │  │       CHOOSE TRIGGER        ████    │                           ││
│  │  │  Name                                                           ││
│  │  │  POST-QUERY                                                     ││
│  │  ┌──────────────────────────────────────────────────────────────┐ │
│  │  │ Seq #  ▋         TRIGGER STEP         Label ████████           │ │
│  │  │ SELECT cust_no, booking_no,                                    │ │
│  │  │        model_name, registra │    TRIGGER STEP ATTRIBUTES        │ │
│  │  │ INTO :bookings.cust_no, :bo │                                   │ │
│  │  │      :bookings.date_rent_st │  *Abort trigger when step fails   │ │
│  │  │      :bookings.model_name,  │   Reverse return code             │ │
│  │  │ Message if trigger step fai │  *Return success when aborting trigger│
│  │  │ Unable to retrieve any book │   Separate cursor data area    ▋  │ │
│  │  │ Actions:                                                       │ │
│  │  │    CREATE        COPY        Success label ████████████████     │ │
│  │  │    FORWARD       BACKWARD    Failure label                      │ │
│  │  └──────────────────────────────────────────────────────────────┘ │
│                                                                       │
│ ████████████████████████████████████████████████████████████████████ │
│ Form: cust_book   Block: customers   Page: 1   SELECT: B  Char Mode: Replace│
└─────────────────────────────────────────────────────────────────────┘
```

**Figure 8.24**   Trigger step attributes.

a trigger which is executing a SQL data manipulation statement fails, any uncommitted transactions will be rolled back and the trigger aborted. For a full list of possible outcomes, refer to the SQL*Forms reference guide.

## Summary: Triggers

☐ Much of the power of SQL*Forms derives from the use of triggers. They contain SQL statements and other commands.

☐ The syntax of SQL in triggers is extended with the INTO clause.

☐ There are two fundamental types of trigger. Event triggers are actioned when particular events occur. Key triggers are actioned when function keys are pressed.

☐ Triggers have a defined scope. They can act for the whole of a form, for a block or just for a field.

☐ A trigger defined at a lower level has precedence over the same trigger defined at a higher level.

☐ User-named triggers are used for actions which are needed in several different triggers (a sort of trigger subroutine).

☐ Triggers can sometimes fail for quite mundane reasons. There are several features for dealing with trigger errors.

---

**EXERCISE 8.3**

1. Modify the customer bookings form to include a field to hold the total amount due for a customer's bookings. It should be displayed but not input, updated or deleted and not derived from the database. Call this field `total_bookings`.

2. Create a `post-query` trigger to display the total number of bookings for each customer in this field.

---

## 8.5 MACROs

SQL*Forms has a number of special commands which can be invoked as trigger steps. One of these commands activates macro functions, which can be used to do such things as define the function keys, carry out actions normally done by the user (like execute queries) or move from one block to another. Other SQL*Forms commands allow you to manipulate variables, pass values from one form to another and to invoke other forms. Some of these facilities will be used to implement an automatic help facility for the BOOKINGS form.

There are four SQL*Forms commands to achieve all this. They all begin with a hash mark. They are all used in triggers together with, or instead of, SQL statements.

#EXEMACRO executes a series of macro functions. This is most commonly used of the commands. #COPY copies the contents of a form field into a variable and vice versa. #ERASE erases the contents of a variable. #HOST temporarily suspends the execution of the current form to execute a host operating system command.

### 8.5.1 Using #EXEMACRO

There is only a minimum amount of synchronization between the block of the example form as it has been developed so far. The customer number is copied into the bookings block so that a query in this block will bring out data for the correct customer. But there is no automatic display of the booking details when the customer block is queried. To achieve this, we are going to redefine the action of the [*Execute query*] key to bring the data into the bookings block.

What we will do is to define a key trigger for the customer number field that will redefine the action of the [*Execute query*] key so that it brings up the information we want. Get the DEFINE BLOCK window and select the TRIG-GER option. The trigger type is KEY-EXEQRY (Figure 8.25). Enter this trigger type and select CREATE. Then enter the #EXEMACRO statement:

```
┌──────────────────────────────────────────────────────────────────┐
│ CUSTOMER │                                                         │
│  ┌─────────────────────────────────────────────┐                  │
│  │     DEFINE BLOCK          Seq #  ▋ │ ntact: ████████████        │
│  │  Name  customers                                                │
│  │  ┌──────────────────────────────┐                              │
│  │  │     CHOOSE TRIGGER      ████ │    Pay method: ▐              │
│  │  │  Name                        │                              │
│  │  │  KEY-EXEQRY                  │                              │
│ ┌──────────────────────────────────────────────────────────────┐  │
│ │ Seq # ▋            TRIGGER STEP        Label ████               │
│ │ #EXEMACRO ENTQRY; NXTBLK; EXEQRY; PRVBLK;                       │
│ │                                                                │
│ │                                                                │
│ │ Message if trigger step fails:                                 │
│ │ ████████████████████████████████████████████                  │
│ │ Actions:                                                       │
│ │   CREATE        COPY         DROP          ATTRIBUTES  COMMENT  │
│ │   FORWARD       BACKWARD     PREV STEP     NEXT STEP            │
│ └──────────────────────────────────────────────────────────────┘  │
│ Form: cust_book   Block: customers   Page: 1   SELECT: B  Char Mode: Replace │
└──────────────────────────────────────────────────────────────────┘
```

**Figure 8.25** The KEY–EXEQRY trigger.

#EXEMACRO EXEQRY; NXTBLK; EXEQRY; PRVBLK;

#EXEMACRO will execute all the macro functions listed as parameters and separated (and terminated) by semicolons.

The command will be fired when the user of the form has set up a query and pressed the [*Execute query*] key. The effect is to execute the query in the customers block with the EXEQRY function, retrieving the appropriate row(s). Next, control will be transferred to the next block (the BOOKINGS block) with the NXTBLK function and a query executed in this block with the EXEQRY function. This will retrieve all the relevant bookings details for the customer. Then it returns control to the previous block (the CUSTOMERS block) with the PRVBLK function.

### 8.5.2 Variables

The #COPY and #ERASE commands are provided so that global variables can be used. These variables do not have to be defined in advance of their use. A common use of global variables is to pass the contents of fields from one form to another. This is usually the method employed when calling context-sensitive Help screens using the CALL or CALLQRY functions (see below).

#COPY allows us to copy the contents of a field into a global variable. For example:

    #COPY customers.cust_no GLOBAL.customer

copies the contents of the field `cust_no`, from the customer bookings enquiry screen, into a global variable called `customer`. Notice that the `cust_no` field name is preceded by the block name and the global variable has the keyword `GLOBAL` before its name. It will then be available to any form called after this assignment. `#COPY` can also be used to copy the contents of system variables to global ones. SQL*Forms provides several system variables; a complete list is in Appendix D. These variables are maintained by SQL*Forms; their values cannot be assigned any other way and their contents can only be read, not altered. Some of the most commonly used are:

- `SYSTEM.CURRENT_FORM` contains the name of the form currently being used.

- `SYSTEM.CURSOR_BLOCK` contains the name of the block in which the cursor is placed.

- `SYSTEM.CURSOR_FIELD` contains the name of the field in which the cursor is currently placed. The name is in the format *blockname.fieldname*.

- `SYSTEM.CURSOR_VALUE` contains the value of the field where the cursor is currently placed.

For example: `#COPY SYSTEM.CURSOR_FIELD GLOBAL.curfield` assigns the current field name held in the system variable to a global variable called `curfield`.

`#ERASE` removes the contents of a global variable and releases the memory it occupied. Once erased, the variable name is no longer valid, although on some systems a 'feature' of this command means that it can still be referred to. `#ERASE` cannot be used to erase the contents of a system variable. If the variable contents have already been erased or the variable was empty, the `#ERASE` command is ignored.

## Summary: Macros and SQL*Forms commands

☐ SQL*Forms provides four commands which can form steps in triggers. Of these, `#EXEMACRO` is the most commonly used. It is used to invoke a number of macro functions.

☐ Macro functions can mimic the actions of a person operating a form, moving the cursor from block to block, performing queries and so on.

☐ They can also invoke user-named triggers and call other forms.

☐ Other SQL*Forms commands deal with variables. There are system variables used to access the name and contents of the current form, block and field. Global user variables can be defined. The commands allow data to be copied to and from these variables.

☐ Other commands allow variables to be erased and operating system commands to be executed without leaving SQL*Forms.

---

**EXERCISE 8.4**

1.  Build the help screen to provide a list of customer numbers in the previous sections.

2.  Create the trigger to redefine the [*List of values*] key to display the help form.

3.  Execute the BOOKINGS form and enter a query by supplying a value for customer number and pressing the [*Execute query*] key. What happens?

4.  Define a default ORDER BY clause for the help form so that customers are always displayed in ascending sequence of customer number.

---

## 8.6   Nested forms

Realistic applications built with SQL\*Forms are usually made up of many different forms with control passing from one to another in a hierarchical structure, so you will often want to call one form from another. This can be done using the CALL and CALLQRY macro functions. They can be used in both event and key triggers and are invoked by the #EXEMACRO command.

When calling a form with the CALL function, the called form can be used just like any other form to query, insert, update or delete. If you use the CALLQRY function, then the called form can only be used to query. One of the most common uses for CALLQRY is to display forms used for active help screens.

### 8.6.1   Providing automatic help

The CALLQRY macro function will now be used to implement a help screen to assist the user of the example form to identify the customers who currently exist in the database. A screen that shows this information will be linked to the action of the [*List of values*] key in the example form.

First, the screen to be used to provide this help must be built. It can be quite simple; we need to look at the customers table and bring out the customer number and the customer name. We want to display as many customers as we can at a time, so we have a single, multi-record block. We have already covered how to build a simple form like this, so we will not go through it again. Build your own version as part of the next set of exercises.

The help form is linked by defining a new trigger which will call the form when the [*List of values*] key is pressed. The help to be provided is on what is a valid customer number, so this is a field-level trigger associated with the customer number field. Get the BOOKINGS form loaded and ready to modify. Call up the DEFINE FIELD window for the customer number field in the CUSTOMERS block. Select triggers and enter KEY-LISTVAL as the trigger name. Create the trigger. The trigger step will invoke CALLQRY to call the help screen in query-only mode. Type in the #EXEMACRO statement:

    #EXEMACRO CALLQRY custhelp;

You can see that, by defining the [*List of values*] key trigger in this way, the user has to query the help form explicitly when it appears. It would be nice if it could do this automatically for us. Use the KEY-STARTUP trigger to do this.

### 8.6.2   The KEY-STARTUP trigger

This trigger is fired whenever a form is first entered, either directly by running the form or indirectly when a form is called from another form. All SQL*Forms and macro functions can be used in the trigger. It is always best to define it at form level and it should only be defined once per form. To implement the rest of our help system, this trigger is defined to perform a query whenever the help form is called.

Load the help form and get the DEFINE FORM window. Select the trigger option. Give the trigger the KEY-STARTUP name, select CREATE and enter the trigger step (Figure 8.26):

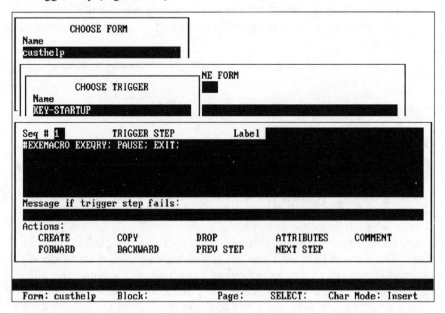

**Figure 8.26**   The help form KEY-STARTUP trigger.

```
#EXEMACRO EXEQRY; PAUSE; EXIT;
```

This trigger will execute a query to retrieve all the rows from the customers table. The PAUSE functions will wait until the user presses any key to continue. EXIT then returns control to the calling form, the BOOKINGS form.

## Summary: Nested forms

☐ Nested forms are implemented with the CALL and CALLQRY macro functions.

☐ CALLQRY insists that the called form is used for querying only. Forms called with CALL can be used for insert and update as well.

---

**EXERCISE 8.5**

1. Build the help screen to provide a list of customer numbers, in the previous sections.

2. Create the trigger to redefine the [*List of values*] key to display the help form.

3. Execute the BOOKINGS form and enter a query by supplying a value for customer number and pressing the [*Execute query*] key. What happens?

4. Define a default ORDER BY clause for the help form so that customers are always displayed in ascending sequence of customer number.

---

## 8.7   User exits

User exits are a way of integrating procedural code, written in a traditional third-generation programming language, into a SQL\*Forms application. The sorts of things you might need them for are check-digit or other complex validation, complex computations and so on where SQL cannot do what you need or where it is excessively inefficient.

Sometimes user exits are written just to increase the performance of a form. They are called from any level and type of trigger. Any detailed treatment of user exits is really beyond the scope of this book. In outline, though, once you have written and compiled your code, it can be called from a trigger by quoting the name of the compiled routine preceded by a hash mark. The example

```
#VALIDATE 10 25 var1
```

calls the procedure VALIDATE, passing as parameters the numbers 10 and 25 and the variable called var1. Parameters may be literals or variables.

## 8.8 Testing and debugging

SQL*Forms has several features to help with testing and debugging forms. Firstly, a form can be executed from within the SQL*Forms designer environment, thereby avoiding the need to exit from the designer to do a separate run. This is the way all the examples and exercises have been done. This facility is useful to show up and correct simple errors very quickly.

If you are unsure whether a field has been defined correctly you can get this information, whilst the form is still running, by using the advanced help screen. This is invoked by pressing the [*Help*] key twice.

If an Oracle error message is displayed on the status line, the [*Display error*] key will give more information by displaying the statement which caused the error and an indication as to its cause.

The next level of testing is provided by running the form in debug mode. This is accessed by pressing the [*Run-options*] key at any time while designing the form. Debug mode will display processing information about triggers and other states of the form. All run options selected from within SQL*Forms remain in force only for the duration of that run of SQL*Forms.

## 8.9 Multi-user considerations

When designing and building a form, it is necessary to take into account how it will behave when used by several users at the same time. This brief section considers COMMIT processing, table locking and runtime options that control how the form will work on a multi-user system.

### 8.9.1 COMMIT processing

When changes are made to the fields on a form or when records are inserted or deleted, the modifications only take place on the copy of the data held in memory. The database is not modified until the user presses the [*Commit*] key or until a trigger executes the COMMIT function.

The processing gone through when a COMMIT is actioned is:

```
For each block
    for each record
        for each field
            If field has been changed then
                validate field
For each block
    for each deleted record
        execute pre-delete trigger
        delete row from database
        execute post-delete trigger
    for each inserted record
        execute pre-insert trigger
        insert row in database
        execute post-insert trigger
        if record updated then
            execute pre-update trigger
            update row in database
            execute post-update trigger
COMMIT transaction
```

This sequence is followed for every block of the form each time a commit is requested. Should **any** of the operations fail, the commit for the whole form fails and the database remains unchanged. This strategy is rather drastic, but is the simplest to implement and control.

### 8.9.2  Locking

Before any changes can be applied to the database, SQL\*Forms has to take out locks on the tables or rows it is going to update. This is to prevent several users trying to update the same rows at the same time and overwriting one another's changes. For the most part, SQL\*Forms automatically handles the locking and you do not have to worry about its details. It is, however, important to understand the principles of how locking is handled so that you can design forms which fit with the way the locking is done and which, therefore, make efficient use of system resources in a multi-user environment.

First and most important, querying the data does not require any locks. Oracle automatically makes sure that all users see the same version of the data even while other users are in the process of updating it. Locks are required, however, when data is updated. There are detailed differences in the way the locking operates between those systems with the Transaction Processing Option and those without it. You may also come across SQL\*Forms version 2.3 running against version 5 of the database and this behaves in a similar way to version 6 without the option.

- With the Transaction Processing Option: when a row is updated on the screen, a lock is taken on the row, which prevents other users from updating it. They can still query that row and can query and update other rows in the same table. When the updates are committed, the lock remains just on the row and is released when the commit cycle has completed.

- Without the Transaction Processing Option: when a row is updated on the screen, a lock is taken out on the row, as before. Again, users can query the row and can query or update other rows in the same table. When the changes are committed, however, the lock is escalated to apply to the whole table. During the commit process, other users can continue to modify the rows on their form but their commits are queued up.

When several users are accessing and updating the same rows at the same time, they can change the values on the screen without having to worry about what other users are doing. When one user (*A*) commits, however, it is possible that the changes made by another user (*B*) have got in first and that the original values in the row, as seen by *A* when she first queried the data, have been changed. In this case, user *A* is warned of the change and is invited to re-query the data. Because he committed first, user *B* is unaware of user *A*'s involvement.

This locking process applies to the base tables of all the blocks in a form and is handled entirely automatically by SQL*Forms. If you update other tables in trigger processing and you are using Oracle without the Transaction Processing Option, you should explicitly specify the type of locking to be used with the SQL LOCK TABLE statement in the trigger code:

```
LOCK TABLE tablename IN ROW SHARE MODE;
```

# 8.10 Portability

Version 2.3 of SQL*Forms runs on both character and block-mode screens. Within each of these classes, the forms you generate are virtually device independent. You can design and build a form on one make of terminal and run it on another. In most cases, though, the form will need to be regenerated when you move it to new hardware. Forms can also be made to be portable across different styles of terminal but you will need to design such portability in from the start. The most usual case will be to build forms on character screens for later use on block-mode screens.

## 8.10.1 Block-mode screens

While asynchronous (or character) screens handle data a character at a time, block-mode screens transmit and receive whole screensful of data at a time. Terminals like the IBM 3270 and its derivatives use block-mode transmission, while the terminals on Unix machines, DEC VAX and so on are almost always asynchronous.

With async connections, the machine has complete control over what is going on at the terminal. The software knows every time a key is pressed. This gives SQL*Forms much more control over what is displayed and much more awareness of what the operator is doing.

Block mode is intended to minimize the transmission of data to and from the terminal. The mainframe usually knows very little of what is going on on the screen. It does not know where the cursor is, for instance. This means that field-level triggers do not normally fire. It is sometimes possible to force the terminal to behave asynchronously and, in this case, triggers will fire; there is a performance penalty, however, because you are creating more traffic on the network between the terminal and the computer.

Therefore, when designing a form to run on block-mode terminals, you should use block-level triggers to perform all of the field-level processing of the block together. You should also set the validation unit of the forms to be a block. If you are developing in a block-mode environment, this will be the default. But, if you are developing in a character-mode environment for later use in block mode, you should use SQL*Forms' runtime option to set block-level validation.

Because SQL*Forms cannot keep track of where the cursor is on block-mode terminals, fields cannot automatically scroll horizontally when the space on the screen is full, so always leave enough space for the full size of the fields. Vertical scrolling in multi-row blocks will scroll up the captions as well as the variable data on block mode terminals, so avoid scrolling multi-row blocks.

Finally, always make sure that there is at least one space between the caption and the field and between the field and the edge of the screen. Block-mode terminals need this space for field attributes, such as reverse video or blink attributes.

### 8.10.2 Runtime options

A form can be run with a set of options which will determine how it behaves and the memory resources it will use. These options become important when defining how the form should operate in a multi-user environment.

The options can be set up when the form is built. They are selected in the RUN OPTIONS window. In this case they remain in force only temporarily while SQL*Forms is run. The options can also be specified on the command line when executing the form with the RUNFORM command.

The important options to consider are those to do with memory management.

- The BUFFER RECORDS WITH FILE option will cause all records selected from the database to be buffered in a file rather than holding them in memory. This slows down processing, but allows more users to work in a limited amount of memory.

- The OPTIMIZE SQL AND TRANSACTION PROCESSING option governs how SQL statements are held in memory. By default, each SQL statement is allocated its own memory area. When this option is selected, the system will re-use areas of memory for several SQL statements. The latter is obviously better in terms of store occupancy but not so good for response times.

  Other options include:

- Display Menu – which will display a block menu when the form is first invoked, allowing the user to go directly to the block of his or her choice.

- Quiet Mode – switches off the terminal bell, which normally sounds when error messages are displayed.

- Statistics – displays information about memory utilization of triggers. This is normally used during performance tuning.

*Nine*
# SQL*Menu

Almost every serious application system will need some sort of front-end system to control access to the various functions of the system. SQL*Menu provides a menuing system which allows users of the application to invoke its various functions. It also provides access security by limiting the functions which can be invoked by various classes of users. The actions invoked from the menus can be used to run Oracle tools or any other applications or operating system commands.

Menu structures implemented by SQL*Menu can be quite intricate. For most applications, they require careful design and may reflect the way in which the whole company operates, rather than just how one computer application system works. For this reason, it is often sensible to have a person nominated as the SQL*Menu administrator, whose responsibility it is to coordinate all the uses of SQL*Menu.

This chapter describes SQL*Menu version 5, which provides a close integration with SQL*Forms version 3.

## 9.1 SQL*Menu basics

Menus are designed and built in very much the same sort of way as an application is built with SQL*Forms or SQL*ReportWriter: the various components of the menu structure are defined, the menu system is generated and then it is run. SQL*Menu keeps the definition of the menu system in a series of tables in the database.

### 9.1.1 Running SQL*Menu

SQL*Menu is made up of four distinct components which **design**, **generate**, **run** and **document** menus. The design component acts as an umbrella environment from which all the others can be started. It is invoked from the operating system command line with SQLMENU (or in lower case, depending on operating system). As usual, you can put the username and password on the command line. There are various other, optional and less important parameters on the command line as well. When loaded, SQL*Menu displays its main menu

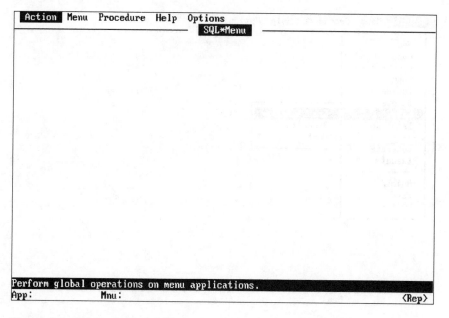

**Figure 9.1** The main menu bar.

screen (Figure 9.1). The format is very similar to the main menu screen of SQL\*Forms. The options are in a bar across the top of the screen and the system is controlled by function keys in the same way as SQL\*Forms. There is also a help service which can be invoked from the main menu bar or by pressing [*Help*]. If the latter, it is context-sensitive, taking you to the section of the help information which is relevant to the task you are carrying out.

### 9.1.2 Access privileges
Even though a user may have access rights to the database, he or she will not be able to use SQL\*Menu unless the appropriate privileges have been given. This may only be done by someone with DBA privilege and is done using one of the options on the *Action* submenu (Figure 9.2).

Privileges are: **execute**, to allow a user to operate the finished menu system; **design**, to allow a user to design and build menus; **administrate**, to define a user as the administrator of SQL\*Menu. Each level also gives the user the previous level of privilege. Thus design privilege also confers execute privilege.

### 9.1.3 Roles
The concept of *roles* is used to define the classes of users who may use an application. Roles correspond roughly to job function. The roles are defined and then the usernames of the people with that role are specified. For instance,

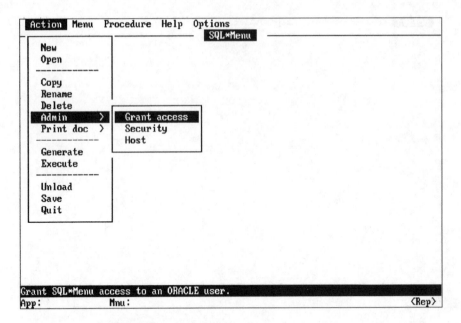

**Figure 9.2**   Menu selection to grant access.

you might set up a role with the name `Counter_staff` associated with the usernames of the people who regularly manned the counter and could accept bookings. However this role would not, for instance, be able to get to the part of the system used to enter details of new cars. A single user may have more than one role.

### 9.1.4   Styles of menu

By default, SQL\*Menu generates menus which look very much like its own menu structure. In this **pull-down style** there is a menu bar with submenus which pull down from it.

Menus can be generated in two other styles. **Bar style** menus rely entirely on the menu bar at the top of the screen to present the options. Submenus are presented as another menu bar, replacing the original. **Full-screen** menus (Figure 9.3) present the options down the screen. Submenus are shown on separate screens. Full-screen menus have more room at the top and bottom of the screen to show fixed information.

## 9.2   An example menu structure

As a way of showing how SQL\*Menu operates, a menu structure will be developed for 50K Cars' computer applications. The menus cover all of

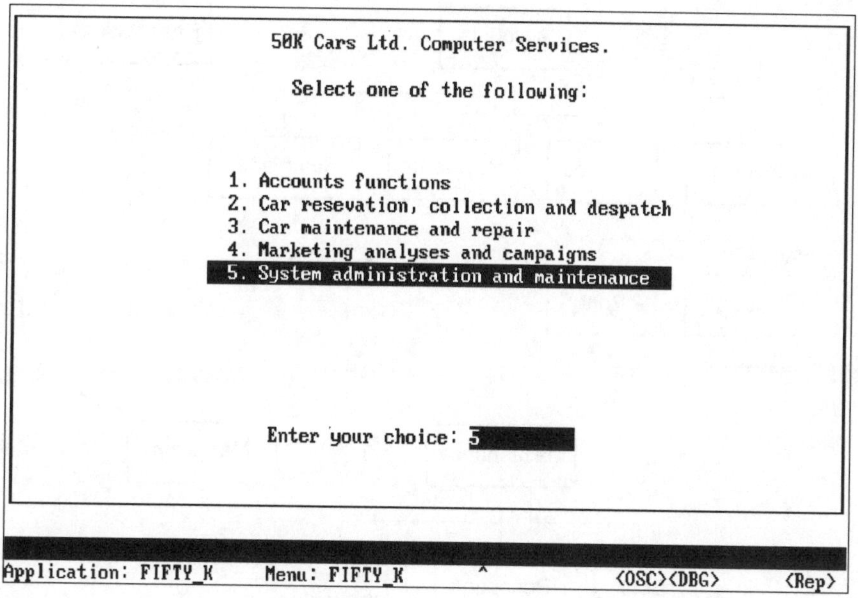

```
┌─────────────────────────────────────────────────────────────┐
│  ┌───────────────────────────────────────────────────────┐  │
│  │                                                       │  │
│  │           50K Cars Ltd. Computer Services.            │  │
│  │                                                       │  │
│  │            Select one of the following:               │  │
│  │                                                       │  │
│  │                                                       │  │
│  │         1. Accounts functions                         │  │
│  │         2. Car resevation, collection and despatch    │  │
│  │         3. Car maintenance and repair                 │  │
│  │         4. Marketing analyses and campaigns           │  │
│  │         5. System administration and maintenance      │  │
│  │                                                       │  │
│  │                                                       │  │
│  │                                                       │  │
│  │                                                       │  │
│  │            Enter your choice: 5                       │  │
│  │                                                       │  │
│  │                                                       │  │
│  └───────────────────────────────────────────────────────┘  │
│                                                             │
├─────────────────────────────────────────────────────────────┤
│ Application: FIFTY_K    Menu: FIFTY_K        ^    <OSC><DBG>    <Rep> │
└─────────────────────────────────────────────────────────────┘
```

**Figure 9.3**　Full-screen style menu.

the areas in which they use their computers, some of which have been developed as examples in other chapters.

## 9.2.1　The menu structure

The structure of the computer service is reflected in the structure of the menus for 50K Cars. Figure 9.4 shows the structure. At the top level, the service is split between accounts, car reservation, car maintenance, marketing and system administration. Each of these, in turn, is divided into separate sections. Each of the boxes with lines below it corresponds to a menu and each of the lines out of a box corresponds to a menu choice.

Different people will need to be able to access different parts of the service. The roles are:

- **Front-of-house**. These are the people who accept reservations and book cars out on rental and back in again. They need access to the car reservation section of the service.

- **Accounts**. Theses are the people who deal with routine accounting and queries about customers' accounts. They need only to have access to the accounting section of the service.

- **Maintenance**. These are the people who look after the maintenance of the cars. They can use the car maintenance section of the service.

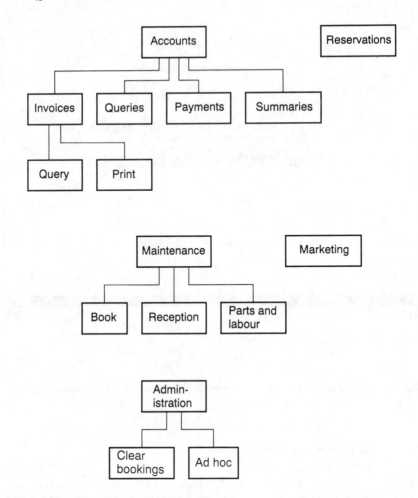

**Figure 9.4**   The menu structure of the example.

- **Marketing**. They have access to various marketing functions, doing mail-shots and other campaigns.

- **System administration**. These are the technicians who look after the service. They have access to all the services with the exception of account-ing and personnel.

- **Managers**. They have unrestricted access.

To define these roles, use *AdminD* and *Security* on the *Action* menu. This displays a spread table showing all the roles defined so far. Just like SQL\*Forms (V3), data like this can be displayed as a spread table with a single spread showing all the roles or as a form-based display with a single screen for

```
 Action  Menu  Procedure  Help  Options
                          Role Definition
 ┌──────────────────────────┬─────────┬────────┬─────────┬──────────┐
 │            Role          │ Select  │ Debug  │   OS    │ Backgr.  │
 │            Name          │ Users   │ Mode   │ Command │  Menu    │
 │                          │         │        │         │          │
 │  FRONT_OF_HOUSE          │ ( * )   │ [   ]  │ [   ]   │ [ X ]    │
 │  ACCOUNTS                │ ( * )   │ [   ]  │ [   ]   │ [ X ]    │
 │  MAINTENANCE             │ ( * )   │ [   ]  │ [   ]   │ [ X ]    │
 │  MARKETING               │ ( * )   │ [   ]  │ [   ]   │ [ X ]    │
 │  SYSTEM_ADMIN            │ ( * )   │ [ X ]  │ [ X ]   │ [ X ]    │
 │  MANAGERS                │ ( * )   │ [   ]  │ [   ]   │ [ X ]    │
 │                          │         │        │         │          │
 │                          │         │        │         │          │
 │                          ├─────────┴────────┴─────────┴──────────┤
 │                          │                                     > │
 └──────────────────────────┴───────────────────────────────────────┘
 Enter the name of the role.
 App:            Mnu:                                          <Rep>
```

**Figure 9.5**  The role definition spread table.

each role. The [*Alter display*] toggles from one style of display to the other. You can define which is to be used as default using the *Options* menu.

Figure 9.5 shows the spread table for these roles. Notice that only the system administration role has access to debug mode and to operating system commands. To define the users which have each of these roles, move the cursor to the *Select users* box and press [*Select*]; then enter the usernames.

## 9.2.2  Defining the applications and menus

It is quite possible to put all of the menus for the whole of the computer services into one structure. It is sometimes better, however, to split them into **applications** to provide a top-level partitioning of the totality of the available services. The example is not really complex enough to warrant this division into separate applications and it will be built as a single application.

The application is named by selecting *New* on the *Action* menu and then defined using the *Application* option under *Menu* to change any of the default details (Figure 9.6).

Each menu in the application is defined using the *Menu* option on the *Menu* submenu. Each option on a menu is defined using the *Item* option on the *Menu* submenu (the terminology needed to describe how to use a menu-based system to define another menu-based system gets rather repetitive). The top-level menu of an application has to have the same name as the application.

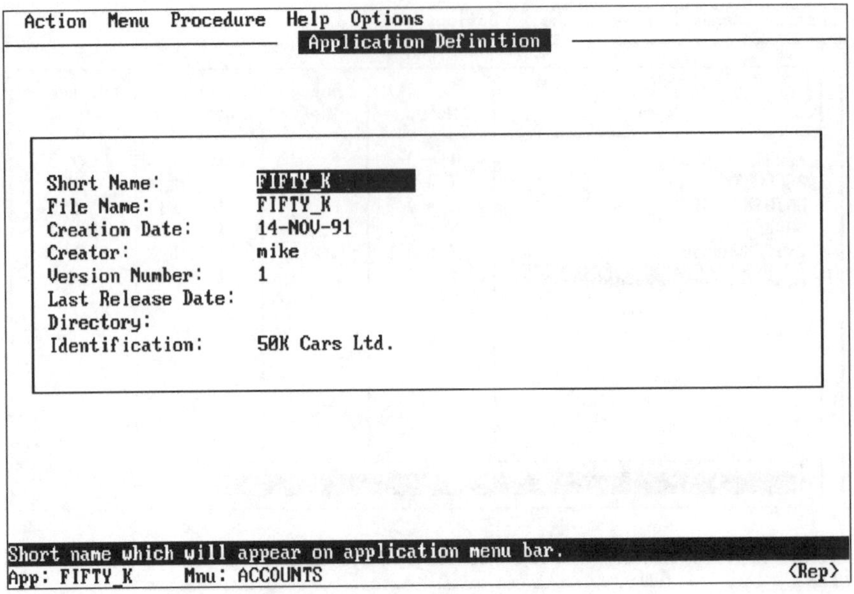

```
 Action  Menu  Procedure  Help  Options
 ─────────────────────────────┤ Application Definition ├──────────────
│
│
│
│  ┌─────────────────────────────────────────────────────────────┐
│  │                                                             │
│  │   Short Name:        FIFTY_K▓▓▓▓▓▓▓▓▓▓                       │
│  │   File Name:         FIFTY_K                                 │
│  │   Creation Date:     14-NOV-91                               │
│  │   Creator:           mike                                    │
│  │   Version Number:    1                                       │
│  │   Last Release Date:                                         │
│  │   Directory:                                                 │
│  │   Identification:    50K Cars Ltd.                           │
│  │                                                             │
│  └─────────────────────────────────────────────────────────────┘
│
│
│
 ──────────────────────────────────────────────────────────────────
 Short name which will appear on application menu bar.
 App: FIFTY_K     Mnu: ACCOUNTS                              <Rep>
```

**Figure 9.6**   The application definition screen.

In just the same way as SQL\*Forms (V3), spread tables are used to display
the details of all the menus and of all options on a menu (Figure 9.7).
Full-screen displays of a single menu or menu option can be obtained by
pressing [*Change display type*] (Figure 9.8).

[*Zoom in*] moves from application definition to menu definition to menu item
definition. [*Zoom out*] goes the other way. [*Navigate*] allows you to specify
exactly which bit of the application or menu definition you want to look at.

Use [*Insert record*] to get a blank record in which to specify the menu and
[*Accept*] when you have finished defining all the menus. When filling in the
menu definition, you must define a menu title and subtitle even though these
will not appear if you use the pull-down or bar menu styles. The bottom title
is optional and it, too, only appears on full-screen menus.

### 9.2.3   Defining the menu items
Having defined all the menus, the next task is to define all the options on each
menu. Again, either spread table or full-screen displays are available.

Use [*Insert record*] to get a blank record in which to define the menu item
and [*Accept*] when you have finished defining the items.

Figure 9.9 shows the full-screen display for the first item on the top-level
menu. The item number is just the sequence of the option within the menu.
It can be resequenced by changing the number. The Command Type specifies
what action this option is to perform. It can call another menu, issue an

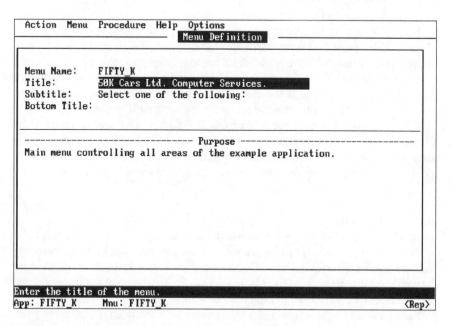

```
  Action   Menu   Procedure   Help   Options
  ─────────────────────────┤ Menu Definition ├─────────────────

           Menu                                                   Bottom
           Name              Title           Subtitle             Title

        ACCOUNTS          Accounting functi  Select one of the
        ADMIN             Systems administr  Select one of the
        FIFTY_K           50K Cars Ltd. Com  Select one of the
        INVOICES          Invoice preparati  Select one of the
        MAINTENANCE       Car maintenance    Select one of the
        MARKETING         Marketing jobs     Select one of the




                                                                          ⟩

  Enter the name of the menu.
  App: FIFTY_K      Mnu: FIFTY_K                                    ⟨Rep⟩
```

**Figure 9.7**   The menu definition spread table.

```
  Action   Menu   Procedure   Help   Options
  ─────────────────────────┤ Menu Definition ├─────────────────

   Menu Name:    FIFTY_K
   Title:        50K Cars Ltd. Computer Services.
   Subtitle:     Select one of the following:
   Bottom Title:

   ──────────────────────────── Purpose ────────────────────────────
   Main menu controlling all areas of the example application.






  Enter the title of the menu.
  App: FIFTY_K      Mnu: FIFTY_K                                    ⟨Rep⟩
```

**Figure 9.8**   Definition screen for top-level menu.

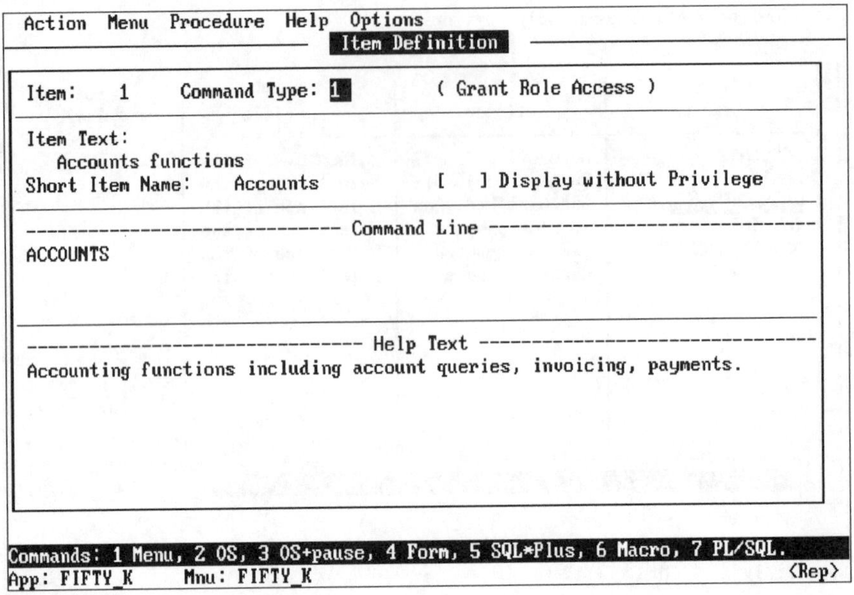

```
 Action  Menu  Procedure  Help  Options
 ──────────────────────────────────┃ Item Definition ┃──────────────
 ┌───────────────────────────────────────────────────────────────┐
 │ Item:   1      Command Type: ▓      ( Grant Role Access )       │
 │ ─────────────────────────────────────────────────────────────  │
 │ Item Text:                                                      │
 │     Accounts functions                                         │
 │ Short Item Name:    Accounts            [   ] Display without Privilege │
 │ ─────────────────────────────────────────────────────────────  │
 │ ───────────────────────────── Command Line ─────────────────── │
 │ ACCOUNTS                                                        │
 │                                                                 │
 │                                                                 │
 │ ───────────────────────────── Help Text ────────────────────── │
 │ Accounting functions including account queries, invoicing, payments. │
 │                                                                 │
 │                                                                 │
 │                                                                 │
 └───────────────────────────────────────────────────────────────┘
 Commands: 1 Menu, 2 OS, 3 OS+pause, 4 Form, 5 SQL*Plus, 6 Macro, 7 PL/SQL.
 App: FIFTY_K    Mnu: FIFTY_K                                    <Rep>
```

**Figure 9.9** Item definition screen.

operating system command, invoke a form and so on. The example in Figure 9.9 calls another menu, `accounts`.

Select `Grant Role Access` to define which roles have access to this option (Figure 9.10). Initially, no roles will have access; use [*Insert record*] and [*List of values*] to see what roles have been defined and to give access to the appropriate ones.

The `Item text` is the text which appears against this item on full-screen menus. The `Short Item Name` is the name which appears for this item on pull-down and bar menus. Normally, menu items are not displayed if the user logged on to SQL\*Menu does not have the role access to the item. This can be changed by checking the `Display without Privilege` box. The `Command Line` is used to specify the action to be taken when the option is chosen. If the action is to go to another menu, the command line just quotes the name of the menu.

### 9.2.4 Parameters

It is often useful to be able to have parameters in the command line. For instance, you might want to invoke SQL\*Plus and pass the current username and password as parameters. SQL\*Menu provides a number of predefined parameters of which the username and password are the most commonly used. You may define your own parameters, as well.

Parameter names have two letters. They may be referenced in command lines or in PL/SQL procedures. In command lines the parameter name is preceded

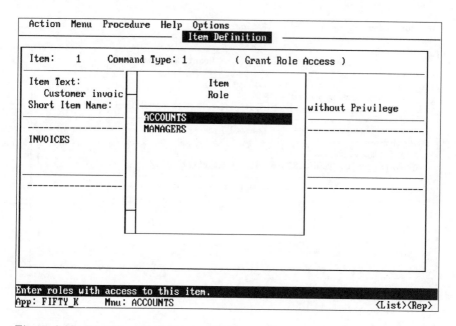

**Figure 9.10**   The *Grant Role Access* window.

by an ampersand (&) and in PL/SQL it is preceded by a colon (:). Thus an example command line might be: `sqlplus &UN/&PW`. User parameters are defined using the *Parameter* option on the *Menu* submenu. They are prompted for when the menu item which references the parameter is invoked.

### 9.2.5   PL/SQL in menus

The action of a menu item may be to carry out a PL/SQL program. The PL/SQL code is entered as an anonymous block (i.e. one not starting with `PROCEDURE procname IS`) in the `Command Line` section of the menu item definition. In the example, one of the options on the system administration menu is to clear out old bookings from the bookings table. This is done with PL/SQL code, the start of which is shown in Figure 9.11.

### 9.2.6   Runtime

Application menus are generated and run using options on the *Action* menu. Once generated, they may also be invoked as a separate run of RUNREP quoting the application name as a parameter.

The style of menus used depends on what has been set up using the *Options* menu or on a parameter on the RUNREP command line. Figure 9.12 shows the target menu system in the example with three levels of selection activated.

```
 Action   Menu   Procedure   Help   Options
┌───────────────────────────── Item Definition ──────────────────────────┐
│                                                                         │
│  Item:    █    Command Type: 7        ( Grant Role Access )             │
│ ──────────────────────────────────────────────────────────────────────│
│  Item Text:                                                             │
│     Clear old booking data                                              │
│  Short Item Name:   Clear bookings    [  ] Display without Privilege    │
│                                                                         │
│ ───────────────────────────── Command Line ─────────────────────────── │
│  BEGIN                                                                   │
│    DELETE FROM bookings                                                  │
│    WHERE MONTHS_BETWEEN(SYSDATE, date_rent_start) > 12;                  │
│                                                                         │
│ ───────────────────────────── Help Text ──────────────────────────────│
│                                                                         │
│                                                                         │
│                                                                         │
│                                                                         │
│                                                                         │
│                                                                         │
└─────────────────────────────────────────────────────────────────────────┘
 Enter the item number for this item.
 App: FIFTY_K    Mnu: ADMIN                                        ⟨Ins⟩
```

**Figure 9.11** *Clear Bookings* item definition.

```
┌─────────────────────────────────────────────────────────────────────────┐
│ ▐Accounts▌ Reservations   Maintenance   Marketing   Admin               │
│ ┌──────────┬─────────┐        50K Cars Ltd. ──────────────────           │
│ │ Invoices > │▐Query ▌│                                                  │
│ │ Queries    │ Print  │                                                  │
│ │ Payments   └────────┘                                                  │
│ │ Summaries  │                                                           │
│ └────────────┘                                                           │
│                                                                         │
│                                                                         │
│                                                                         │
│                                                                         │
│                                                                         │
│                                                                         │
│                                                                         │
│                                                                         │
│                                                                         │
│                                                                         │
│ Query customer invoice details              •                           │
│ Application: FIFTY_K                    ⟨OSC⟩⟨DBG⟩            ⟨Rep⟩       │
└─────────────────────────────────────────────────────────────────────────┘
```

**Figure 9.12** The target menu system.

*Part 4*

*Reports*

*Ten*
# Report writing products

This part of the book describes the most important Oracle tools for building applications which produce reports from the database. Normally, when you use the word 'report', you think of printed reports on paper, but all the products allow you to direct the data to the screen, to a printer or to a file.

There is a wide spectrum in the complexity of reporting requirements. At the simple end of the spectrum there are straightforward listings, while at the complex end there are multi-dimensional matrix reports. You would not expect a single product to satisfy this whole range of requirements efficiently, so Oracle provides a number of tools to cover the whole of the spectrum. The most appropriate one depends on the type of report you want to produce. The two products which are described in the next two chapters are intended to satisfy the centre of the spectrum.

- SQL*Plus, described in Part 2, is very useful for producing straightforward reports. A command file can be built to produce the report. By default, output will be to the screen but it can be directed to a text file which is then spooled out.

- SQL*QMX is really an end-user tool, intended for non-technical people, but it could be useful for simple reports. However, SQL*QMX was bought in by Oracle, rather than developed in-house, and they have had trouble supporting it. It is likely that they will either withdraw support altogether or to hand support over to the original developers of the product. Either way, it might be wise to use the product only for *ad hoc* applications rather than for crucial production systems.

- SQL*ReportWriter is the subject of the next chapter. It is intended to cope with the reporting requirements of the majority of routine commercial applications. Its approach is very similar to that of SQL*Forms, with extensive use of defaults. This results in fast development of applications provided that they conform to one of the report models handled by the system.

- SQL*Report is the subject of Chapter 12. It is Oracle's old reporting product, which was supposed to be replaced by SQL*ReportWriter. It is intricate and labour intensive to use, but it does have many features which SQL*ReportWriter does not. It is likely to be around for some time yet.

■ For the most complicated reports it could be necessary to retreat into using a third-generation language and to access the database through Oracle's 3GL interfaces, the PRO*... series. These are beyond the scope of this book.

SQL*ReportWriter is the product you will use for that middle-ground of reasonably complicated reports, but which do not have any specialist or highly complex requirements. And within this scope, it is very effective.

For a long time SQL*Report was Oracle's only heavyweight report writer. It was supposed to have been totally superseded by the new, long-awaited SQL*ReportWriter. This has not happened for two main reasons. Firstly, SQL*Report is a powerful system which, if you have the time and the expertise, can be made to produce almost any report you could want. The problem is having the time and the expertise. SQL*ReportWriter, on the other hand, is quick but not so capable.

The second reason is that SQL*Report's procedural constructs (it has `IF...THEN...ELSE` and `GOTO`) and the fact that you can use `INSERT` and `UPDATE` as well as `SELECT` statements have meant that it has been used for all sorts of jobs not directly related to reports. Batch updating is the main example. Though many of the extra jobs pressed on SQL*Report can now be done in PL/SQL, many of Oracle's customers have already made a big investment in programs based on SQL*Report.

The result is that Oracle has decided to continue to support SQL*Report for the moment, though they say it will not be further developed. It is described in some detail but some of the more complicated facilities are omitted.

*Eleven*
# SQL*ReportWriter

## 11.1 SQL*ReportWriter basics

The philosophy behind SQL*ReportWriter has much in common with that of SQL*Forms. They both use a system of menus and point-and-select for users to specify their needs. They both use system-generated defaults to minimize the work needed from the user. The style of the user interface is almost exactly the same as SQL*Forms version 3. Although version 1.1 of SQL*ReportWriter does not use screen painting to lay out the report, an upcoming version will do so, as does SQL*Forms.

SQL*Forms, however, produces interactive applications while SQL*ReportWriter produces essentially passive ones which just display data. It is, therefore, rather simpler.

### 11.1.1 Structure of a report

The whole operation of SQL*ReportWriter revolves around a number of simple concepts. Get these straight and the system is very easy to understand.

First, the report is made up of the components in Figure 11.1. At the outer level, there is a report title and report trailer page. The report itself starts with a report header and ends with a report footer. Within these is the body of the report.

The body of the report is divided up into groups. A group is any subdivision of the report which corresponds to a logical structure of the data in the report: all the data for one customer, for instance. Each group may have a group header, group body and group footer. These might contain, respectively, the identity of the customer, several detail lines about the customer's rental bookings and the total of her rental charges for the current month.

The whole of the report is presented in pages. Each of these has a page header and a page footer. Sometimes a report will be wider than can be fitted on one page, in which case it is defined in several *panels*, each of which will fit on a page. Spreadsheet users will be familiar with this method of printing wide documents.

This structure is not always rigidly followed, of course. Many reports will have only some of these components. Often there will be no page footers, for instance.

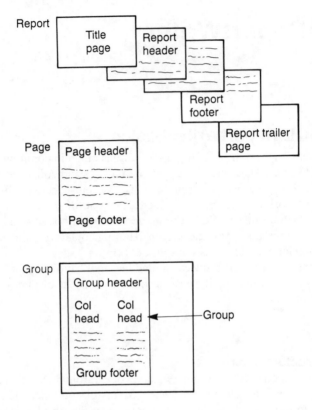

**Figure 11.1**  Report components.

### 11.1.2  Report objects

A number of 'Report Objects' are used to define each element of this structure. Do not be fooled by the use of the word 'object' here. This is not an object-oriented system; nor does it claim to be. The report objects are:

- **Groups** are defined in terms of control breaks and their relationships with other groups. Each group has an associated query.

- **Queries** define the data to be included in the report. There may be several queries associated with a report and they may be interrelated. Queries are associated with groups.

- **Fields** are areas in which to display data from the database or other data derived with the SELECT statement of a query.

- **Summaries** are like fields, but are used to display totals or other summary data, rather than data from the SELECT. They can be associated with footers, for instance to show carried-forward totals, headers (brought-for-ward totals), groups (group totals) and so on.

- **Text** objects are the fixed text for headings, captions etc.

Finally, the definition of the report is rounded off by describing page size, destination device and any parameters which govern the way the report executes at runtime.

You can see from this structure that report objects are associated with one another. Each *group* is associated with a *query*. A *group* may be associated with another *group*. A *group* will have associated *fields*, *summaries* and *text*. This linking can be important when you come to modify report structures, as we shall see later.

### 11.1.3   SQL*ReportWriter components

SQL*ReportWriter is made up of a number of components which look after the design and definition of the report, the generation of the report program and the actual execution of the report program. All these components can be accessed from within a single environment, SQLREP. The components to generate and run the report program are also available directly from the operating system command line.

The definition of the report is held in tables in the database, and it is these tables which SQLREP uses when you define the report. There is nothing special about these tables. They are available under your user name and you can use SQL*Plus to explore their structure. Obviously you should not attempt to alter their contents because, in doing so, you will mess up the report definition.

The program to generate the report program, GENREP, reads the report definition in the database and produces a coded, semi-compiled format of the report program. This is not held in the database but in a separate file. RUNREP interprets this coded form of the report program, accesses the data in the database and produces the report. It uses a definition of the capabilities of the printer to be used which is held in another free-standing file. This printer definition file is maintained by another component of the system, PRINTDEF.

Finally, there are two utility programs which are used primarily to move report definitions from one system to another. DUMPREP takes a report definition in the database and dumps it out to an ASCII file which can be carried across to another system. LOADREP copies a report definition into the database from the ASCII file produced by DUMPREP.

### 11.1.4   Use of function keys

As in the previous chapters, the various keys are not referred to by the label on the keytop but by the function they carry out. For example, [*Previous field*] is the key or key combination which moves the cursor to the previous field on the screen. The mapping of which function is carried out by which key (or combination of keys) depends on the type of hardware being used.

A new structure for key usage has been implemented which is intended to be common to both SQL\*ReportWriter and SQL\*Forms version 3. Note, however, that earlier versions of SQL\*Forms have an entirely different scheme. The new scheme splits the key functions into three groups:

- **Text editing** keys, which are used, when designing forms, to enter headings, captions, boilerplate text and so on.

- **Navigation** keys, which are also used during the design phase to move around the screen and from one screen to another.

- **General** keys for all the miscellaneous jobs, like screen dumps, printing and so on.

Within each of these categories, the key sequences for each operation are build in a logical way. Apparently, this new structure is to be used in all Oracle products from now on. It is an improvement on the old hotch-potch of key allocations, but there are still annoying differences in the key allocations as they are set up when you first install the products. Fortunately, there is a utility program, SQL\*Terminal, which can be used to redefine the key allocations so that you (or your DBA) can build your own consistent set.

### 11.1.5   The main menu bar

SQL\*ReportWriter is controlled using a number of menus. The top level of this menu structure is the menu bar which appears across the top of the screen when the system is loaded (Figure 11.2). The other menus 'pull-down' from the various options on the main menu bar when you select the option. You will see how the menus are used as we work through an example. In outline, though, the options on the main menu bar are:

- **Action** deals with the housekeeping functions of managing reports and report definitions. It has options to open, rename, execute a report and so on.

- **Query** is used to specify the queries which will generate the data for the report.

- **Group** is used to define how the groups of data, returned by the query, are to be formatted.

- **Field** is used to define the format and position of each field within the group.

- **Summary** is used to specify totals and other summary information.

- **Text** is used to specify fixed text for report header, page header, footers etc.

- **Report** is used to define the destination and overall shape of the report.

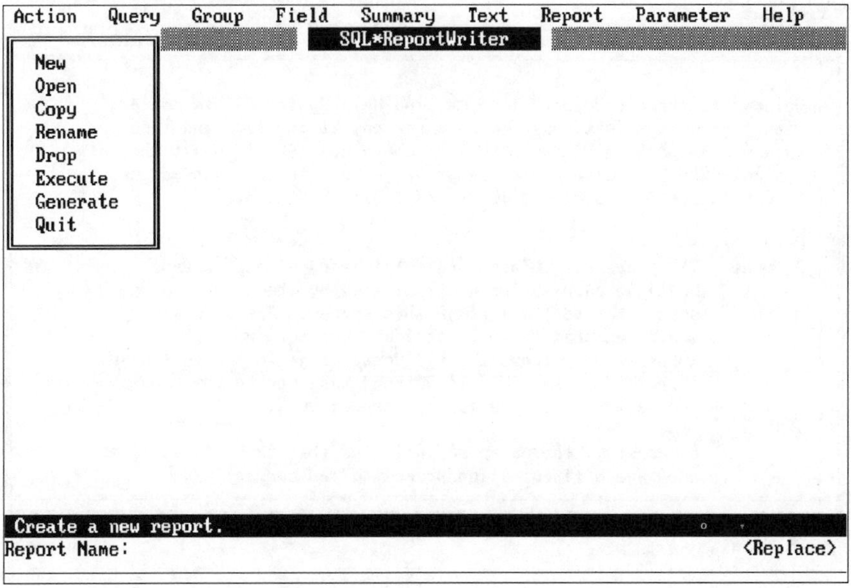

```
Action    Query    Group    Field    Summary   Text    Report   Parameter   Help
                                 SQL*ReportWriter
 ┌─────────────┐
 │ New         │
 │ Open        │
 │ Copy        │
 │ Rename      │
 │ Drop        │
 │ Execute     │
 │ Generate    │
 │ Quit        │
 └─────────────┘




Create a new report.                                            o    ,
Report Name:                                                        <Replace>
```

**Figure 11.2**   The main menu bar.

- **Parameter** is used to specify runtime parameters, which can be used in the query which generates the data for a report.

- **Help** provides access to the help service.

## 11.1.6   The HELP system

There is a very comprehensive on-line help service. Selecting the *Help* option on the main menu bar gets you into the introductory help screen (Figure 11.3). You can also get help by pressing the [*Help*] key at any time. If you use the [*Help*] key, the help you get will be context-sensitive, that is it will be tailored to what you are currently trying to do.

This useful service is largely self-documenting and easy to use. Each help screen has a menu bar across the top which is used to navigate around amongst the help information. You will see that some words in each screen of information are highlighted. These highlighted keywords are buttons to take you on to further information. Use the cursor keys to pick out the keyword about which you want more information (it will go into reverse video or change colour, depending on your terminal) and press [*Select*]. The help service will follow the link associated with the keyword and will display the appropriate screen of information. There are many useful examples in the help system and it is well worth exploring it fully.

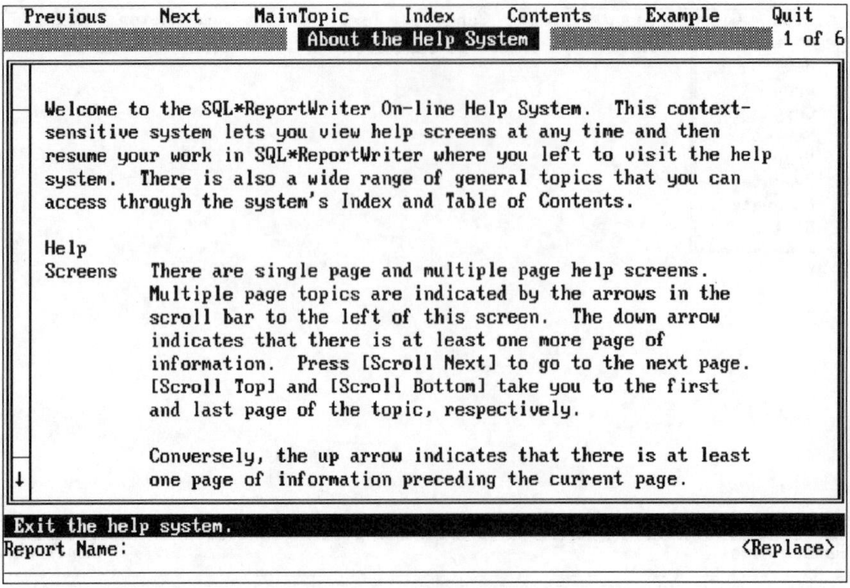

```
 Previous    Next    MainTopic    Index    Contents    Example    Quit
                      About the Help System                       1 of 6
```
```
    Welcome to the SQL*ReportWriter On-line Help System.  This context-
    sensitive system lets you view help screens at any time and then
    resume your work in SQL*ReportWriter where you left to visit the help
    system.  There is also a wide range of general topics that you can
    access through the system's Index and Table of Contents.

    Help
    Screens    There are single page and multiple page help screens.
               Multiple page topics are indicated by the arrows in the
               scroll bar to the left of this screen.  The down arrow
               indicates that there is at least one more page of
               information.  Press [Scroll Next] to go to the next page.
               [Scroll Top] and [Scroll Bottom] take you to the first
               and last page of the topic, respectively.

               Conversely, the up arrow indicates that there is at least
               one page of information preceding the current page.
```
```
 Exit the help system.
Report Name:                                                <Replace>
```

**Figure 11.3**   The help service introductory screen.

### 11.1.7   Running SQL*ReportWriter

SQL*ReportWriter can be invoked with a range of parameter values with a command of the form:

```
sqlrep keyword1=value keyword2=value ...
```

The parameters define the detail of how SQL*ReportWriter will run. They are all optional; defaults will be used for missing parameters. To start with, the only one needed is the username and password. Even these will be prompted for if you do not provide them. For example:

```
sqlrep USERID=mike/cornucopia
```

The other possible parameters are described in Section 11.6

## Summary: SQL*ReportWriter basics

☐ The product is intended for mainstream reporting requirements. Very simple reports can often be achieved more quickly with other Oracle products. Some complex reports will be beyond SQL*ReportWriter's capabilities.

☐ The product is similar in concept to SQL*Forms, using defaults to minimize the work needed from the developer. The user interface is almost identical to SQL*Forms version 3.

☐  A report is defined in terms of 'report objects' which specify queries, data groups, summary data (totals etc.), text elements and so on.

☐  There is a useful context-sensitive help service with a system of buttons which lets you explore related topics automatically.

## 11.2   Building a default report

To start with, we go through the building of a report using the default options. This and several of the subsequent sections are written as if you have SQL*ReportWriter running in front of you. Invoke `sqlrep` and log on.

The report will be a simple list of the bookings table showing those bookings with payment still outstanding. An example page from the report is shown in Figure 11.4. In later sections, we will come back and modify the report to make it look better and to give it more functionality.

### 11.2.1   The Action menu

The main menu bar is displayed when you log on. Use the [*Next choice*] and [*Previous choice*] keys (these are usually the cursor keys) to move across the

| 03-OCT-92 | | Unpaid Bookings | | | | | Page 1 | of 1 |
|---|---|---|---|---|---|---|---|---|
| Booking | Cust | Date Start | Period | Model | Registration | Miles | Amount |
| 502 | 1553 | 20-DEC-90 | 015 | BMW 750 | G123RMR | 02545 | 04002.00 |
| 118 | 8979 | 23-JAN-91 | 004 | JAG XJS | H626RPG | 00892 | 01123.80 |
| 265 | 2029 | 04-MAY-91 | 016 | RR SSPIR | E246WFC | 00556 | 01366.60 |
| 504 | 1553 | 12-APR-91 | 001 | JAG XJ6 | G551JBA | 00284 | 00476.95 |
| 811 | 701 | 05-SEP-91 | 008 | P944 T | G202XRP | 00636 | 01279.80 |
| 812 | 2338 | 15-OCT-91 | 015 | MERC 560 | J644TNR | 01416 | 02477.85 |
| 2123 | 667 | 19-SEP-91 | 005 | FERR TR | H935CSA | 02091 | 00501.80 |
| 2124 | 667 | 19-SEP-91 | 005 | BMW 750 | G123RMR | 10780 | 01823.00 |
| 2126 | 667 | 02-OCT-91 | 010 | ASTON V8 | H266MHU | 00671 | 00873.60 |
| 2127 | 668 | 01-OCT-91 | 001 | MERC 560 | J644TNR | 00133 | 00106.00 |
| 2128 | 701 | 14-APR-91 | 010 | LAMB COU | H235BMA | 00765 | 00512.00 |

**Figure 11.4**   A page from the finished report.

menu bar; each option is highlighted when the cursor is on it. Note that, at the bottom of the screen, there is an explanation of what the option does. The name of the report currently being worked on is also displayed. At the moment it will be blank because we have neither opened an existing report definition nor created a new one. The system also indicates whether the keystrokes on the keyboard are to be *insert*ed in front of the current cursor position or to *replace* the character at the cursor position. The [*Insert/replace*] toggles between the two.

As well as positioning the cursor on an option and pressing [*Select*], an option can be selected by just typing the first letter of the option, as in Lotus 1-2-3. This applies both across the top menu and within the subsidiary menus.

The *Action* option is already highlighted when you get into SQL\*Report-Writer; press [*Select*]. This pulls down the menu (Figure 11.5). It is reasonably self-evident what each of these options does. *New* creates a new report definition. *Open* opens an existing report definition.

Select *New*. The system prompts for a name for the report. We will call this one bookings; enter the name and press [*Accept*].

### 11.2.2 Error messages

In the course of specifying the various options for the example report, you will probably make mistakes. An error message is displayed at the bottom of the screen and, in contrast with SQL\*Forms, you must always acknowledge and

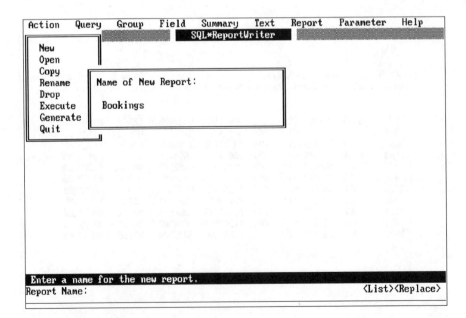

**Figure 11.5** The *Action* submenu.

clear this message by pressing any key before you can continue. Press [*Help*] to get an explanation of the error message. When the error derives from the use of incorrect SQL syntax, pressing [*Next line*] displays more detail.

### 11.2.3 Lists of values
At many points as you specify the options you will also see that the <*List*> indicator appears on the status line at the bottom of the screen. This indicates that a list of possible values is available for this item. To see the list, press [*List of values*]. You can select the one you want and transfer it into the original screen by using the cursor keys to highlight the one you want, then pressing [*Select*].

This list-of-values indicator appears in many circumstances and is very useful to prompt you about what you are required to enter.

### 11.2.4 The Report menu
The next thing to do is to define the physical characteristics of the report and to specify the report options. Move across to *Report* on the main menu bar and press [*Select*]. This displays the *Report Settings* screen (Figure 11.6). Use [*Next field*] and [*Previous field*] to move the cursor around on the screen. *Page* and *Margins* define the size of the medium on which the report is to be produced. The example report will be directed to the screen, so the page height should be reduced to 20 lines. The width can stay at 80.

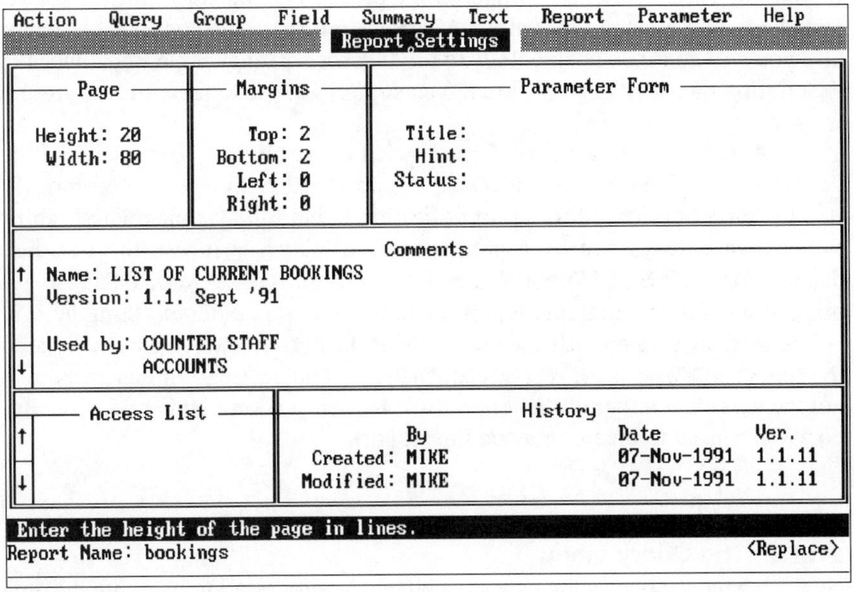

```
 Action    Query    Group    Field    Summary   Text    Report    Parameter    Help
                               Report Settings

 +-- Page --+--- Margins ---+-------- Parameter Form --------+
 |          |               |                                |
 | Height: 20|    Top: 2    |  Title:                        |
 | Width: 80 | Bottom: 2    |   Hint:                        |
 |           |   Left: 0    | Status:                        |
 |           |  Right: 0    |                                |
 +-----------+--------------+---------------------------------
                          -- Comments --
  ↑  Name: LIST OF CURRENT BOOKINGS
  ─  Version: 1.1. Sept '91

  ─  Used by: COUNTER STAFF
  ↓          ACCOUNTS

 +--- Access List ---+-------------- History --------------+
 ↑|                  |         By          Date       Ver. |
  |                  | Created: MIKE    07-Nov-1991  1.1.11 |
 ↓|                  | Modified: MIKE   07-Nov-1991  1.1.11 |
 +-------------------+-------------------------------------+
 Enter the height of the page in lines.
 Report Name: bookings                              <Replace>
```

**Figure 11.6** The report definition screen.

When the finished report is executed, a runtime parameter form will be displayed, prompting the initiator of the report to specify where the report should be directed (screen, printer, file etc.), the number of copies and various other information. The *Parameter form* section of the report settings screen allows you to specify a title, hint line text and status line text for this runtime parameter form. The example report will use default values for these, so they can be ignored for this example.

The *Comments* area is used for a description of the report. It is important always to fill in at least a minimum level of documentation here. Most installations will have their own standards about what to enter. Consider including these as a minimum:

- An official name for the report.

- A version number for the report.

- Who uses the report, in terms of job function rather than name.

- What it is used for.

- The tables accessed.

- A description of what the report consists of.

The comments panel can be used to enter quite a large amount of text. It automatically scrolls both horizontally and vertically. The panel is, in effect, a window on a large area of text which extends both horizontally and vertically. If you are used to using a proper word processor, you may find this a bit awkward. You must put in your own carriage returns at the end of each line or else you will continue horizontally to produce a very long single line. Once the description has been entered, use the cursor keys to move the window around over the text.

The *Access List* area of the form is used to specify the usernames of the people who will be able to access the report, either to run it or to modify it. This only applies if the report definition is held in system-owned tables rather than ones owned by a particular user. Which is in use in your case depends on how SQL\*ReportWriter was installed; talk to your database administrator. For the example report, there is no need to enter anything here.

The *History* area records the username of the person who originally created the report and who most recently amended it. The version number in here is not the version number of the report itself but the version number of SQL\*ReportWriter used to create or amend the report.

### 11.2.5 The Query menu
Next we have to specify the query which will be processed to generate the data which will appear in the report. Almost everything else about the report can be

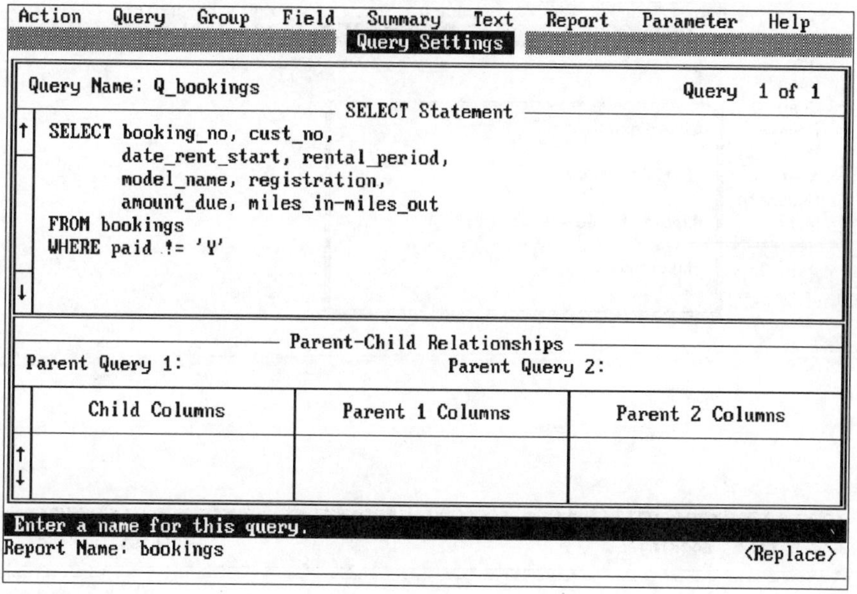

```
Action    Query    Group    Field    Summary    Text    Report    Parameter    Help
                                   Query Settings

  Query Name: Q_bookings                                    Query  1 of 1
  ─────────────────────── SELECT Statement ───────────────
  ↑ SELECT booking_no, cust_no,
            date_rent_start, rental_period,
            model_name, registration,
            amount_due, miles_in-miles_out
     FROM bookings
     WHERE paid != 'Y'

  ↓

  ─────────────────── Parent-Child Relationships ───────────────
   Parent Query 1:                      Parent Query 2:

      Child Columns      │  Parent 1 Columns   │   Parent 2 Columns
  ↑                      │                     │
  ↓                      │                     │

  Enter a name for this query.
  Report Name: bookings                                       <Replace>
```

**Figure 11.7**   The query definition screen.

left to SQL*ReportWriter's default settings, but you must at least provide a query. Select the *Query* option. You have to give the query a name, as a single report may have several queries and they may be referred to by name elsewhere as the report is defined. There is just one query in this example and it is called Q_bookings. The query, shown in Figure 11.7, just selects a few columns for those bookings which have not been paid for. Enter the query as shown and press [*Accept*]. Note that not only is the semicolon at the end of the SQL statement not required, an error is generated if it is entered.

A report could have more than one query. They could be completely unrelated or could have a parent–child relationship, where the data resulting from one query is used to carry out the subsidiary query, for a master–detail report, for instance. The top half of the *Query* screen is used to define the queries themselves. Notice that when the cursor is in the *Query name* field, the list-of-values flag is displayed. You can display the names of the queries of the report with the [*List of values*] key or you can skip through the queries by using [*Next record*] and [*Previous record*].

Queries can be inserted using [*Insert record above*] and [*Insert record below*]. Update them by just typing in the new version. A query name can be changed by just typing over the old name with the new. A query can be deleted using [*Delete record*], but this can introduce complications, which will be discussed later.

The bottom half of the *Query* screen is used to define the relationship between the queries. This is not relevant for this simple report; we come back

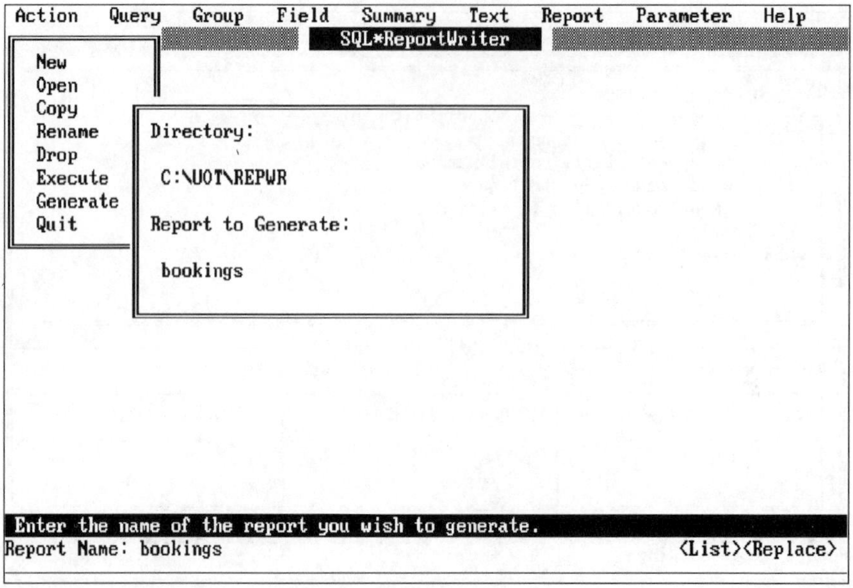

```
Action    Query    Group    Field    Summary    Text    Report    Parameter    Help
░░░░░░░░░░░░░░░░░░░░░░░░░░  SQL*ReportWriter  ░░░░░░░░░░░░░░
┌──────────┐
│ New      ║
│ Open     ║
│ Copy     │─────────────────────────────────────────────────
│ Rename   │ Directory:
│ Drop     │                \
│ Execute  │   C:\UOT\REPWR
│ Generate │
│ Quit     │ Report to Generate:
└──────────┘
               bookings



▐ Enter the name of the report you wish to generate. ▌
Report Name: bookings                                        <List><Replace>
```

**Figure 11.8**   The *Generate* screen.

to it later on. Another important feature, which you should be aware of but which is not relevant for this example, is that parameters can be used in the definition of the queries. This can result in a general purpose report, tailored by supplying the value of the parameters at runtime. We will illustrate this later on, too.

### 11.2.6   Generate and run the report

We have now done enough to allow a working report to be generated. Press [*Accept*] to finish with the *Query* menu and go back to the *Action* menu. Select *Generate* (Figure 11.8). The system prompts for the name of the directory and the file to hold the generated form of the report program, but has already inserted a default filename in the current directory. Press [*Accept*] to use these defaults. Next select *Execute* on the *Action* menu to run the report. Again, the name and directory have already been set up so press [*Accept*].

The *Parameter* form, displayed next (Figure 11.9), can be used to override any of the settings previously set up using the *Report* option on the main menu bar. Note that the display of this form can be suppressed by supplying the parameter PARAMFORM=NO when SQL*ReportWriter is invoked (see Section 11.6). In this case, nothing needs to be changed so press [*Accept*] and the report will be run.

```
▓▓▓▓▓▓▓▓▓▓▓▓▓▓▓▓█ Parameter Values █▓▓▓▓▓▓▓▓▓▓▓▓▓▓▓
┌──────────────────────────────┬────────────────────────────────┐
│ Parameter                    │ Value                          │
│                              │                                │
│ Destination Type             │ Screen                         │
│ File Name / Spool Device     │ bookings.lis                   │
│ Printer Description File      │ dflt                           │
│ Number of Copies             │ 1                              │
│                              │                                │
│                              │                                │
│                              │                                │
│                              │                                │
│                              │                                │
│                              │                                │
│                              │                                │
│                              │                                │
│                              │                                │
│                              │                                │
└──────────────────────────────┴────────────────────────────────┘
█ Enter the desired value for each parameter. █
Report Name: bookings                                    〈Replace〉
```

**Figure 11.9**   Runtime parameter form.

To produce the report, SQL*ReportWriter has used default headings and
default field formats for the data (Figure 11.10). The headings are a bit smarter
than just using the column names from the dictionary; words are capitalized
and underscore is converted to space. But the layout is pretty crude and splits
the details for each booking on to two lines, though there is, in fact, plenty of
room to fit it all on a single line.

```
Booking No  Cust No  Date Rent Start  Rental Period  Model Name  Registration
----------  -------  ---------------  -------------  ----------  ------------
Amount Due                            Miles In Miles Out
----------                           -------------------
       502    1553   20-DEC-90               015  BMW 750    G123RMR
   4002.00                                   2545
       118    8979   23-JAN-91               004  JAG XJS    H626RPG
   1123.80                                   0892
       265    2029   04-MAY-91               016  RR SSPIR   E246WFC
   1366.60                                   0556
       504    1553   12-APR-91               001  JAG XJ6    G551JBA
   0476.95                                   0284
       811     701   05-SEP-91               008  P944 T     G202XRP
   1279.80                                   0636
       812    2338   15-OCT-91               015  MERC 560   J644TNR
   2477.85                                   1416
```

**Figure 11.10**   Untailored default report.

## Summary: Generating a simple report

☐ It is possible to generate a simple report very quickly, relying on SQL*ReportWriter's defaults.

☐ As a minimum, you must supply a SQL query to select the data to appear in the report. All the rest can be left to defaults.

☐ Although SQL*ReportWriter does not insist on it, it is good practice to provide a minimum level of documentation for each report definition using the *Report* option.

☐ Reports like this one, generated using defaults, are rather crude and sometimes wasteful of space on the paper (or screen). But they are often quite adequate for one-off reports.

---

**EXERCISE 11.1**

1. Modify the example report to include the mileage for the bookings.

2. Generate and run the modified report.

---

## 11.3   Tailoring the report

The report we have generated shows the data we wanted, but the layout is ugly and the format of the data items is inadequate. The `amount_due` fields, for example, do not always show two digits of pence. Next, we will tailor the layout by providing:

• a page heading with a title, date and page number

• revised column headings which allow the fields to be placed closer together

• definitions of the print formats for the numeric fields to improve readability and to allow the fields to be placed closer together.

### 11.3.1   The Fields option

The *Fields* option is used to define the details of the fields to be printed. When the query for the report was specified, the system automatically generated a series of field definitions using the column names in the query and the datatypes

```
Action   Query   Group   Field   Summary   Text   Report   Parameter   Help
                              Field Settings

     Field Name           Source               Group            Label

↑  BOOKING_NO           BOOKING_NO           G_bookings       Booking No
   CUST_NO              CUST_NO              G_bookings       Cust No
   DATE_RENT_START      DATE_RENT_START      G_bookings       Date Rent Start
   RENTAL_PERIOD        RENTAL_PERIOD        G_bookings       Rental Period
   MODEL_NAME           MODEL_NAME           G_bookings       Model Name
   REGISTRATION         REGISTRATION         G_bookings       Registration
   AMOUNT_DUE           AMOUNT_DUE           G_bookings       Amount Due
   MILES_IN_MILES_O     MILES_IN-MILES_O     G_bookings       Miles In Miles Ou

↓
                                                                          >

 Enter the field label for this field.
Report Name: bookings                                          <Replace>
```

**Figure 11.11**    Leftmost page of field definitions.

in Oracle's data dictionary. Select the *Fields* option on the main menu bar and you will see that all the fields in the report are listed vertically arranged in the *groups* in which they appear (Figure 11.11). The sequence of the list is the sequence in which the fields will be printed.

The structure of the *Fields* display is quite involved. It is very similar to the *spread table* format used by SQL*Forms (V3) but, for some reason, the same terminology is not used in SQL*ReportWriter. It spans three pages, extending horizontally. There is a horizontal scroll bar at the bottom of the screen to indicate which portion of the table is displayed. Use [*Next screen*] and [*Previous screen*] to move across from one page to another. Use [*Next line*] and [*Previous line*] to go vertically from one field definition to another and [*Next field*] and [*Previous field*] to go horizontally from one element of the definition to another. If you tab across off the edge of one page, the next page is automatically brought on to the screen.

You may find that navigation around this set of screens is rather slow, particularly on a PC. There is a lot of work going on in the background, processing field definitions held in the database. Watch the little Work-ing... indicator in the status bar at the bottom right of the screen to see if the system is busy.

In the example report, field definitions have been automatically created for each of the items selected in the query defined for the report. The areas on the screen which hold the field name, source columns etc. all scroll horizontally to accommodate longer entries.

| Action    Query    Group    Field    Summary    Text    Report    Parameter    Help |
|---|

Field Settings

| Field Name | Data Type | Field Width | Display Format | Relative Position | Lines Before | Spaces Before |
|---|---|---|---|---|---|---|
| BOOKING_NO | NUM | 7 | | | | |
| CUST_NO | NUM | 7 | | | | |
| DATE_RENT_START | DATE | 9 | | | | |
| RENTAL_PERIOD | NUM | 5 | 999 | | | |
| MODEL_NAME | CHAR | 8 | | | | |
| REGISTRATION | CHAR | 7 | | | | |
| AMOUNT_DUE | NUM | 8 | 99999.99 | | | |
| MILES_IN_MILES_0 | NUM | 5 | 99999 | | | |

Enter the width of this field in spaces.
Report Name: bookings                                          ⟨Insert⟩

**Figure 11.12**   Modified display formats.

The fields have been assigned to a default group, also generated by the system, called G_bookings. The label, which will be placed at the head of the column displaying the data, has been generated from the database column name. The concatenation of all these labels forms the column heading for the fields in a group. They need to be changed to make them more understandable and to reduce the amount of space used. In normal circumstances, it is best to modify each of these labels using the *Fields* option. It is also possible to modify the complete column heading text object for the group using the *Text* option, and this method is easier to use because you can see all the labels together. However, there is a restriction which makes it difficult to modify the text object more than once. So it is wise to avoid modifying it until the report definition is nearly complete and you are therefore unlikely to need to modify it again. We have nearly finished this example report and we shall, in fact, use the *Text* option to modify the labels in the next section.

Move to the miles_in-miles_out field and move horizontally to the second page to define the field size and display format, as shown in Figure 11.12. Likewise, set up field size and display format for rental_period and amount_due as shown. The format specifications are the same as those used in SQL\*Plus. A complete description of them is given in Appendix B.

### 11.3.2   The Text option

*Text* is used to define all the text which can appear in the report. We will now use it to modify some of the captions which have been generated as defaults.

**Table 11.1**  Use of text items.

| Text object | Example use |
|---|---|
| `Page header` | Appears at the top of each page of the body of the report. Usually contains page number among other items. |
| `Page footer` | Appears at the bottom of each page of the body of the report. Often used to show carried forward totals. |
| `Report title page` | A whole page which appears once at the beginning of the report. Often shows the report name as a banner. |
| `Report trailer page` | A whole page which appears at the end of the report. |
| `Report header` | Appears at the start of the body of the report. Often used to show the values of any parameters submitted to the report run. |
| `Report footer` | Appears at the end of the body of the report. Often used to show overall summaries or totals. |
| `Group header` | Appears at the start of each group in the report. Often used to show the name of the group or data which is the same throughout the group. |
| `Group footer` | Appears at the end of each group in the report. Often used for group totals or other summaries. |
| `Group column heading` | Appears at the top of the group. Usually used to provide captions for the columns of the report. |
| `Group body` | The text printed for each record of the group. Usually a mixture of fixed text and text derived from database values. |

Select the *text* option. The screen displayed is used to define the position and content of all text objects. There is one screen for each item of text: one for page headers, one for page footers, one for the report title page and so on; Table 11.1 has a complete list of the text items which can be defined. Use [*Next screen*] and [*Previous screen*] to move between the text items. Use [*Next field*] and [*Previous field*] to move between aspects of the text definition for the current text object.

Navigation through this set of screens can be rather slow as well – there is a lot of processing going on to retrieve text definitions from the database. The top section of each screen is used to define where the text is to appear in relation to the page and to the other fields on the page. The prompts are fairly self-explanatory and most have a set of valid entries which can be accessed with [*List of values*]. Use this, the short help line at the bottom of the screen and the full help service to make your way around the top section.

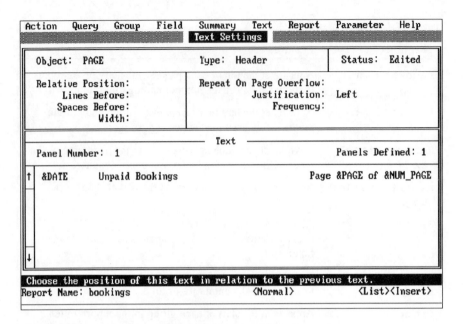

**Figure 11.13**   The page header definition screen.

The bottom section of the screen is used to enter the text itself. The area of the screen acts as a window on the underlying text, which can be larger than the window itself. The window scrolls over the text as the cursor comes to the margins of the window. There are three system variables which are available to be included in the text. They are used in the example in the illustration. &PAGE contains the current page number, &NUM_PAGES contains the total number of pages in the report and &DATE contains today's date. Type in the heading as shown (in Figure 11.13).

We shall not use any other text associated with the page or report. Use [*Next screen*] to skip forward to the text associated with the G_Bookings group. This group has been generated as a default by SQL*ReportWriter to hold the detail bookings items. Move forward to the column headings text for the group and rearrange the headings to look like the illustration in Figure 11.12. By shortening the headings in this way, all the text (and the data) can be fitted on one line.

Next, move on to the definition of the body of the group G_Bookings (Figure 11.14). In the lower section of the screen are the columns which are to appear in the report, with the column name preceded by an ampersand. The horizontal positioning of these fields has been partly dictated by the length of the column names which have been used, by default, for headings. We have already changed the headings; now change the spacing between the fields to correspond to the headings.

```
 Action    Query    Group    Field    Summary    Text    Report    Parameter    Help
                                    ▐Text Settings▌
 ┌─────────────────────────────────────────────────────────────────────────────┐
 │  Object:  G_bookings            Type:  Body                 Status:  Edited   │
 │                                                                               │
 │  Relative Position:            Repeat On Page Overflow:  X                     │
 │        Lines Before:                    Justification:  Left                   │
 │       Spaces Before:                        Frequency:                         │
 │              Width:                                                            │
 ├───────────────────────────────── Text ───────────────────────────────────────┤
 │  Panel Number:  1                                       Panels Defined:  1     │
 │ ┌─┬─────────────────────────────────────────────────────────────────────────┐│
 │ │↑│ &BOOKING_NO &CUST_NO  &DATE_RENT_START  &RENTAL_PERIOD  &MODEL_NAME  &REGI ││
 │ │ │                                                                           ││
 │ │ │                                                                           ││
 │ │ │                                                                           ││
 │ │↓│                                                                           ││
 │ └─┴─────────────────────────────────────────────────────────────────────────┘│
 ├───────────────────────────────────────────────────────────────────────────────
 │ Choose the position of this text in relation to the previous text.            │
 │Report Name: bookings                  <Normal>              <List><Insert>     │
 └─────────────────────────────────────────────────────────────────────────────┘
```

**Figure 11.14**   Group body definition for bookings.

The report should now have a more useful layout and be easier to read. Select *Generate* and then *Execute* to see the results.

## Summary: Building a default report

☐   With just simple tailoring, the default report can be much improved.

☐   Use the *Fields* option to change the display format of fields, for instance to provide two digits of pence.

☐   Use the *Text* option to revise the position or content of text items.

☐   System variables can be used to display the date, the total number of pages in the report and the page number of the current page.

☐   Navigation around the screens which define *Text* and *Field* items is slow. Keep an eye on the 'Working...' indicator.

## 11.4   A nested report

The report built in the previous section was quite simple and was implemented by letting the system use defaults wherever possible. We now move on to tackle a more complicated master–detail report. It serves a similar

```
Customer:  G G WHITTAKER & CO
           WHEATLEY ROAD
           DONCASTER
           YORKSHIRE
           DN5 8AA


Booking No  Rental Start Days Model    Registration Amount Due
----------  ------------ ---- -------- ------------ ----------
      2123     19/09/91    5 FERR TR   H935CSA        501.80
      2124     19/09/91    5 BMW 750   G123RMR       1023.00
      2126     02/10/91   10 ASTON V8  H266MHU        873.60
                                                    ----------
                                       Total due:    2398.40
```

**Figure 11.15**   A page from the finished report.

function to the previous report, showing unpaid accounts. This time, though, the report shows the customer details as well as the unpaid bookings for the customer.

### 11.4.1   The report layout

The body of this report has two report groups: the first containing the details of the customer and the second containing the details of the unpaid bookings for the customer. Each customer starts on a new page and there is a total of the amount outstanding at the end of the bookings details. Figure 11.15 shows a sample page of the report.

Use the *Action* menu to create the report; call it Cust_Accs. Go to the *Report* menu to provide some documentation of the purpose of the report.

### 11.4.2   The queries

Each of the report groups has an associated query which defines the data to print in the group. The report shows unpaid bills for customers who pay on account. So the query for the customers group selects customers who pay on account. The query for the bookings group selects bookings which are unpaid. The relationship between the two queries is defined by specifying a column returned by one query as being the *parent* of a column returned by the other query (the *child*). This is just another way of expressing a join (an outer join, in fact).

Set up the queries as shown in Figures 11.16 and 11.17. Use [*Insert record below*] to insert a blank entry into which to write the query.

### 11.4.3   Groups

In the previous example, there was no need to use the *Group* option; default values were adequate. This time we do need to define group characteristics, so

```
Action    Query    Group    Field    Summary    Text    Report    Parameter    Help
                                  ·Query Settings
┌──────────────────────────────────────────────────────────────────────────────┐
│ Query Name: Q_Customers                                      Query  1 of 2     │
│ ┌───────────────────────── SELECT Statement ──────────────────────────────┐   │
│↑│ SELECT cust_no, cust_name, address, town, county, post_code             │   │
│ │ FROM customers                                                          │   │
│ │                                                                         │   │
│ │                                                                         │   │
│↓│                                                                         │   │
│ └─────────────────────────────────────────────────────────────────────────┘  │
│ ┌───────────────────── Parent-Child Relationships ───────────────────────┐    │
│ Parent Query 1:                        Parent Query 2:                         │
│ ┌──────────────────┬──────────────────────┬──────────────────────┐            │
│ │   Child Columns  │   Parent 1 Columns   │   Parent 2 Columns   │            │
│↑├──────────────────┼──────────────────────┼──────────────────────┤           │
│↓│                  │                      │                      │            │
│ └──────────────────┴──────────────────────┴──────────────────────┘            │
├────────────────────────────────────────────────────────────────────────────────┤
│ Enter a name for this query.                                                   │
│ Report Name: Cust_accs                                          <Replace>      │
└────────────────────────────────────────────────────────────────────────────────┘
```

**Figure 11.16**   The parent query.

```
Action    Query    Group    Field    Summary    Text    Report    Parameter    Help
                                  Query Settings
┌──────────────────────────────────────────────────────────────────────────────┐
│ Query Name: Q_bookings                                       Query  2 of 2     │
│ ┌───────────────────────── SELECT Statement ──────────────────────────────┐   │
│↑│ SELECT booking_no, cust_no, date_rent_start, rental_period, registration,│  │
│ │    model_name, amount_due                                               │   │
│ │ FROM bookings                                                           │   │
│ │ WHERE paid!='Y'                                                         │   │
│ │                                                                         │   │
│↓│                                                                         │   │
│ └─────────────────────────────────────────────────────────────────────────┘  │
│ ┌───────────────────── Parent-Child Relationships ───────────────────────┐    │
│ Parent Query 1: Q_Customers            Parent Query 2:                         │
│ ┌──────────────────┬──────────────────────┬──────────────────────┐            │
│ │   Child Columns  │   Parent 1 Columns   │   Parent 2 Columns   │            │
│↑├──────────────────┼──────────────────────┼──────────────────────┤           │
│↓│ CUST_NO          │ CUST_NO              │                      │            │
│ └──────────────────┴──────────────────────┴──────────────────────┘            │
├────────────────────────────────────────────────────────────────────────────────┤
│ Enter a name for this query.                                                   │
│ Report Name: Cust_accs                                          <Replace>      │
└────────────────────────────────────────────────────────────────────────────────┘
```

**Figure 11.17**   The child query.

select the *Group* option. The group screen has one line for each group which you have defined (or which the system has defined for you, as in our case) and three pages horizontally to define the characteristics of each group. The structure is somewhat similar to the *Fields* screen. As with the other screens with this sort of format, use [*Next record*] and [*Previous record*] to move vertically from group to group, [*Next screen*] and [*Previous screen*] to move horizontally between screens and [*Next field*] and [*Previous field*] to move horizontally between fields.

Each customer should start on a new page in the report so move to the *page break* field for the G_Customers, use the [*List of values*] key to show the possible values and select *Always*. We need line spacing between the two groups so go across to the *Lines before* field on the next screen and set one line before the customers group and two before the bookings group. Finally, we need to put the captions on the left of the data in the customers group; go across to the *Label position* field on the next page, use the list of values to show the options and select *label on left*. This will put all the labels in the customers group on the left of the data. In the report, though, some of the data, like the address, does not need a label; it is obvious what it is. This will be sorted out in a moment.

### 11.4.4   Field sequence and attributes

By default, fields are displayed in the same sequence as they are selected by the query. Starting at the top left of the group, they go down and to the right with a specified horizontal and vertical spacing. In this case, we want the displayed fields to be in a different sequence than in the query, with the contact name following the customer name on the top line of the customers group.

Fields can be resequenced using the *Fields* option. You temporarily delete a field and then re-insert it in its new sequence. Move the cursor to the name of the field to move and press [*Delete record*]. The *Verify delete* panel is displayed. Move the cursor to show that you want to delete only this object and press [Select]. Then move the cursor to the fieldname of the field in front of which you want to insert the field you have just deleted; press [*Undelete record*] and the field is re-inserted in its new position. The process of deleting report objects can sometimes be a bit more involved than this; see Section 11.5.

Set up the other field attributes as shown in Figure 11.18. By default, every field will have been given a caption (label). For the address fields, get rid of the captions using [*Delete line*]. Note that the report does not contain the customer number, just the customer's name. This field is skipped by putting an 'X' in the *Skip* indicator, on page 3 of the fields definition.

### 11.4.5   Totals

The report has a summary line for each customer, showing the total amount due from the customer. This is specified using the *Summary* option. The summary screen (Figure 11.19) has a line for each summary defined in the

| Action | Query | Group | Field | Summary | Text | Report | Parameter | Help |
|---|---|---|---|---|---|---|---|---|

**Field Settings**

| | Field Name | Data Type | Field Width | Display Format | Relative Position | Lines Before | Spaces Before |
|---|---|---|---|---|---|---|---|
| ↑ | CUST_NO | NUM | 7 | | | | |
| | CUST_NAME | CHAR | 20 | | Below | | 2 |
| | ADDRESS | CHAR | 20 | | Below | | 13 |
| | TOWN | CHAR | 20 | | Below | | 13 |
| | COUNTY | CHAR | 20 | | Below | | 13 |
| | POST_CODE | CHAR | 10 | | Below | | 13 |
| | BOOKING_NO | NUM | 7 | | | | |
| | DATE_RENT_START | DATE | 8 | dd/mm/yy | | | |
| | RENTAL_PERIOD | NUM | 3 | | | | 1 |
| | MODEL_NAME | CHAR | 8 | | | | 1 |
| | REGISTRATION | CHAR | 7 | | | | 1 |
| | AMOUNT_DUE | NUM | 8 | ZZZZ9.99 | | | 1 |
| ↓ | CUST_NO2 | NUM | 7 | | | | 1 |

Enter the width of this field in spaces.

Report Name: Cust_accs        ⟨Replace⟩

**Figure 11.18**    Middle page of fields definition.

| Action | Query | Group | Field | Summary | Text | Report | Parameter | Help |
|---|---|---|---|---|---|---|---|---|

**Summary Settings**

| | Summary Name | Field | Function | Data Type | Width | Display Format |
|---|---|---|---|---|---|---|
| ↑ | Customer_total | AMOUNT_DUE | Sum | NUM | 8 | ZZZZ9.99 |
| ↓ | | | | | | |

Enter a name for this summary field.

Report Name: Cust_accs        ⟨Replace⟩

**Figure 11.19**    The summary screen.

report and extends over two pages horizontally to define the characteristics of each summary. Navigate around the screen as before. Fill in the definition of the `Customer_total` shown in Figure 11.20.

Each summary is given a name by which it is referenced elsewhere in the report definition and the field on which the summary operates is identified. This must be a simple field name, one of the items selected in a query. Arithmetic statements like `amount_due*1.1` are not allowed here; if you need to operate on an arithmetic derivative like this, incorporate the arithmetic in the SELECT statement in the relevant query for the report or use a computed field.

The summary function used here is *Sum*. Other functions available include maximum, minimum, average and percentage of total. Use [*List of values*] to see the options.

The print group is the group within which this summary is to be printed. It can be any of the groups defined, or can be *Report* to indicate that the summary is to appear at the end of the whole report. The summary has to be reset periodically (unless the print group is *Report*, in which case there is no point in resetting) and this is defined by specifying the reset group. The summary is reset at the end of the processing of each instance of the reset group. The reset group defaults to the group one level up from the group which contains the group to be summarized. This is the sensible setting for producing single-level totals etc. It can be set to be the group which contains the field or any group at a higher level. The [*List of values*] key will give you the valid options.

```
 Action    Query    Group    Field    Summary    Text    Report    Parameter    Help
░░░░░░░░░░░░░░░░░░░░░░░░░░░░░░░░░█ Text Settings █░░░░░░░░░░░░░░░░░░░░░░░░░░░░
┌──────────────────────────────────────────────────────────────────────────┐
│  Object:  G_bookings          Type:  Footer          Status:  Default     │
├──────────────────────────────────────────────────────────────────────────┤
│  Relative Position:        Repeat On Page Overflow:                        │
│       Lines Before:                 Justification:  Left                   │
│      Spaces Before:                    Frequency:                          │
│             Width:                                                         │
├─────────────────────────────────── Text ──────────────────────────────────┤
│  Panel Number:  1                                  Panels Defined:  1      │
│ ↑                                                                          │
│                                 Total due:          &Customer_total        │
│                                                                            │
│                                                                            │
│                                                                            │
│ ↓                                                                          │
├──────────────────────────────────────────────────────────────────────────┤
│█ Edit the text.                                                            │
│ Report Name:  Cust_accs                <Normal>               <Replace>    │
└──────────────────────────────────────────────────────────────────────────┘
```

**Figure 11.20**  Definition of the summary.

```
Action    Query    Group    Field    Summary    Text    Report    Parameter    Help
                                    Text Settings
┌──────────────────────────────────────────────────────────────────────────────┐
│  Object:  G_bookings              Type:  Column Heading    Status:   Edited     │
├────────────────────────────────┬───────────────────────────────────────────────┤
│  Relative Position:             │  Repeat On Page Overflow:  X                  │
│       Lines Before:             │          Justification:  Left                 │
│      Spaces Before:             │             Frequency:                        │
│             Width:              │                                               │
├────────────────────────── Text ──────────────────────────────────────────────┤
│  Panel Number:  1                                    Panels Defined: 1          │
│ ┌─┬──────────────────────────────────────────────────────────────────────────┐ │
│ │↑│ Booking  Cust  Date Start  Period  Model  Registration  Miles  Amount     │ │
│ │ │                                                                            │ │
│ │ │                                                                            │ │
│ │ │                                                                            │ │
│ │↓│                                                                            │ │
└─┴─┴──────────────────────────────────────────────────────────────────────────┘
 Choose the position of this text in relation to the previous text.
 Report Name: bookings                      <Normal>              <List><Replace>
```

**Figure 11.21**   Text definition.

Using *print group* and *reset group* carefully, you can build up multi-level summaries. Defining the summary like this just creates the summary field; it does not define where it is to be printed. For this, use the *Text* option to set up the footer for the G_bookings group.

### 11.4.6   Finishing off the report

The report still needs to be tidied up to shorten the captions and to line up captions and data. Use the *Text* option to do this as shown in Figure 11.21. Generate and run the report.

## Summary: A nested report

☐  Nested reports usually have more than one group and each of them has its associated query.

☐  The structure of the nesting is defined by specifying a parent–child relationship between the groups. This is just like specifying a join.

☐  The position of each group is specified relative to the page and relative to the preceding elements of the report.

☐ Field positions are specified relative to the preceding field. To rearrange fields, it may be necessary to re-order the fields on the *Fields* definition screen.

☐ Totals and other summary information can be associated with a group, often as a group footer. Summaries are usually reset at the next higher level group.

---

**EXERCISE 11.2**

1. You will notice that there is a deliberate mistake in the report just developed. It will display customer details even if there are no outstanding unpaid bookings. Modify the report so that only customers with unpaid bookings are displayed.

2. Modify the report to display the total number of days rental which is unpaid. This should be on the same line as the total amount due; give it some suitable caption.

---

## 11.5  Clearing up

In one of the earlier examples, we used the delete operation to temporarily delete a field record prior to re-inserting in a different order. It was a simple operation because it was just a temporary delete. Sometimes, however, it gets more complicated. The problem is that a report object can contain other report objects. For instance, a *Group* may contain *Fields* and *Summaries*. If the group is to be deleted, what should happen to the fields and summaries? SQL*ReportWriter always prompts to determine how you want to perform the delete (Figure 11.22).

If you are doing radical surgery to a report, you may well want to get rid of all the component report objects as well as the original object. This is a cascaded delete. But beware: the cascade can reach further than you might expect. For instance, if you cascade delete a query, you will also delete all the groups based on the query, all the fields in those groups, all the summaries based on those fields, all the summaries whose print group is one of the groups just deleted and, finally, any text objects associated with any of the deleted objects!

If you were just doing minor changes to a report, such a delete might well rub out many objects which you really just wanted to relink into a slightly different structure. In this case (or if in doubt), it is sensible to delete only the specified report object.

This type of delete could leave other report objects which refer to the one just deleted in a sort of limbo. They have been defined but do not link into the

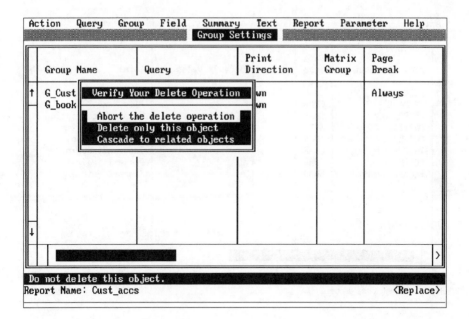

**Figure 11.22**    The verify delete panel.

rest of the report in any way. SQL*ReportWriter will not let you leave the report in an untidy state, though. Any references to non-existent (deleted) objects are flagged as *undefined* and the report will not generate successfully and cannot be run.

# 11.6  Runtime

## 11.6.1  User parameters

The usefulness of a report can be greatly extended by allowing the operation of the report to be modified by supplying parameters at runtime. These parameters are defined with the *Parameter* option on the main menu (see Figure 11.23) and are used in queries. The values for the parameters are supplied on the parameter form displayed at the start of the execution of the report.

To illustrate the way this is done, the example will be modified so that the report can show the unpaid rentals for customers who have accounts and those who are supposed to pay by cash. To do this pay_method will be provided as a parameter.

You can define more than one parameter. There is a line for each one on the parameter screen. The name given to the parameter can be the same as the name of the column for which it provides a value. It may not conflict with any of the

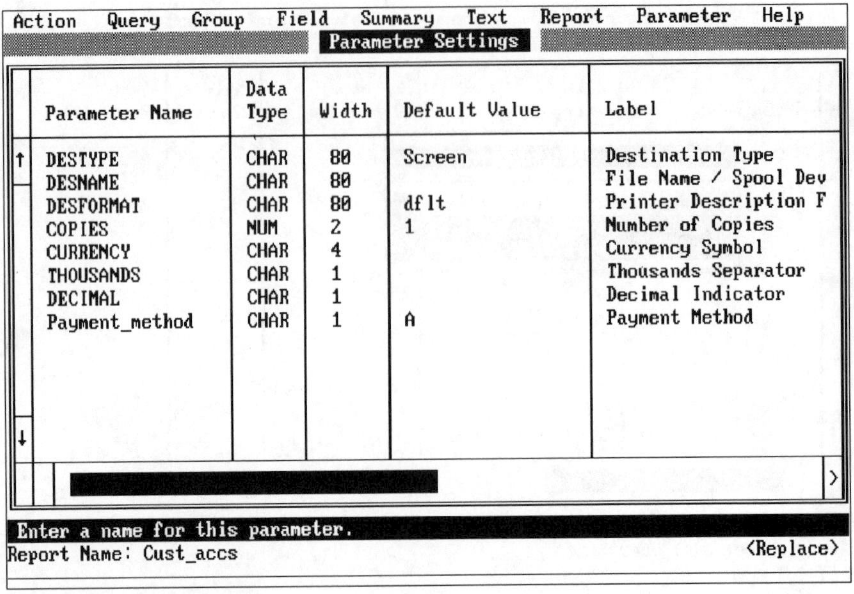

```
Action   Query   Group   Field   Summary   Text   Report   Parameter   Help
                          Parameter Settings

┌──────────────────┬───────┬───────┬───────────────┬─────────────────────────┐
│                  │ Data  │       │               │                         │
│  Parameter Name  │ Type  │ Width │ Default Value │ Label                   │
├──────────────────┼───────┼───────┼───────────────┼─────────────────────────┤
│↑ DESTYPE         │ CHAR  │  80   │ Screen        │ Destination Type        │
│  DESNAME         │ CHAR  │  80   │               │ File Name / Spool Dev   │
│  DESFORMAT       │ CHAR  │  80   │ dflt          │ Printer Description F    │
│  COPIES          │ NUM   │   2   │ 1             │ Number of Copies        │
│  CURRENCY        │ CHAR  │   4   │               │ Currency Symbol         │
│  THOUSANDS       │ CHAR  │   1   │               │ Thousands Separator     │
│  DECIMAL         │ CHAR  │   1   │               │ Decimal Indicator       │
│  Payment_method  │ CHAR  │   1   │ A             │ Payment Method          │
│                  │       │       │               │                         │
│↓                 │       │       │               │                         │
└──────────────────┴───────┴───────┴───────────────┴─────────────────────────┘

Enter a name for this parameter.
Report Name: Cust_accs                                           <Replace>
```

**Figure 11.23**   Parameter definition screen.

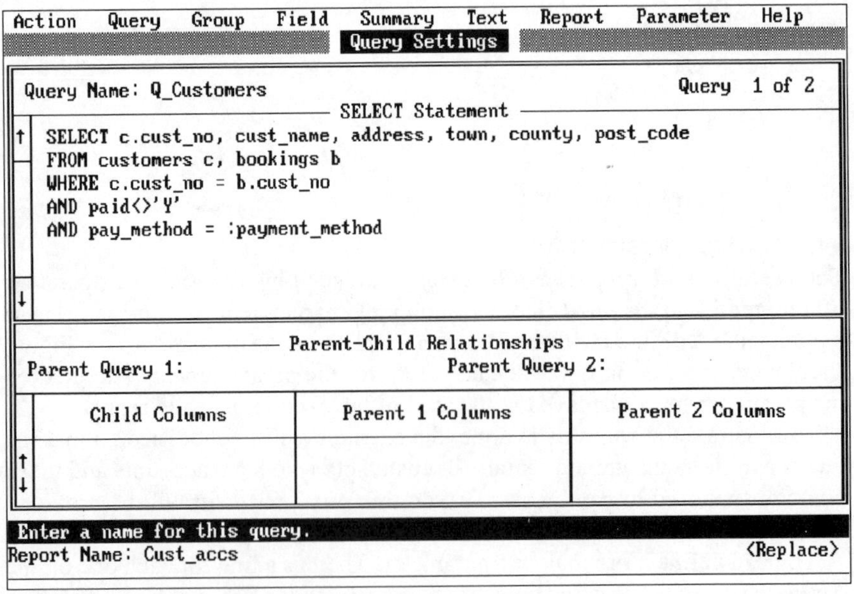

```
Action   Query   Group   Field   Summary   Text   Report   Parameter   Help
                          Query Settings

Query Name: Q_Customers                                  Query  1 of 2
────────────────────── SELECT Statement ──────────────────────
↑ SELECT c.cust_no, cust_name, address, town, county, post_code
  FROM customers c, bookings b
  WHERE c.cust_no = b.cust_no
  AND paid<>'Y'
  AND pay_method = :payment_method

↓

──────────────── Parent-Child Relationships ────────────────
Parent Query 1:                   Parent Query 2:
┌──────────────────┬─────────────────────┬─────────────────────┐
│  Child Columns   │  Parent 1 Columns   │  Parent 2 Columns   │
├──────────────────┼─────────────────────┼─────────────────────┤
│↑                 │                     │                     │
│↓                 │                     │                     │
└──────────────────┴─────────────────────┴─────────────────────┘

Enter a name for this query.
Report Name: Cust_accs                                           <Replace>
```

**Figure 11.24**   The parametrized query.

names of the system parameters which may be provided on the command line, like DESNAME (see below). The datatype and size of a parameter defaults to CHAR(40). In this case, we want it to be CHAR(1). The default value should be 'A' so that if the parameter is not specified at runtime, the report will show account customers. The label field specifies the label used in the prompt on the parameter form.

Having set up the definition of the parameter, it must now be included in the query to extract the customer records. The parameter name is quoted preceded by a colon, as in Figure 11.24. Note that the query originally had a line

```
WHERE pay_method = 'A'
```

with the value in literals. When supplying the value via a parameter, do not put the parameter name in literals or quote the value for the parameter in literals on the parameter form.

Parameters can be used in the query wherever you would expect to find an expression, i.e. in WHERE, GROUP BY, ORDER BY, HAVING, CONNECT BY clauses. Parameters are not allowed anywhere else. For instance,

```
SELECT *
FROM :tablename
```

is illegal because it uses a parameter in a FROM clause.

Parameters like this which are replaced by a single value (a literal, number, string or date) are known as *bind* parameters. It is also possible to specify

```
┌──────────────────────────────────────────────────────────────────────┐
│                          ▓ Parameter Values ▓                          │
│  ┌──────────────────────────────┬──────────────────────────────────┐  │
│  │ Parameter                    │ Value                            │  │
│  ├──────────────────────────────┼──────────────────────────────────┤  │
│  │ Destination Type             │ Screen                           │  │
│  │ File Name / Spool Device     │ Cust_acc.lis                     │  │
│  │ Printer Description File     │ dflt                             │  │
│  │ Number of Copies             │ 1                                │  │
│  │ Payment Method               │ A                                │  │
│  │                              │                                  │  │
│  │                              │                                  │  │
│  │                              │                                  │  │
│  │                              │                                  │  │
│  │                              │                                  │  │
│  │                              │                                  │  │
│  │                              │                                  │  │
│  └──────────────────────────────┴──────────────────────────────────┘  │
│  ▓ Enter the desired value for each parameter.                         │
│  Report Name: Cust_accs                                   <Replace>    │
└──────────────────────────────────────────────────────────────────────┘
```

**Figure 11.25**   The runtime parameter form.

parameters which can be replaced by a SQL expression as well as a value. These are known as *lexical* parameters. Lexical parameters start with an ampersand; they must be defined on the *Parameter* screen and given a default value before they are used. They may appear in WHERE, GROUP BY, ORDER BY and HAVING clauses of a SELECT statement. For example, the query for a group could be defined as

```
SELECT registration, car_group, cost
FROM cars
WHERE &condition
```

When the report is run, the parameter form will be displayed to prompt for the values of all the parameters (Figure 11.25). The display of this form can be suppressed by setting the system parameter PARAMFORM off, in which case default values will be used; see below. There is a line for each of the user parameters; any which are not supplied will be given their default values. The system validates the value entered to make sure that it conforms with the length and datatype specified for the parameter.

*Twelve*

# SQL*Report

## 12.1 SQL*Report basics

### 12.1.1 Structure and components

SQL*Report is a command-driven report writer. You write command files which specify what data to extract and how to format it. This is in complete contrast with SQL*ReportWriter, which is based on screen painting and point-and-select.

You use your system's text editor to write the command or script file. It contains two classes of command: those which control how to extract the data from the database and those which control how this data is to be merged with fixed text and laid out on the page. These two classes of command are processed by the two components which work together to produce the report: the report generator, RPT, and the report formatter, RPF (Figure 12.1).

**RPT** reads a command file containing a mix of RPT commands, text and RPF commands. It executes its own commands and extracts data from the database. Fixed text and RPF commands are copied on. The result is an interim file of extracted data, fixed text and RPF formatting commands.

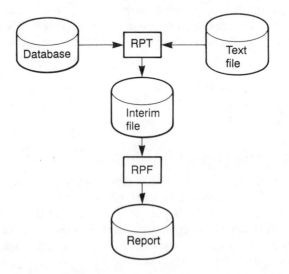

**Figure 12.1**   SQL*Report components.

**RPF** reads the interim file produced by RPT and positions the text and database values found in the file on each page of the report. RPF produces a print file which is then spooled to the printer.

### 12.1.2   Running SQL*Report
SQL\*Report is executed in two discrete stages. RPT is invoked first from the operating system command line. The format is:

```
RPT comm-file interim-file user/pass [-switches]
```

where `comm_file` is the name of the command file produced with the system editor. The default extension for this file is `.RPT`, but any valid file extension can be used instead. `Interim_file` is the interim file to be output for later processing by RPF. The default file extension here is `.RPF`, although once again any valid extension can be used. `User/pass` is the Oracle username and password, separated by a solidus(/), which will be checked before any access to the database is allowed. There are also a number of switches which can be invoked to control processing. They are not important to the understanding of how RPT works and are listed in Appendix E.

RPF is invoked from the operating system command line with the syntax:

```
RPF interim-file output-file [-switches]
```

where `interim_file` is the interim file produced by RPT. The file extension can be omitted if the default of `.RPF` is used. `Output_file` can either be a print file or an output device, such as a logical name for a terminal or printer. The default for the file extension of a print file is either `.LIS` or `.LST` depending on the operating system. There are optional switches which affect output. A list of them can be obtained by entering RPF without any parameters. They are described later on.

## 12.2   RPF, the report formatter
The report formatter is covered first as it is easier to learn and less involved than RPT. RPF is a report formatting program which reads an input file containing a mixture of fixed text and variable text derived from the database together with RPF formatting commands. RPF acts on these commands and produces a print file. This file contains the formatted report which includes headings, underlined and tabulated text, page breaks etc. RPF does not have to be used in conjunction with RPT. It can be used on its own to format any text file.

**Table 12.1** Simple letter command file.

```
#DT 1 13 73 #
#PAGE 6 58
#T 1
#S 3
January 13, 1989
#S 3
Mr John Savage              #N
52 Cleveland Drive #N Camberley, Surrey
#S 1
Dear Mr Savage,
#S 1   #P
Thank you for renting a car from 50K Cars Ltd
recently.
#S 1
#P I am happy to tell you of a new promotion we are
running from 1 February. If you rent a car from us
any time between 1 February and 31 March, we will
give you 10 per cent discount on your booking fee
and include a Michelin map of the road ABSOLUTELY
FREE.
#B #P
This offer is only open to our valued customers and
must close on 31 March. So hurry to claim your
discount NOW!
#S 1
Sincerely, #S 4 Stuart Holland #N Branch Manager
#TE
```

## 12.2.1  A simple letter

The command file shown in Table 12.1 produces a simple letter. It does no more than a standard word processor or text editor could do, but it illustrates the workings of RPF quite clearly. You can see that the letter contains standard text and RPF formatting commands freely interspersed. This letter would have been created by entering the lines, as you see them, into a file using a text editor, and then submitting them to RPF for processing.

#DT defines a format template within which the text is to be formatted. Just to cause confusion, this template is called a *table*, but it is quite different from a database table. The command defines the columns of the table into which the text is to be placed. In the example letter, the text should begin at column position 13 and end at position 73. As this command can be used to specify several such columns and therefore may contain any number of parameters, it must be terminated by a hash. The '1' simply identifies the table.

#DT just defines a table and gives it an identifying number. #Tn (where n is the table number) activates the table previously defined with the #DT command. Several tables can have been defined so the table identifier is used to denote which table we wish to activate. #TE deactivates the table previously activated with #T.

#PAGE specifies the top and bottom margins of each page. In the example, there will be a six-line margin at the top and the last line printed will be line 58. #S specifies lines to be skipped. For instance, #S 3 causes three lines to be skipped. #B puts one blank line between text lines (same as #S 1). #N causes the following text to be placed on a new line and #P causes the following text to begin as a new paragraph, the first line of which will be indented 5 spaces.

### 12.2.2   RPF commands

The example letter uses some of the more common RPF commands. There are many more. They all start with either a full stop (.) or hash sign (#). These may be used interchangeably without affecting the meaning of the command. However, in order to make it easy to distinguish between RPF commands, RPT commands and ordinary text, we will always use the hash sign to start RPF commands. You are recommended to use this convention, too. You will see later on that RPT commands start with a full stop.

Commands can be entered in either upper or lower case together with one or more parameters separated by a space. A single full stop or hash is used to terminate a command which has a variable number of parameters. Again, we will always use the hash sign.

The most commonly used commands are shown in Table 12.2.

### 12.2.3   Tables

RPF puts all text and data into a format defined as a *table*, quite different from a database table. It is simply a window into which text is arranged. The width and number of columns (print columns, not database columns) in a table are defined using the #DT command. More than one table can be defined and up to 30 can be used in one RPF file, each one uniquely identified by a number in the range 0 to 29. A table must be explicitly invoked before its definition takes effect. More than one table can be in use at any point in time. If no tables are defined, RPF uses a default one which contains a single column starting at position 1 and ending at position 255.

Thus each RPF input file has a simple basic structure containing the following sequence of commands:

- Table definitions using #DT command

- Table invocation(s) as required

- Text and formatting commands

**Table 12.2** RPF command summary.

| Command | Effect |
|---------|--------|
| #B | Insert a blank line. |
| #CEN | Centre following text. Needed for each line of text to be centred. Text is terminated by #. |
| #CUL | Centre and underline following text. Needed for each line of text to be centred and underlined. Text is terminated by #. |
| #DT | Define a table (format template) and its constituent print columns. Last column specification is terminated by #. |
| #I | Indent the following line by a specified number of places. |
| #N | Put the following text at the start of a new line. |
| #NC | Put the following text in the next column defined for the currently active table. |
| #NP | Start a new page. |
| #PAGE | Define the borders at the top and bottom of each page. |
| #R | Right-justify all text, leaving a ragged left margin. Right-justification remains in force until another #R is encountered. |
| #S | Skip a specified number of lines. |
| #T | Invoke the specified table. |
| #TE | Terminate the most recently invoked table and revert to the previously invoked one. |
| #TTL | Specify the title to be printed at the centre top of each page. Text of the title is teminated with a #. |
| #TTLU | As for #TTL, but the title is underlined. |
| #UL | Underline the following text. Underlining remains in force until a single # switches it off again. |

- Termination of table(s) at the end of the file or when it is necessary to deactivate a table.

This basic structure is far from rigid; for example, it is possible to invoke and terminate a table anywhere in the file. This structure merely shows the constituent parts of any input file required by RPF.

This structure is illustrated with the next example, which is more complicated. It produces a tabular report and makes use of more than one table definition to control its layout. The report command file, called TABRPT.EX, is listed in Appendix E.

This program makes use of the fact that more than one table definition can exist in a single RPF input file. These tables can be invoked in any order and may be nested. A maximum of 30 tables may be in effect at any time, with table identifiers 0 to 29. These table definitions may define more than one column in a single statement by using additional parameters in the #DT command. In order to control the placement of text within these columns we make use of special commands. Additional RPF commands allow us to control the appearance of text in the final output such as underlining, centring etc.

Looking at the contents of the file TABRPT.EX, you can see that two tables have been defined using the #DT command:

```
#DT 1 13 73 #
#DT 2 1 5 9 28 32 39 42 49 52 0 #
```

The first one, identified by the number 1, is the same one used in the previous example and defines the overall width of the page. The second one, table 2, defines the table which will control the placement of text into columns.

In this second table, five columns are defined, the relative positions of which are determined by each pair of numbers. The final pair, 52 0, specifies a column starting in relative position 52 and ending in the last position of the right-hand margin as defined by a previously invoked table. This table will be nested within the first (i.e. it will be invoked using the #T command whilst table 1 is still active). The column positions defined in table 2 will therefore be relative to the start of table 1. For example, the first column defined as relative positions 1 to 5 will be placed in absolute print positions 13–17.

Note that a nested table must fit entirely within the table in which it has been invoked; otherwise a runtime error occurs.

### 12.2.4  Placing text within columns

Once the second table has been invoked, using the #T 2 command, RPF is told which columns to place the text in (see Figure 12.2). This is done using the #NC command. For example:

```
#T 2
Item #N No #NC
#CEN Car # #N #CEN Registration # #NC
#R Miles #N Used # #NC #N
```

sets up the headings for the report. It invokes table 2 and then uses a series of #NC commands interspersed with text. Each time an #NC is encountered, RPF places the following text into the next column. When the last column is reached, a subsequent next column command will place text in the first column again.

Having reached the appropriate column, text is inserted and formatted using other commands. In the example, the #CEN and #R commands are used to affect the way text is positioned. #CEN centres the following text within the column. #R causes any text placed within the column to be right-justified.

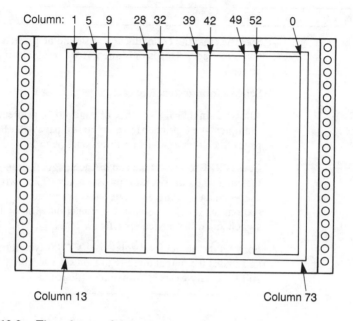

**Figure 12.2** The columns of the report.

Right- (and left-) justification commands remain in effect for a column even after an #NC command has been used to move to the next column.

Justification within a column remains in force even when the column is no longer current. All text inserted into the column will be justified until justification is turned off by executing a # for the column. If any text is too long to fit on a single line within a column, RPF will automatically adjust it so it is spread over two or more lines without splitting any words.

### 12.2.5 Additional features

When entering text into an RPF input file, it is permissible to have as many spaces as you wish between words and commands. When RPF processes the file, however, it will only ever place one space between each word. It will ignore special characters like tab characters or form feeds. If you require a form feed, insert the #NP command. Sometimes this feature can pose a problem if you want to insert several spaces between words to distinguish them from other text. To achieve this you must use the backslash (\) followed by a space, thus:

```
#CEN Customer    No: \ \ \ \ 13224 #
```

In this example, the words 'Customer' and 'No:' have been separated with five spaces but this will be output with just one space between the words. In

**Table 12.3**   RPF switches.

| Switch | Effect |
|--------|--------|
| A | Specifies that the entire document should be printed in bold type face. This is only supported for Diablo-type printers. |
| F | Sends a form feed before each page is printed. |
| P | Allows a single page or range of pages to be printed. For example: $-P:8$ prints page 8 to the last page; $-P:8:10$, pages 8 to 10, and $-P:1:1$ prints only page 1. |
| W | Causes RPF to wait at the end of each page. Printing is resumed when the operator presses a key. This switch is useful when printing on single sheet pre-printed stationery. It only operates in conjunction with the D:V switch and other device-specific switches. |
| D:V | Formats the output for display on a VT100-type terminal and routes the output directly to the user's terminal. It is still necessary to specify an output file name. |

order to insert five spaces between the customer number and the text, four backslashes have been inserted, each separated by one space. Each backslash will cause RPF to output an additional space, thereby achieving the desired effect.

To print a backslash character as text you must enter two, without a space between them.

### 12.2.6   RPF switches

Switches can be specified when invoking RPF. These switches control the execution of RPF and specify various print options. The common ones are shown in Table 12.3. There are other switches that can be used, and these can be found in Appendix E. RPF switches are specified in any order in lower or upper case. Spaces are not allowed between switches (though this does vary on some ports). The string of switches is preceded by a single minus sign. For example:

```
RPF invoices.rpf invprint.lst -d:vw
```

outputs to a VT100, pausing between pages.

## Summary: Report formatter

☐ RPF, the report formatter, works in conjunction with RPT, the report generator. It reads an input file containing a mixture of RPF formatting commands and text, to produce a file suitable for printing.

☐ 'Tables' are used as templates into which the text is placed. These tables are quite different from database tables.

☐ Tables may be nested and several tables can be in use at one time. Various commands specify where text is to be placed within the scope of the table.

☐ RPF commands can specify horizontal and vertical margins, centring and underlining, tabulation etc.

---

**EXERCISE 12.1**

1. Use your system's text editor to modify the promotion letter used in the first example. (a) Add an additional paragraph offering an additional discount to those customers replying by a certain date. (b) Underline the paragraph you add to highlight it.

2. Save the file and, using RPF, format the file into a print file called PROMO.LIS.

3. Produce your own marketing letter from 50K Cars Ltd using the commands covered so far. Print your output file after it has been processed by RPF.

4. Modify the second example, TABRPT.EX, to print the customer address. Run the new version.

5. Create a command file to produce an invoice from 50K Cars Ltd. Invent the customer name, address and any other data you may need. Run the report.

---

## 12.3 RPT outline

All the exercises and examples of RPF input files so far have had fixed text embedded amongst RPF commands. RPT allows variable text, derived from the database, to be inserted.

RPT interprets commands and SQL statements, ignoring any RPF-specific commands, and produces an interim file. This file includes the data retrieved by the SQL statements together with RPF formatting commands.

### 12.3.1 RPT program structure

There are few enforced rules for the structure of an RPT program. RPT just goes through the command file, interpreting the relevant commands as it comes across them. Logically, however, it is structured in three main sections: data declaration, macro definition and procedure sections. These sections are not introduced formally as they would be in, say COBOL. The grouping is purely to help provide clarity and make program maintenance easier, and you are recommended to structure the program this way physically as well as logically. You will see that all the examples are written this way.

The data declaration section contains the definition of all variables to be used to store values from the database. The macro definition section names and defines macros. Macros can be thought of as the equivalent of program modules or subroutines in a 3GL. There are two types:

- SELECT macros which define SQL SELECT statements to retrieve data from database tables.

- Procedural macros which containing RPF statements.

The procedure section contains executable RPT statements which make up the main body of the program. Within this section macros may be explicitly or implicitly executed. Remember that there are no restrictions on the positioning of these types of statement within a program. The only rule is that variables must be defined before they are used. With such a loose structure it is possible to produce very messy and unmanageable RPT programs, so programming discipline is more than usually important.

All RPT identifiers, i.e. macro names, variable names and statement labels, must start with an alphabetical character and consist only of letters, digits, underscore ( _ ) and hash (#). You are recommended not to use hash so as to avoid confusion with RPF commands. RPT ignores the case of identifiers so, for example, CUST is the same as CUst . Identifiers can be of any length but only the first 30 characters are treated as significant.

Like RPF, RPT commands can be prefixed with either a full stop or a hash. To help distinguish between RPF and RPT commands, we use a full stop to start all RPT commands and reserve the hash to introduce RPF commands. You are recommended to follow this convention as well.

You can divide any report into three major parts: the *report head*, the *report body* and the *report foot* (Figure 12.3). Each of these parts, in turn, could have a head, a body and a foot. This nested structure can describe complex reports, like master–detail. It provides a good framework around which to structure RPT programs. In the next sections we will examine an example report containing the three basic parts without nesting. This will then be developed to show more complex structures involving nesting of these sections.

### 12.3.2 Error handling

Generally all errors found in an RPT script file are directed to the standard error output device for the system, normally a terminal. RPT can also write errors to an error file.

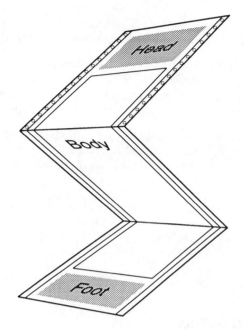

**Figure 12.3**   Report components.

Before RPT executes the commands found in the source file, it scans the entire file searching for syntax errors. If errors are found it will display them (if the output device is a terminal), but will not produce the interim report file. RPT can be forced to ignore syntax errors and produce the interim file by using a switch (-X) on the RPT command line. For example:

```
RPT input output user/pass -X
```

By entering the -X switch, RPT will still flag syntax errors, but when it executes it will ignore those statements which contain syntax errors and therefore the interim file produced will not be complete. This switch is entered on the command line after the username and password.

RPT is unable to detect statements which will cause runtime errors until execution time, i.e. they are not detected during syntax checking. If a runtime error does occur RPT will abort execution and display an error message on the terminal. Runtime errors are not written to an error file.

## Summary: RPT outline

☐ RPT uses SQL statements to access data in the database, which it then merges with RPF formatting commands in an intermediate file to be processed by RPF. There are a number of RPT commands to control the extraction of the data and its processing.

☐ RPT commands can start with a full stop or a hash. You are strongly recommended only to use the full stop, saving hash for RPF commands.

☐ Logically, an RPT program contains three sections: data declaration, macro definition and procedure sections. RPT enforces very few rules on program structure, but you are strongly recommended to structure your programs into these three sections – physically as well as logically.

☐ Macros are an important feature of RPT. There are two types. SELECT macros contain SQL statements to extract data from the database. Procedural macros contain RPT commands, perhaps including the invoking of other macros.

☐ RPT is able to detect syntax errors prior to report generation. These errors are written to an error file together with the source statement which caused it. Any errors detected at runtime will abort the report process.

## 12.4   RPT commands

RPT commands fall into six categories. **Declarative** statements define and initialize program variables. **Macro definition** statements define both SELECT and procedural macros. **Macro execution** statements invoke macros. **General RPT commands** control the printing of variables and message displays on the terminal. **Program control** statements determine the report processing. Finally, there are **Arithmetic** statements.

The example command file TABRPT.EX is used to illustrate this section. It is listed in Appendix E. You can see that this example is quite different from the RPF file used earlier. To help guide you through the complexities of RPT, each major feature of this file is discussed separately, starting with RPT's declarative statements.

All RPT commands have the same syntactical structure. It consists of an RPT command followed by one or more arguments, thus:

```
command arg1 [arg2[ ... argn]]
```

Commands can be entered in upper or lower case and may begin anywhere on the input line. Each command must be on a new line and the line should not contain anything other than the command and its arguments. All the arguments must appear on the same line as the command.

### 12.4.1   Declarative statements

There are three declarative statements in the command set: .DECLARE, .SET and .EQUAL. The .DECLARE command declares a program variable and defines its format using a format mask. These masks are the same as those used by SQL*Plus and are described in Chapter 2 and Appendix B. There are two exceptions. Firstly, a zero to denote leading zeros (e.g. 09999) will fill the mask out to its maximum size with leading zeros. Secondly, V is used to align the decimal point (in SQL*Plus, V is used to raise the number to a power). For example:

```
.DECLARE charge $9,999.99
```

declares a numeric variable charge which can hold a maximum value of 9,999.99. The variable will be displayed with a leading dollar sign. As in SQL*Plus, the pound sign can replace the dollar, but then dollar is no longer available.

When a variable is first declared, RPT automatically sets it to NULL. It may be necessary to initialize these variables prior to their use, for example, to set numeric variables to zero. This is achieved by using the .SET command. For instance:

```
.SET charge 0
```

will assign the value zero to the numeric program variable charge. It is also possible to copy the value of one program variable to another. For example, the statement:

```
.EQUAL charge amount
```

causes the value held in the variable amount to be copied to the variable charge. So there is an implied := operator between the two variables. Both variables must be of the same datatype.

### 12.4.2 Macros and SQL

RPT functions depend heavily on macros. A macro is simply a set of statements which carries out a particular function. Within RPT there are two types, a SELECT macro which can only contain a SQL statement, and a procedural macro which contains all other RPT commands.

SELECT macros and procedural macros are specified in exactly the same way. RPT distinguishes between them by the way they are invoked. To define a macro the .DEFINE statement is used followed by a macro name. For example:

```
.DEFINE selrow
```

defines a macro called selrow. Subsequent statements list the contents of the macro. RPT stores the complete macro definition for later execution.

Looking at the enhanced Statement of Account report, you can see how we have defined macros. Note that all macro definitions are ended with two full stops (..) which must be placed on their own line.

---

**EXERCISE 12.2**

1. Which of the following RPT identifiers are legal and which illegal? Why?

   ```
   147889
   this_is_an_RPT_identifier_which_could_be_used
   176-a
   CD899x
   this_is_an_RPT_identifier_which_could_also_be_used
   ```

2. Define the following program variables:

   | Variable name | Format |
   |---|---|
   | `Customer_number` | Numeric, max. 5 digits |
   | `Post_code` | Alphanumeric, max. 10 characters |
   | `amount_paid` | Numeric displaying the $ sign, maximum size sufficient to hold $10,000.00 with two decimal places |

3. Initialize the numeric variables above to zero and the character variable to NULL.

4. Initialize the variable `charge` to the value of the contents of the variable `running_total`. Now reset `charge` to NULL.

---

A SELECT macro contains the text of a SQL query. Only one query may be specified within each SELECT macro, although two or more SQL statements may be joined using the UNION, INTERSECT or MINUS commands, or by the use of subqueries. The macro may include any SQL statement.

There are two ways in which a macro may be executed. A SELECT macro can be explicitly executed using the EXECUTE command. For example:

```
.EXECUTE selrow
```

Executing a SELECT macro in this way only makes the first row available for the report. If the macro is re-executed the same row will be returned. This method of execution should only be used if the SELECT statement is expected to retrieve a single row. But note that if the macro contains, for instance, a DELETE statement, *all* relevant rows will be deleted, not just the first one. Beware.

A procedural macro is explicitly executed by preceding its name with a full stop (period). For instance,

```
.printline
```

will execute a procedural macro called `printline`. This type of macro can be executed in this way from anywhere within an RPT program, including other procedural macros. The macro must have been defined prior to its execution. When processing of the macro is complete, the next sequential statement in the file is executed.

The second way in which macros can be invoked is by using the REPORT statement, described below. Examples of macro invocation can be seen in the example RPT report file `TABRPT.EX3`.

### 12.4.3  SQL syntax in SELECT macros

In addition to standard SQL clauses, a SELECT macro SQL query must use the INTO clause in order to assign the column values returned to pre-defined program variables. If the INTO statement is missing, a syntax error occurs. The program variables into which the values are to be placed must be of the same datatype as the columns or expressions in the SELECT clause.

Contents of program variables can be used in a SQL statement in the WHERE clause. The variable name must be preceded by an ampersand (&). For example:

```
SELECT      cust_name, address
INTO        customer_name, customer_address
FROM        customers
WHERE       cust_no = &which_cust
```

will retrieve customer name and address from the customers table where the customer number in the table is equal to the value contained in the `cust_no` program variable. The program variable must have been declared before being used.

### 12.4.4  The REPORT command

The REPORT statement controls the execution of the entire report by automatically invoking the SELECT macro and procedural macros when they are required to process a new row. The syntax of the statement is:

```
.REPORT select-macro body-macro
[head-macro[foot-macro]]
```

where `select-macro` is the name of the main SELECT macro to be used to select the information for the report from the database. `Body-macro` is the name of a procedural macro used for the body of the report. `Head-macro` is the name of the procedural macro to be executed at the start of the report. This macro would normally supply report titles. `Foot-macro` is the name of a procedural macro executed once at the end of the report. It is normally used to print a report footer.

The head and foot macros are optional parameters. A foot macro may not be specified without a head macro.

Unlike the `.EXECUTE` statement, the `.REPORT` command will cause every row returned by the `SELECT` macro to be processed. The head macro is executed when the first row of the `SELECT` macro is returned. The body macro, however, is not executed for the first row if a head macro is specified. So, in these circumstances, it should be explicitly executed within the head macro, otherwise the first row will not appear in the body of the report. Once again, an example of this can be found in the example.

The foot macro is executed **after** the last row has been processed. `.REPORT` statements may be invoked within the head, body or foot macro of another report and this means it is possible to produce very complex reports which involve nesting whole report programs and structures within other report structures. The most common application of this is master–detail reports where the master row is created using one `REPORT` statement and the detail rows are processed using another.

To illustrate this there is an example master–detail report, a car maintenance report. The RPT command file is called `NESTRPT.EX` (see Appendix E).

### 12.4.5  General RPT commands

There are a number of important general purpose commands. `.PRINT` outputs the values of program variables in the report. The positions of the values are determined by the RPF table and formatting commands. `.REM` indicates a comment line. These can be anywhere in the RPT input file. Examples can be found in the example reports.

`.ROLLBACK` and `.COMMIT` have the same effects as their SQL counterparts. `ROLLBACK` undoes any modifications made to the database tables after the last commit, `COMMIT` makes any changes permanent.

### 12.4.6  Accepting user input

Very often it is necessary to input various parameters, such as a date range, to limit the data required on a report. RPT provides two statements to accept this information and display error messages if the format is input incorrectly: `.ASK` and `.TELL`. `.ASK` will display a prompt and wait for the user to input a value. The format is:

```
.ASK promptfield input_variable
```

Once the value has been input, you may validate it using an `IF` statement. For example:

```
.&askcust
.ASK "Please enter the customer number:" cust_no
.IF "&cust_no <=0" THEN askcust
```

will ask the user to enter a customer number. RPT will store the value input in cust_no. The .IF statement then checks to see if the value input is less than or equal to zero and, if so, returns control to the label askcust, prompting the user to re-enter. Special care is needed if you are prompting for a date; see the section on date handling below.

If you wish to display an error message before re-prompting for input, use the .TELL command. For example:

.TELL "Invalid Customer Number, please re-enter"

could be used in the earlier example before branching to &askcust. Note that .TELL can only output a literal. It is not possible to insert the contents of a variable in the message to be output, for instance to repeat the incorrect customer number.

---

**EXERCISE 12.3**

1. Use your system editor to write an RPT script file, CUSTRPT.RPT, which contains a SELECT macro to retrieve customer number, name and postcode from the customers table. Do not forget to terminate the macro correctly.

2. Define a procedural macro in the same script file which takes each row returned from your SELECT macro, and, using RPF commands, prints it out in a tabular format.

3. Add all the required commands to your SELECT and procedural macros in order to produce printed output of the customer information. This will include RPF statements such as #DT to define your tables and RPT statements such as .REPORT to execute your report. Don't forget to include a heading and footer to your report and any additional text you feel is necessary.

4. Run your report program to get printed output, executing RPT followed by RPF. Choose your own filenames.

---

### 12.4.7 Program control statements

RPT has several procedural statements which control the flow of processing through the program. These program control statements bypass lines of code and jump to routines dependent upon values found in program variables. This type of conditional processing is mainly achieved by using the .IF statement.

The .IF statement allows a branch to a specified macro label dependent upon the evaluation of an expression. The syntax of the command is:

```
.IF expression THEN label [ELSE label]
```

The expression may compare the contents of one program variable with
another, or with a literal constant. Program variable names must be preceded
by an ampersand (&). If the ampersand is omitted, an 'Invalid Column Name'
error message is displayed. Any expression permitted within a WHERE clause
of a SQL statement can be used as an expression in an .IF statement. If the
expression includes spaces, it must be surrounded by double quotation marks
("). For example:

```
.IF "&cust_name = 'YM Marketing Ltd'" THEN
discount ELSE normal
```

Some other valid IF expressions are:

```
&amount*2<10000
"&miles_out IS NULL"
"&group='A' or &group='B'"
```

The .IF statement should be used with care, as it is very intensive on
processing and hence can affect the performance of the report generation
process. Before coding an .IF statement, check whether the same thing could
be achieved by using a SQL statement in a SELECT macro.

There is another form of the .IF statement specifically for dealing with
nulls. .IFNULL branches to the specified label if the variable is null. For
instance:

```
.IFNULL cust_name unknown_cust
```

branches to the label unknown_cust if the customer name is null. This is a
commonly used statement and, in contrast to .IF, is executed very efficiently. Both the .IF and .IFNULL statements require a branch to a label
within the macro. Labels are defined when they are required and are
indicated by a full stop followed by an ampersand and the label name. For
example:

```
.&unknown_cust
```

A label name must conform to the RPT naming conventions for identifiers. It
may only be referenced within the macro in which it has been defined, therefore
it is possible (but not recommended) to use the same label name in several
macros without conflict.

It is possible to specify unconditional branching by using the .GOTO
statement in the format:

```
.GOTO label-name
```

The label must be within the same macro as the .GOTO command.

To stop the processing of a report the .STOP command is used. This
normally appears on the very last line of an RPT file. If omitted, the report

**Table 12.4** RPT arithmetic functions.

| Function | Description |
|---|---|
| `.ADD dest_var`<br>`var1 var2` | Adds the contents of `var1` and `var2` and places the result in `dest-var`. |
| `.SUB dest_var`<br>`var1 var2` | Subtracts the contents of `var2` from `var1` and stores the result in the destination variable, `dest-var`. |
| `.MUL dest_var`<br>`var1 var2` | Multiplies the contents of `var1` by the contents of `var2` and stores the result in `dest-var`. |
| `.DIV dest_var`<br>`var1 var2` | Divides the contents of `var1` by the contents of `var2` storing the result in `dest-var`. If `var2` contains a zero, a fatal 'Divide by zero' error occurs and the report will be terminated. |

program will stop when it has processed the last line in the file. `.STOP` can be used to terminate processing anywhere in a file and is also used to test parts of the RPT code whilst debugging.

### 12.4.8 Arithmetical functions
Several arithmetical functions are provided in the RPT command language, shown in Table 12.4. All of these functions can use literals in place of the source variables, `var1` and `var2`.

## Summary: RPT commands

☐ Program variables are defined and initialized with declarative statements `.DECLARE`, `.SET` and `.EQUAL`. Each variable has a datatype, defined by a format mask in the `.DECLARE` statement.

☐ Any SQL statement can be used in a `SELECT` macro. The `INTO` clause is used to insert the values into the named program variables. Program variables can be used anywhere that SQL syntax would allow a column name or literal.

☐ The `.COMMIT` and `.ROLLBACK` statements allow any changes to the database to be made permanent or undone. They can appear anywhere in the command file.

☐ A `SELECT` macro can be executed either by using the `.EXECUTE` statement or from a `.REPORT` statement; a procedural macro by preceding its name with a full stop, or within a `.REPORT` statement.

☐ Invoking a SELECT macro with .EXECUTE will only ever return a single row. The .REPORT statement will automatically execute its macros for all rows returned.

☐ There are procedural statements, .IF, .IFNULL, .GOTO, STOP and program labels which can be used to control the flow of processing. Beware of the .IF statement; it is executed very inefficiently.

☐ The .TELL and .ASK statements are used to communicate with the user, for instance to get parameters for the print run.

---

**EXERCISE 12.4**

1. The following section of RPT code contains deliberate errors. Find them, explain why they are incorrect and then correct them.

```
#DT 30 1 5 7 9 11 21 23 30 #
.DECLARE cust_no number(5)
.DECLARE model a(8)
.DECLARE registration a8
#T 1
.DEFINE selcust
SELECT cust_no,model,registration
FROM bookings
INTO   :cust_no,registration,model
.PRINT cust_no #NC
.PRINT model #NC
.PRINT car_registration #NC
#TE
```

2. Write an .IF statement which tests the program variable cust_name to see if it is equal to the name 'WATSON' and if not branches to a label called notwatson.

3. Write an .IF statement which tests a program variable to see if it is less than 10 000. If it is, branch to a label called lessthan; if not, branch to a label called greaterthan; and if the variable contains a null value branch to error. The code at error prints out a message on the terminal which reads 'Error: NULL value'. Write the procedure error.

4. Write a statement, or series of statements, to add the contents of the variable amount to the variable totalamount. Ten per cent should then be deducted from totalamount and stored in a variable called discount.

5.  Write an `.IF` statement to test which group a car is in. If it is in groups 'A1', 'A2', 'A3' or 'A4' then branch to a label called `correctgroup`, otherwise branch to `wrongroup`.

## 12.5    Date manipulation in RPT

Date handling in RPT can be rather erratic, producing some unexpected results. Furthermore, the results obtained on one hardware range may be different from those obtained on another hardware range (i.e. results can be port-specific). In these circumstances, it is sensible to use defensive programming and follow two simple rules which will give predictable results:

*   Treat dates in RPT as character strings. Get them into this format as soon as you can.

*   Do all your date manipulation as part of the SELECT statement in macros.

These rules ensure that the date processing is done in the database software, which is reliable and predictable, rather than in RPT. It will not always be possible to stick to these rules, so this section describes how RPT deals with dates.

### 12.5.1    Date variables

Date variables are declared in the normal way with the `.DECLARE` command. There are three date datatypes that can be used to define the format of the variable:

*   DATE, which uses the MM/DD/YY display format

*   EDATE, which uses the DD/MM/YY display format

*   YYMMDD, which uses the display format you would expect

None of these date datatypes can hold a time as well as a date. Internally, all dates are held in a Julian format. It is possible to subtract dates from one another leaving a number of days, but you must use `.DSUB` for this:

```
.DSUB days date1 date2
```

This subtracts the contents of `date2` from `date1` and stores the result in the numeric variable `days`. The date variables may not be replaced by literals in the .DSUB command. Move the literal into a variable first. Avoid adding numbers to (or subtracting them from) variables of any of the date datatypes. It is safest to do date arithmetic in a SELECT macro.

RPT date variables of any datatype may be initialized by assigning a literal value. For example:

```
.SET edate_var 24/12/91
```

assigns the date to a variable with datatype edate. Date variables of any datatype may also be initialized by setting them equal to the value of another RPT date variable using the .EQUAL command.

### 12.5.2  Relation of RPT dates to Oracle dates

A particular area of unpredictability is ascribing date values from the database to RPT variables. The only completely reliable thing to do is to define RPT character variables and use them to hold date values in the database. Convert the dates to character strings using the TO_CHAR function in the SELECT macro.

YYMMDD variables can only accept dates from the database if they are held there as 6-digit numbers (holding the date as YYMMDD).

SELECTing a database date into an RPT variable in any other way may not work the way you may expect. Test the results carefully and re-test if you move the program to another hardware platform.

### 12.5.3  Date keyword constants

A special keyword constant, $$DATE$$, is available in RPT to assign the current date to program variables. Again, this area is unreliable and appears to be port-specific.

$$DATE$$ can be used to set a program variable to the current date. In many cases this operates as you would expect. If assigned to a character string variable, the date will be stored as a character string in the format MM/DD/YY. If assigned to an edate field, it will be stored as DD/MM/YY. If assigned to a date field, it will be stored as MM/DD/YY. If it is a YYMMDD field, it will be stored as YYMMDD (no solidi).

Do not rely on it working this way, though. Always check the effect of setting a variable equal to $$DATE$$, as it can be quite unexpected, depending on the datatype of the variable and on the port of RPT.

Another keyword constant, $$TIME$$, is available to assign the time to a variable. It returns the time as an 8-digit character string, in 24-hour format (e.g. 15:23:30). This area works reliably.

Note that both $$DATE$$ and $$TIME$$ are set when RPT starts running. Their values are not updated while RPT is running.

### 12.5.4 Prompting for dates

If a date is required as user input, using the .ASK command, make sure that the date datatype of the receiving field is the same as the format of the date which the user expects to enter. It is sensible always to specify the format of the date expected in the prompt. For instance:

```
.ASK "Enter booking date (DD/MM/YY): " book_date
```

In this case book_date must have been defined as an edate variable. RPT looks after the validation of dates and re-prompts the user if necessary.

## Summary: Dates in RPT

☐ The manipulation of dates within RPT can be unreliable and port-specific. As far as possible, do all date handling within SELECT statements so that it is the database, not RPT, which does the work.

☐ There are three date datatypes, corresponding to different external date formats. Internally, all are held as Julian dates. None of these datatypes includes time of day with the date.

☐ Date arithmetic is not as simple as in SQL. Use .DSUB to get the difference between two dates. Do not add or subtract numbers to or from dates except in SELECT statements.

☐ RPT provides two constants, $$DATE$$ and $$TIME$$, containing today's date and the time of day. These are set once at start of run and then not updated.

*Part 5*

*Appendices and
reference information*

*Appendix A*
# The example database

A ll the exercises and examples in the book deal with the same mythical
company, 50K Cars Ltd, who rent out expensive cars. An extract from
the company's database is used for all the exercises and examples. The
structure of these sample tables is described in this appendix.

## A.1 Tables
### A.1.1 Cars

| Column | Type | Description |
|---|---|---|
| Registration | CHAR(7) NOT NULL | The registration number of the car. This is the primary key of the table. |
| Model_name | CHAR(8) | The model of the car. Used as a foreign key into the *MODEL* table. |
| Car_group_name | CHAR(2) | Group code defining type of car and rental cost. Used as a foreign key into the *CARGROUP* table. |
| Date_bought | DATE | The date the car was bought by 50K Cars. |
| Cost | NUMBER(8,2) | The original cost of the car. |
| Miles_to_date | NUMBER(6) | The current mileage of the car as read when last brought in at the end of a rental period. |
| Miles_last_service | NUMBER(6) | The mileage of the car as read when last serviced. |
| Status | CHAR(1) | The current status of the car. 'A' for available, 'H' for on hire, 'S' for being serviced, 'X' for in need of repair or service. |

## A.1.2 CarGroup

| Column | Type | Description |
|---|---|---|
| Car_group_name | CHAR(2) NOT NULL | The car group code. This will be one of the following values: 'A1', 'A2', 'A3', 'A4', 'B1', 'B2', 'B3', 'B4'. |
| Rate_per_mile | NUMBER(3) | The charge per mile for cars in this group. In pence. |
| Rate_per_day | NUMBER(5,2) | The rental charge per day for cars of this group. In pounds and pence. |

## A.1.3 Models

| Column | Type | Description |
|---|---|---|
| Model_name | CHAR(8) NOT NULL | The model name (an abbreviation of the full name). This is the primary key for the table. |
| Car_group_name | CHAR(2) | The group to which this mod•: of car belongs. |
| Description | CHAR(30) | A full description of the car model. |
| Maint_int | NUMBER(5) | The number of miles between regular services. |

## A.1.4 Customers

| Column | Type | Description |
|---|---|---|
| Cust_no | NUMBER(5) NOT NULL | The customer/account number. This is the primary key for the table. |
| Cust_name | CHAR(20) | The name of the customer. |
| Address | CHAR(20) | This and the next three columns contain the customer's address. |
| Town | CHAR(20) | |
| County | CHAR(20) | |
| Post_code | CHAR(10) | Postcode (or zip code). |

| Column | Type | Description |
|---|---|---|
| Contact | CHAR(20) | Name of person to contact. |
| Pay_method | CHAR(1) | Code to indicate how this customer usually pays. 'A' for payment on account, 'C' for cash, or null. |

## A.1.5 Bookings

| Column | Type | Description |
|---|---|---|
| Booking_no | NUMBER(5) NOT NULL | A serial number used to uniquely identify the booking. |
| Cust_no | NUMBER(5) | Customer number of the customer making the booking. |
| Date_reserved | DATE | The date on which the booking was made. |
| Reserved_by | CHAR(12) | Name of the person who took the reservation. |
| Date_rent_start | DATE | The date on which the rental commences. |
| Rental_period | NUMBER(3) | Length of rental period in days. |
| Registration | CHAR(7) | Registration of car actually rented. |
| Model_name | CHAR(8) | The model of car rented. |
| Miles_out | NUMBER(6) | Miles on clock at rental start. |
| Miles_in | NUMBER(6) | Miles on the clock at rental end. |
| Amount_due | NUMBER(6,2) | The cost of the rental. Calculated when the car is returned. |
| Paid | CHAR(1) | Indicator to show if this rental has been paid for. 'Y' for paid, 'N' for not yet paid. |

## A.1.6 Models of cars in the database

| Model | Description |
|-------|-------------|
| ASTON V8 | Aston Martin V8 |
| BMW 635 | BMW 635 CSi |
| BMW 750 | BMW 750 iL |
| FERR TR | Ferrari Testarossa |
| JAG XJS | Jaguar XJS V12 |
| JAG XJ6 | Jaguar XJ6 Sovereign |
| LAMB COU | Lamborghini Countach |
| MERC 560 | Mercedes 560 SEL |
| P911 TC | Porsche 911 Turbo Cabriolet |
| P944 T | Porsche 944 Turbo |
| RR SSPIR | Rolls Royce Silver Spirit |

## A.1.7 Database on disk

The author can provide copies of SQL command files to build the example database on IBM PC floppy disk. Get in touch via Compuserve (ID 100015, 3306) or via Addison-Wesley in the UK.

*Appendix B*
# SQL and SQL*Plus: reference information

## B.1 SQL commands

| Command | Description |
|---|---|
| /*...*/ | Comment |
| ALTER PARTITION | Alters a database partition |
| ALTER SPACE | Alters a database space definition |
| ALTER TABLE | Changes the definition of an existing table |
| AUDIT | Switches on audit trail on use of system resources |
| COMMENT | Records a comment about a table or column |
| CREATE CLUSTER | Creates a cluster to make tables physically adjacent on disk |
| CREATE DATABASE LINK | Sets up a link to another, usually remote, database |
| CREATE INDEX | Creates an index to a table |
| CREATE PARTITION | Creates a new partition in the database |
| CREATE SPACE | Creates a space definition for the placement of a table |
| CREATE SYNONYM | Sets up a synonym for a table or view |
| CREATE TABLE | Creates a table and defines its columns |
| CREATE VIEW | Defines a view on a table(s) |
| DELETE | Deletes rows from a table |
| DROP | Removes database objects (tables, indexes, views etc.) from the database |
| GRANT | Assigns user IDs, passwords and access rights |
| INSERT | Inserts rows into a table |

| Command | Description |
|---|---|
| LOCK TABLE | Locks a table to avoid conflict from several users wanting to access it |
| NOAUDIT | Switches off audit trail of system resources |
| RENAME | Changes the name of a table, view or synonym |
| REVOKE | Takes away access rights |
| SELECT | Queries the database to extract data |
| UPDATE | Updates fields in a table |
| VALIDATE INDEX | Checks the validity of and rebuilds an index to a table |

## B.2   SQL*Plus commands

| Command | Description |
|---|---|
| @ | Runs a file containing SQL*Plus commands |
| # | Ends a block of comment started by DOCUMENT command |
| $ | Executes an operating system command from within SQL*Plus |
| / | Executes the statement in the SQL buffer |
| ACCEPT | Prompts for the value of a variable |
| APPEND | Appends text to the end of the current line in the SQL buffer |
| BREAK | Specifies control breaks for reports and action to be taken |
| BTITLE | Specifies text to go at the bottom of each page of a report |
| CHANGE | Changes contents of current line in the SQL buffer |
| CLEAR | Clears break definitions, etc. |
| COLUMN | Specifies layout and heading of columns in a report |
| COMMIT | Makes changes to the database permanent |
| COMPUTE | Carries out calculations on groups of rows |

| Command | Description |
|---------|-------------|
| CONNECT | Logs off Oracle and on again with a different user name |
| COPY | Copies data from one database to another |
| DEFINE | Defines a user variable |
| DEL | Deletes the current line of the SQL buffer |
| DESCRIBE | Displays the description of a table |
| DISCONNECT | Logs off Oracle while remaining connected to SQL\*Plus |
| DOCUMENT | Introduces comment in a command file |
| EDIT | Runs the system editor against the contents of the SQL buffer |
| EXIT | Exits from SQL\*Plus |
| GET | Loads the contents of a file into the SQL buffer |
| HELP | Provides help about commands |
| HOST | The same as $. Executes an operating system command |
| INPUT | Sets line editor into input mode to add lines after current line in the SQL buffer |
| LIST | Lists the contents of the SQL buffer |
| NEWPAGE | Inserts a form-feed in spooled output |
| PAUSE | Outputs a message and waits for the return key to be pressed |
| QUIT | The same as exit. Exits from SQL\*Plus |
| REMARK | The start of a one line comment in a command file |
| ROLLBACK | Undo changes to the database since the last COMMIT command |
| RUN | Displays and runs the contents of the SQL buffer |
| SAVE | Saves the contents of the SQL buffer in a file or in the database |
| SET | Ascribes a value to a SQL parameter |
| SHOW | Displays the value of a SQL parameter |
| SPOOL | Diverts output to a system spool file |
| START | Executes the commands in a command file |
| TIMING | Starts analysing system performance |

| Command | Description |
|---------|-------------|
| TTITLE | Specifies text to appear at the top of each page of a report |
| UNDEFINE | Deletes a user variable |

## B.3   SQL reserved words

The following are treated as reserved words by SQL*Plus. They may not be used for names of database objects.

| | | | |
|---|---|---|---|
| ACCESS | ADD | ALL | ALTER |
| AND | ANY | APPEND | AS |
| ASC | ASSERT | ASSIGN | AUDIT |
| | | | |
| BETWEEN | BY | | |
| | | | |
| CHAR | CLUSTER | COLUMN | COMMENT |
| COMPRESS | CONNECT | CONTAIN | CONTAINS |
| CRASH | CREATE | CURRENT | |
| | | | |
| DATAPAGES | DATE | DBA | DECIMAL |
| DEFAULT | DEFINITION | DELETE | DESC |
| DISTINCT | DOES | DROP | |
| | | | |
| EACH | ELSE | ERASE | EVALUATE |
| EXCLUSIVE | EXISTS | | |
| | | | |
| FILE | FLOAT | FOR | FORMAT |
| FROM | | | |
| | | | |
| GRANT | GRAPHIC | GROUP | |
| | | | |
| IDENTIFIED | IF | IMAGE | IMMEDIATE |
| IN | INCREMENT | INDEX | INDEXED |
| INDEXPAGES | INITIAL | INSERT | INTEGER |
| INTERSECT | INTO | IS | |
| | | | |
| LEVEL | LIKE | LIST | LOCK |
| LONG | | | |
| | | | |
| MAXEXTENTS | MINUS | MODE | MODIFY |
| MOVE | | | |
| | | | |
| NEW | NOAUDIT | NOCOMPRESS | NOLIST |
| NOSYSSORT | NOT | NOWAIT | NULL |
| NUMBER | | | |

| OF | OFFLINE | OLD | ON |
| ONLINE | OPTIMIZE | OPTION | OR |
| ORDER | | | |

| PARTITION | PCTFREE | PRIOR | PRIVILEGES |
| PUBLIC | | | |

| RAW | RENAME | REPLACE | RESOURCE |
| REVOKE | ROW | ROWID | ROWNUM |
| ROWS | RUN | | |

| SELECT | SESSION | SET | SHARE |
| SIZE | SMALLINT | SPACE | START |
| SUCCESSFUL | SYNONYM | SYSDATE | SYSSORT |

| TABLE | TEMPORARY | THEN | TO |
| TRIGGER | | | |

| UID | UNION | UNIQUE | UPDATE |
| USER | USING | | |

| VALIDATE | VALUES | VARCHAR | VARGRAPHIC |
| VIEW | | | |

| WHENEVER | WHERE | WITH | |

# B.4   SQL functions

The following is a list and brief description of the functions available in SQL*Plus. Refer to the SQL*Plus reference guide for complete descriptions. In all these descriptions, the following notation is used:

- *n, m* indicate a numeric column or expression,

- *str* and *chars* indicate a character string column or expression,

- *date, d1, d2* etc. indicates a date column or expression.

Other parameters are explained as they are used.

## B.4.1   Numeric functions

| Function | Value returned |
| --- | --- |
| ABS(n) | The absolute value of *n* |
| CEIL(n) | The smallest integer greater than or equal to *n* |
| FLOOR(n) | The largest integer less then or equal to *n* |

| Function | Value returned |
|---|---|
| MOD(n,m) | The remainder when *n* is divided by *m* |
| POWER(n,m) | *n* to the *m* |
| ROUND(n[,m]) | *n* rounded to *m* decimal places. If *m* is omitted, *n* is rounded to nearest integer |
| SIGN(n) | -1, 0 or 1, depending on whether *n* is negative, zero or positive |
| SQRT(n) | The square root of *n*. NULL if *n* is negative |
| TRUNC(n[,m]) | *n* truncated to *m* decimal places. If *m* is omitted, *n* is truncated to an integer |

## B.4.2  Character functions

| Function | Value returned |
|---|---|
| ASCII(str) | The ASCII value of the first character of *str* |
| CHR(n) | The character whose ASCII numeric value is *n* |
| INITCAP(str) | *str* with the first letter of each word in capitals |
| INSTR(str,chars[,n[,m]]) | The numeric character position of the *m*th occurrence of chars in *str*. The search starts at position *n*. *n* and *m* default to 1 |
| LENGTH(str) | The number of characters in *str* |
| LOWER(str) | *str* with all characters in lower case |
| LPAD(str,n[,chars]) | *str*, padded on the left to length *n* with as many occurrences of *chars* as necessary |
| LTRIM(str,chars) | *str*, with the left-most characters removed up to the first character not found in *chars* |
| RPAD(str,n[,chars]) | *str*, padded on the right to length *n* with as many occurrences of *chars* as necessary |
| RTRIM(str,chars) | *str*, with the right-most characters removed after the last character not found in *chars* |
| SOUNDEX(str) | A coded character string representing the sound of the word in *str* |

| Function | Value returned |
|---|---|
| SUBSTR(str,n[,m]) | A substring from *str*, starting at character *n* and *m* characters long. If *m* is omitted, the substring is to the end of *str* |
| TRANSLATE(str,from,to) | *str*, translated such that each character in *str* that appears in any position in *from* is translated to the character in the corresponding position in *to* |
| UPPER(str) | *str*, with all letters in upper case |
| USERENV(str) | Returns information about the user's environment. Valid contents for *str* are 'ENTRYID' to return an auditing entry identifier, 'SESSIONID' to return the auditing session identifier, 'TERMINAL' to return the terminal identifier and 'LANGUAGE' to return the national language in use |

## B.4.3   Conversion functions

| Function | Value returned |
|---|---|
| CHARTOROWID(str) | The rowid corresponding to the numeric string *str* |
| HEXTORAW(str) | A binary value corresponding to the hexadecimal string *str* |
| RAWTOHEX(raw) | The hexadecimal string corresponding to the binary value *raw* |
| ROWIDTOCHAR(rowid) | The 18 digit numeric string corresponding to *rowid* |
| TO_CHAR(source[,frmt]) | The character representation of source in the format defined by *frmt*. *source* may be a number or a date. If *frmt* is omitted, default layouts are used |
| TO_DATE(str[,frmt]) | The date representation of the date string, *str* held in the format defined by *frmt* |
| TO_NUMBER(str) | The number representation of the numeric string, *str* |

## B.4.4   Date functions

| Function | Value returned |
| --- | --- |
| `ADD_MONTHS(date,n)` | *date* plus *n* months |
| `LAST_DAY(date)` | The date of the last day of the month in which *date* falls |
| `MONTHS_BETWEEN(d1,d2)` | The number of months between dates *d1* and *d2*. Negative if *d1* is earlier than *d2* |
| `NEW_TIME(date,z1,z2)` | The date and time in time zone *z2* contemporaneous with the date and time in *date* in time zone *z1*. *z1* and *z2* are character expressions defining the US time zones and GMT. See Oracle manuals for valid values |
| `NEXT_DAY(date,str)` | The date of the next occurring day of the week specified by *str* |
| `TRUNC(date)` | *date*, truncated to a whole day (time set to 00:00:00) |

## B.4.5   Aggregate functions

All aggregate functions ignore nulls except COUNT(*), which includes nulls because at least one column in each row must be non-null.

All the functions include a specifier to determine whether the function is to operate over all non-null values or over distinct non-null values. This is indicated by spec, below. Valid specifiers are DISTINCT or ALL. ALL is the default if neither is specified.

| Function | Value returned |
| --- | --- |
| `AVG([spec] n)` | The average value of *n* |
| `COUNT([spec] expr)` | The number of rows where *expr* evaluates non-NULL |
| `MAX([spec] expr)` | The maximum value of *expr* |
| `MIN([spec] expr)` | The minimum value of *expr* |
| `STDDEV([spec] n)` | The standard deviation of *n* |
| `SUM([spec] n)` | The sum of values of *n* |
| `VARIANCE([spec] n)` | The variance of *n* |

## B.4.6 Other functions

| Function | Value returned |
|---|---|
| DECODE(expr,s1,r1... sn,rn,[def]) | If *expr* evaluates to any of *s1* to *sn*, then this function returns the corresponding *r1* to *rn*. If not, it returns *def* |
| DUMP(expr[,radix[,start [,len]]]) | The value of *expr* in an internal format. See Oracle manuals for details |
| GREATEST(expr1,expr2... exprn) | Whichever of *expr1* to *exprn* that evaluates to the greatest value |
| LEAST(expr1,expr2... exprn) | Whichever of *expr1* to *exprn* that evaluates to the least value |
| NVL(col, expr) | *expr* if *col* is NULL, otherwise *col* |
| VSIZE(expr) | The number of bytes used to hold *expr* in ORACLE's internal format |

# B.5  Operators
## B.5.1  Logical operators

| Operator | Description |
|---|---|
| = | Equal to; tests for equality |
| !=, ^=, <> | All three mean not equal to; test for inequality |
| > | Greater than |
| >= | Greater than or equal to |
| < | Less than |
| <= | Less than or equal to |
| ALL | Modifies the action of a condition to apply to all members of a list of values |
| ANY | Modifies the action of a condition to apply to any member of a list of values |
| [NOT] BETWEEN...AND... | Greater than or equal to one value and less than or equal to another |

| Operator | Description |
|---|---|
| EXISTS | Evaluates true if the following subquery returns at least one row |
| [NOT] IN | Equal to any member of the set of values |
| IS [NOT] NULL | Tests for NULL |

### B.5.2  Set operators

| Operator | Description |
|---|---|
| INTERSECT | Combines two queries to return only those rows returned by both the queries |
| MINUS | Combines two queries to return only those rows returned by the first query but not by the second |
| UNION | Combines two queries to return the rows returned by either one of the queries |

# B.6   Datatypes

| Datatype | Description |
|---|---|
| CHAR(n) | Character data, *n* characters long. Maximum size is 240 |
| DATE | Date and time |
| DECIMAL | Same as NUMBER, but cannot specify *n* or *m* |
| FLOAT | Same as NUMBER |
| INTEGER | Same as NUMBER(n) |
| LONG | Character data up to 64K characters long. Only one LONG column is allowed in a table. There are restrictions on the use of LONGs |
| LONG RAW | Binary data up to 64K bytes long. Restrictions the same as LONG |
| LONG VARCHAR | Same as LONG |

| Datatype | Description |
|----------|-------------|
| NUMBER | Numeric data with a maximum of 40 digits plus decimal point and sign |
| NUMBER(n) | Numeric data of specified number of digits. Maximum is 105 |
| NUMBER(n,m) | Numeric data of specified number (*n*) of digits, including *m* digits after the decimal point |
| NUMBER(*) | Same as NUMBER |
| RAW(n) | Binary data, *n* bytes long. Maximum is 240 bytes |
| SMALLINT | Same as NUMBER(n) |

# B.7   Format specifications

## B.7.1   Character formats

The display width of character fields is specified as A(n), where n is the number of characters.

## B.7.2   Number formats

Input and display formats for numbers are specified with the following elements:

| Element | Description | Example |
|---------|-------------|---------|
| 9 | The string of 9s shows the number of digits | 9999 |
| 0 | Shows that one or more leading zeros are to be displayed | 00999 |
| $ (£) | Prefixes value with dollar sign. Pound sign may be set up to replace dollar sign | £999 |
| B | Shows that one or more leading zeros are to be displayed as blanks | BB999 |
| MI | Displays a minus sign after negative values | 999MI |
| PR | Displays negative values enclosed in angle brackets | 999PR |

| Element | Description | Example |
|---------|-------------|---------|
| , (comma) | Displays a comma in the position indicated | 99,999 |
| . (period) | Aligns the decimal point to the indicated position | 999.99 |
| V | Multiplies the value of the number by 10 to the power of the number of digits after the V | 9V99 |
| EEEE | Display in scientific notation. Exactly four Es must be used | 9.9999EEEE |

## B.7.3 Date formats

Input and display formats for dates are specified with the following elements:

| Element | Description |
|---------|-------------|
| SSSS | Number of seconds since midnight |
| SS | Number of seconds |
| MI | Number of minutes |
| HH or HH12 | Hours on 12 hour clock |
| HH24 | Hours on 24 hour clock |
| J | The number of days since 31 December 4713 BC (Julian date) |
| DY | Three-letter abbreviation for the name of the day |
| DAY | Name of the day, padded to 9 characters |
| D | Day of the week (1–7) |
| DD | Day of the month (1–28, 29, 30 or 31) |
| DDD | Day of the year (1–364 or 365) |
| W | Week of the month (1–5) |
| WW | Week of the year (1–52) |
| MON | Three-letter abbreviation for the name of the month |
| MONTH | The name of the month, padded to 9 characters |
| MM | The month (1–12) |
| Q | The quarter of the year (1–4) |

| Element | Description |
|---|---|
| Y, YY or YYY | The last one, two or three digits of the year |
| YYYY | The year as a four-digit number |
| YEAR | The year spelled out in words |
| CC | The century as a number (usually two digits) |

Modifiers may also be specified to alter the effect of these elements:

| Modifier | Description |
|---|---|
| fm | Prefix to MONTH and DAY to disable padding and produce a variable length result |
| s | Prefix to CC, YEAR or YYYY to insert a minus sign for BC dates |
| SP | Suffix on any number to spell it out in words (e.g. DDSP) |
| SPTH or THSP | Suffix on any number to produce the ordinal value and to spell it out in words |
| TH | Suffix on any number to produce the ordinal number (i.e. to insert 'TH', 'ST' etc. at the end of the number) |
| upper/lower case | The case in which the elements and modifiers are specified governs the case in which the output is produced. Initial capitals will produce initial capitals in the output (e.g. Day could produce Monday) |
| punctuation | When inserted in the element, comma, full stop, slash etc. will appear at the corresponding position in the output (e.g. A.M. or DD/MM/YY) |
| constants | Character strings, enclosed in double quotes, may be inserted in the format specification and will appear at the appropriate place in the output (e.g. DDth "of" Mon could produce 31st of Mar) |

# SQL*Forms version 3: reference information

## C.1 Triggers

### C.1.1 Key triggers

Key triggers are associated with the pressing of a key or key combination. They fire when the relevant key is pressed.

| Trigger type | Associated function key |
|---|---|
| KEY-CLRBLK | *[Clear block]* |
| KEY-CLRFRM | *[Clear form]* |
| KEY-CLRREC | *[Clear record]* |
| KEY-COMMIT | *[Commit/accept]* |
| KEY-CQUERY | *[Count query hits]* |
| KEY-CREREC | *[Insert record]* |
| KEY-DELREC | *[Delete record]* |
| KEY-DOWN | *[Down]* |
| KEY-DUPFLD | *[Duplicate field]* |
| KEY-DUPREC | *[Duplicate record]* |
| KEY-EDIT | *[Edit]* |
| KEY-ENTER | *[Enter]* |
| KEY-ENTQRY | *[Enter query]* |
| KEY-EXEQRY | *[Execute query]* |
| KEY-EXIT | *[Exit]* |
| KEY-Fn | Programmable function keys 0 to 9 |
| KEY-HELP | *[Help]* |
| KEY-LISTVAL | *[List of values]* |
| KEY-MENU | *[Block menu]* |
| KEY-NXTBLK | *[Next block]* |

| Trigger type | Associated function key |
|---|---|
| KEY-NXTFLD | [*Next field*] |
| KEY-NXTKEY | [*Next primary key field*] |
| KEY-NXTREC | [*Next record*] |
| KEY-NXTSET | [*Next set of records*] |
| KEY-PRINT | [*Print*] |
| KEY-PRVBLK | [*Previous block*] |
| KEY-PRVFLD | [*Previous field*] |
| KEY-PRVREC | [*Previous record*] |
| KEY-SCRDOWN | [*Scroll down*] |
| KEY-SCRUP | [*Scroll up*] |
| KEY-STARTUP | A notional key implicitly pressed when the form is activated |
| KEY-UP | [*Up*] |
| KEY-UPDREC | [*Lock record*] |

## C.1.2 Navigational triggers

| Trigger type | Description |
|---|---|
| POST-BLOCK | Fires when form navigation results in leaving a block. Often used to process together all records in a block. |
| POST-FIELD | Fires when form navigation results in leaving a field. Often used to perform calculations on field values. |
| POST-FORM | Fires when form navigation results in leaving the form. Often used to tidy up (erase global variables, for instance) when exiting a form. |
| POST-RECORD | Fires when form navigation results in leaving a record. Often used to validate combinations of fields in a record. |
| PRE-BLOCK | Fires when form navigation results in entering a block. Often used to generate default values for fields in the block. |
| PRE-FIELD | Fires when form navigation results in entering a field. Often used to set up more complicated default values for the field. |

| Trigger type | Description |
|---|---|
| PRE-FORM | Fires when the form is first entered. Often used to control access to the form. |
| PRE-RECORD | Fires when form navigation results in entering a record. Only fires if the validation unit is field or record. Often used for deriving complex defaults. |

## C.1.3   Transaction triggers

| Trigger type | Description |
|---|---|
| ON-CLEAR-BLOCK | Fires just before the block is flushed. This could be as a result of [*Clear block*], [*Count query*] or [*Enter query*]. |
| ON-DATABASE-RECORD | Fires when a record is recognized as resulting in a change to the database. Often used immediately to update running totals. |
| ON-DELETE | Fires once for each row marked for deletion during *commit* and *post* processing. It replaces the default processing of deleted records and fires after the pre-delete trigger and before the post-delete trigger. |
| ON-ERROR | Fires whenever an error message would normally be displayed. It replaces the default error procedure and is often used to trap and recover from errors or to customize error messages. |
| ON-INSERT | Fires once during *commit* and *post* processing for each row marked for insertion. It replaces the default processing of inserts and fires after the pre-insert trigger and before the post-insert trigger. |
| ON-LOCK | Fires when a row would normally be locked. It replaces the default locking and could be used to impose a special locking strategy. |

| Trigger type | Description |
|---|---|
| ON−MESSAGE | Fires whenever an informative message would normally be displayed. It replaces the normal message display and is often used to customize the messages. |
| ON−NEW−FIELD−INSTANCE | Fires whenever SQL*Forms navigates to a field and is ready for a value to be input (but not when entering a query). Could be used, for example, to provide an automatic list of values for a field. |
| ON−NEW−RECORD | Fires when a new record is created. This could be a result of [Create record] or entering a block which contains only new records. Could be used to set up default values in the fields of new records. |
| ON−REMOVE−RECORD | Fires when a record is deleted or cleared. This could be the result of [Clear record], [Delete record] or [Previous record] from the last (blank) record of a block. Could be used to update a running total. |
| ON−UPDATE | Fires once for each row marked for update during *commit* and *post* processing. It replaces the default processing of updated records and fires after the pre-update trigger and before the post-update trigger. |
| ON−VALIDATE−FIELD | Fires as the last step of validating fields which are marked as new or changed. Often used to provide special validation for the field. |
| ON−VALIDATE−RECORD | Fires as the last step of processing records which are marked as new or changed. Often used to provide special record validation. |
| POST−CHANGE | Fires during field validation when a field is marked as changed and is not null. Also fires when a value is inserted from a list of values or from a fetch. It is not recommended to use this trigger for field validation. Use the on-validate-field trigger instead. |

| Trigger type | Description |
|---|---|
| POST-COMMIT | Fires as the last step of SQL*Forms' commit processing but before the database commit occurs. Could be used to record an audit trail of database changes. |
| POST-DELETE | Fires as part of SQL*Forms' commit processing after each row has been deleted. Often used for auditing. |
| POST-INSERT | Fires as part of SQL*Forms' commit processing after each row is inserted. Often used for auditing. |
| POST-QUERY | Fires each time a record is fetched into a block. Often used to provide totals of values returned by a query. |
| POST-UPDATE | Fires as part of SQL*Forms' commit processing after each row has been updated. Often used for auditing. |
| PRE-COMMIT | Fires as the first step of SQL*Forms' commit processing. Could be used to set up special commit processing. |
| PRE-DELETE | Fires as part of SQL*Forms' commit processing before each row has been deleted. Often used to enforce referential integrity. |
| PRE-INSERT | Fires as part of SQL*Forms' commit processing before each row is inserted. Often used for record validation. |
| PRE-UPDATE | Fires as part of SQL*Forms' commit processing before each row has been updated. Often used for record validation. |

## C.2   Packaged procedures

Packaged procedures fall into two groups: **restricted procedures** fundamentally modify the way in which SQL*Forms operates and may only be used in certain types of trigger; **unrestricted procedures** are less far-reaching in their effect and can be used in any trigger. Restricted procedures should not be used in the following triggers:

- on-delete, on-insert, on-update, on-new-record, on-remove-record, on-validate-field, on-validate-record, on-database-record, on-lock, on-error, on-message

- pre- and post-field, pre- and post-record, pre- and post-block, pre- and post-form, pre- and post-query, pre- and post-insert, pre- and post-update, pre- and post-delete, pre- and post-commit, post-change

- Any user-named trigger which is invoked from these triggers

## C.2.1 Packaged procedures descriptions

| Procedure | Description |
|-----------|-------------|
| ABORT_QUERY | Closes a query open in the current block. Unrestricted. |
| ANCHOR_VIEW | Moves a view of a page to a new position on the screen. Parameters: page number; X-coordinate; Y-coordinate. Unrestricted. |
| BELL | Rings the terminal bell or buzzer when the screen is next synchronized with the internal state of the form. Unrestricted. |
| BLOCK_MENU | Displays the block menu, prompts for a selection and navigates to the selected block. Restricted. |
| BREAK | Only operates in debug mode. Suspends execution and displays the debug options menu. Unrestricted. |
| CALL | Invokes another form while keeping the original form active. Control returns to the original form when the called form is exited. Parameters: called form name; whether or not to clear the screen before displaying the called form; whether or not to use a new default menu application. Unrestricted. |
| CALL_INPUT | Provided for compatibility with version 2; avoid using this procedure. It is used to accept function key input. Restricted. |
| CALL_QUERY | Invokes another form while keeping the original form active. The called form is query only; no updates, inserts or deletes. Parameters: called form name; whether or not to clear the screen before displaying the called form; whether or not to use a new default menu application. Unrestricted. |

| Procedure | Description |
|-----------|-------------|
| CLEAR_BLOCK | Flush the current block. If there are uncommitted changes in the block, a parameter specifies how these changes are to be processed. They can be committed automatically or after prompting. They can be discarded after validating or without validating. Restricted. |
| CLEAR_EOL | Clears the value in the current field from the cursor position to the end of the field. Restricted. |
| CLEAR_FIELD | Clears the value in the current field, setting it to null. Restricted. |
| CLEAR_FORM | Flushes the current form. If there are uncommitted changes in the current form or a called form, a parameter specifies how they are to be processed. They can be rolled back to a savepoint; they can be committed automatically or after prompting; they can be discarded after validating or without validating. Restricted. |
| CLEAR_RECORD | Flushes the current record in a block and, if there is a query open, fetches a new record into the block. Restricted. |
| COMMIT_FORM | Initiates SQL*Forms' commit processing. If there are changes to the database SQL*Forms posts all updates, inserts and deletes for each block and then commits. Restricted. |
| COPY | Writes a specified value to a field. Parameters: the value; the field name. Unrestricted. |
| COPY_REGION | Copies a selected region of the screen into a buffer for subsequent pasting. Restricted. |
| COUNT_QUERY | Counts the number of rows which will be retrieved by a query. If there are uncommitted changes in the block, they will be committed after prompting. Restricted. |
| CREATE_RECORD | Creates a new record after the current record and navigates to the new record. Restricted. |
| CUT_REGION | Cuts a specified region from the screen and stores it in a buffer for subsequent pasting. Restricted. |
| DEFAULT_VALUE | Writes a specified value into a variable if the variable is null. If the variable is not null, the procedure does nothing. Parameters: the value; the variable name. Unrestricted. |
| DELETE_RECORD | Clears the current record from the block and deletes the corresponding row in the database (but does not commit the deletion). Restricted. |

| Procedure | Description |
|---|---|
| DISPLAY_ERROR | Displays the error screen if there is a logged error. The form is redisplayed when the operator presses a function key. Unrestricted. |
| DISPLAY_FIELD | Changes the display attributes of a named field. Parameters: variable name; display attribute. Unrestricted. |
| DISPLAY_PAGE | Changes the display attributes of a page. Parameters: the page number; display attribute. Unrestricted. |
| DO_KEY | Emulates the effect of the operator pressing one of the function keys. If the corresponding key trigger exists, it is executed. Otherwise, the corresponding packaged procedure is executed. Parameter: the packaged procedure name. Restricted. |
| DOWN | Navigates the next instance of the current field in the next record (the one with the next higher sequence number). If necessary, it fetches another record to which to navigate. If a new record has to be created, the procedure navigates to the first field of the record. Restricted. |
| DUPLICATE_FIELD | Copies the value of the instance of the current field in the previous record into the current field. Restricted. |
| DUPLICATE_RECORD | Copies the values of all fields in the previous record (the one with the next lower sequence number) into the current record. An error is generated if the current record corresponds to a database row. Restricted. |
| EDIT_FIELD | Invokes the field editor and puts the form into edit mode. Parameters: X-coordinate; Y-coordinate; width; height of the editor's pop-up window. Restricted. |
| ENTER | Validates the data in the current validation unit. Restricted. |
| ENTER_QUERY | Flushes the current block and puts the form into query mode ready for a query to be entered. If there are changes to the form, they are committed after prompting. A parameter specifies behaviour when the query is executed. The fetch can be for all the selected records. The records can be locked for update. The query can be abandoned if a lock cannot be obtained. Be careful if specifying that all records should be fetched and/or that records should be locked. These are expensive in machine resources. Restricted. |

| Procedure | Description |
|---|---|
| ERASE | Erases a global variable. Parameter: name of global variable. Unrestricted. |
| EXECUTE_QUERY | Executes a query. A parameter specifies behaviour when the query is executed. The fetch can be for all the selected records. The records can be locked for update. The query can be abandoned if a lock cannot be obtained. Be careful if specifying that all records should be fetched and/or that records should be locked. These are expensive in machine resources. Restricted. |
| EXECUTE_TRIGGER | Executes a user-named trigger. Parameter: trigger name. Restricted or unrestricted, depending on the called trigger. |
| EXIT_FORM | Exits from the form. A parameter specifies how to process any changes in the form. They can be committed automatically or after prompting. They can be discarded after validating or without validating. Restricted. |
| FIRST_RECORD | Navigates to the first record in the block's list of records. Restricted. |
| GO_BLOCK | Navigates to a block. Parameter: the target block name. Restricted. |
| GO_FIELD | Navigates to a field. Parameter: target field name. Restricted. |
| GO_RECORD | Navigates to a record. Parameter: target record number (which may be relative or computed). Restricted. |
| HELP | Displays the hint text for the current field. If this is already displayed, it displays the full help screen for the field. Unrestricted. |
| HIDE_MENU | Removes the current menu, if it is displayed. Unrestricted. |
| HIDE_PAGE | Removes a specified page from the screen. You cannot remove the current page. Parameter: page number. Unrestricted. |
| HOST | Executes a host operating system command line, optionally clearing the screen and returning. Parameters: the command; whether or not to clear and return. Unrestricted. |
| LAST_RECORD | Navigates to the last record in the block's list of records. Restricted. |

| Procedure | Description |
|---|---|
| LIST_VALUES | Displays the list of values for the current field. A parameter specifies whether any value in the current field is to be used to restrict the list of values displayed. Restricted. |
| LOCK_RECORD | Tries to take out a row lock for the corresponding row in the database. Unrestricted. |
| MESSAGE | Displays a message. Parameter: message text. Unrestricted. |
| MOVE_VIEW | Changes the section of a page seen by the operator by moving a view of a page to a new location on the page. Parameters: the page number; X-coordinate; Y-coordinate. Unrestricted. |
| NEW_FORM | Exits the current form and executes a new form. Parameter: new form name. Restricted. |
| NEXT_BLOCK | Navigates to the next enterable block or the first block of the form. Restricted. |
| NEXT_FIELD | Navigates to the next enterable field or the first field of the block. Restricted. |
| NEXT_KEY | Navigates to the next primary key field or the first primary key field of the block. An error is generated if there are no primary key fields in the block. Restricted. |
| NEXT_RECORD | Navigates to the next record in the block, fetching or creating a new record if necessary. Restricted. |
| NEXT_SET | Fetches the next set of records from the database and navigates to the first record of the set. Restricted. |
| PASTE_REGION | Pastes an area from the buffer on to the screen, placing the top left corner at the cursor position. Restricted. |
| PAUSE | Suspends processing of the form. It resumes when the operator presses a function key. Unrestricted. |
| POST | Posts any changes from the form to the database but does not commit the changes. Restricted. |
| PREVIOUS_BLOCK | Navigates to the previous block or the last block of the form. Restricted. |
| PREVIOUS_FIELD | Navigates to the previous field or the last field of the record. Restricted. |
| PREVIOUS_RECORD | Navigates to the previous record in the block. Restricted. |

| Procedure | Description |
|---|---|
| PRINT | Writes the contents of the form to a file. The operator is prompted to specify which pages to write, the filename and whether to send the file to the printer. Unrestricted. |
| REDISPLAY | Redisplays the screen. Unrestricted. |
| REPLACE_MENU | Replaces the current SQL*Menu menu with a new one. Parameters specify the name of the new menu application, the display type of the menu, the name of the menu and the security group to use. Unrestricted. |
| RESIZE_VIEW | Changes the size of a view of a page. Parameters: the page number; new width of the view; new height of the view. Unrestricted. |
| SCROLL_DOWN | Scrolls down the records displayed in a block by about 80%, fetching new records if necessary. Restricted. |
| SCROLL_UP | Scrolls up the records displayed in a block by about 80%. Restricted. |
| SET_FIELD | Changes the field attributes of a field. Parameters: the field name; the new attributes. Unrestricted. |
| SET_INPUT_FOCUS | Sets the input focus to the menu of the current form. Unrestricted. |
| SHOW_KEYS | Displays the screen showing key mappings. The form is restarted when the operator presses a function key. Unrestricted. |
| SHOW_MENU | Shows the current menu if not displayed. The menu is not made active and it may be covered in whole or in part by the form. Unrestricted. |
| SHOW_PAGE | Displays a specified page. The page is not made active and may be covered in whole or in part by the active page but it will, itself, cover any other inactive pages. Unrestricted. |
| SYNCHRONIZE | Updates the screen to resynchronize the display with the internal state of the form. Unrestricted. |
| UP | Navigates the previous instance of the current field in the previous record (the one with the next higher sequence number). Restricted. |
| USER_EXIT | Calls a named user-exit. Parameters: the name of the user-exit; the error message to be used if the user-exit fails. Unrestricted. |

# C.3 System variables

| Variable | Description |
|---|---|
| $$DATE$$ | Holds the current date in the format DD-MON-YY. |
| $$DATETIME$$ | Holds the current date and time in the format DD-MON-YY HH:MM:SS. |
| $$TIME$$ | Holds the current time in the format HH:MM:SS. |
| SYSTEM.BLOCK_STATUS | Holds the status of the current block in the form of a character string: CHANGED to indicate that there is at least one changed record, NEW to indicate that the block contains only new records or QUERY to indicate that the block contains records derived from a query. |
| SYSTEM.CURRENT_BLOCK | Holds the name of the current block if the current validation unit is a block, record or field. It is null if the current validation unit is the form. |
| SYSTEM.CURRENT_FIELD | Holds the name of the current field if the current validation unit is a field, otherwise it is null. The field name does not have a block name prefix. |
| SYSTEM.CURRENT_FORM | Holds the name of the form currently being executed. |
| SYSTEM.CURRENT_VALUE | Holds the value of the current field. Provided for compatibility with version 2. You are recommended to use SYSTEM.CURSOR_VALUE. |
| SYSTEM.CURSOR_BLOCK | Holds the name of the block where the cursor currently is. |
| SYSTEM.CURSOR_FIELD | Holds the name of the field where the cursor currently is. |
| SYSTEM.CURSOR_RECORD | Holds the sequence number of the record where the cursor currently is. |
| SYSTEM.CURSOR_VALUE | Holds the value of the field where the cursor currently is. |

| Variable | Description |
|----------|-------------|
| SYSTEM.FORM_STATUS | Holds the status of the current form as a character string: CHANGED to indicate that there is at least one changed record, NEW to indicate that the form contains only new records or QUERY to indicate that a query is open. |
| SYSTEM.LAST_QUERY | Holds the SELECT statement last used to populate a block. |
| SYSTEM.LAST_RECORD | Holds a boolean variable to show whether the current record is the last in a block's list of records. |
| SYSTEM.MESSAGE_LEVEL | Holds the value of the message severity level used to govern error message output. |
| SYSTEM.RECORD_STATUS | Holds the status of the current record in the form of a character string: CHANGED to indicate that the record has been changed, NEW to indicate that the record is a new one, INSERT to indicate that the record has changed and does not exist in the database or QUERY to indicate that the record is valid and derived directly from the database. |
| SYSTEM.TRIGGER_BLOCK | Holds the name of the current block when a trigger was activated. Null for pre- and post-form triggers. |
| SYSTEM.TRIGGER_FIELD | Holds the name of the current field when a trigger was activated. Null for pre- and post record, pre- and post-block and pre- and post-form triggers. The field name has the block name as a prefix. |
| SYSTEM.TRIGGER_RECORD | Holds the sequence number of the current record when a trigger was activated. |

# SQL*Forms version 2: reference information

## D.1 Trigger types

Triggers are categorized according to the level at which they operate. There are triggers which operate at field level, for instance when a field has been changed. There are triggers which operate at block level, for instance when a query is entered. Finally, there are triggers which operate at form level, for instance when the form is first entered. Note that these levels are not necessarily the same as the level at which a trigger is **defined** and which, therefore, determines the trigger's scope. In addition, there are triggers which operate when a function key is pressed. The majority (but not all) of the function keys have corresponding triggers.

### D.1.1 Field triggers

| Trigger | Description |
| --- | --- |
| Post-change | Fires when the cursor leaves a field which has been changed and after normal validation of the field. Often used for additional field validation. |
| Pre-field | Fires when the cursor enters a field. Often used to set up complex default values. |
| Post-field | Fires when the cursor leaves a field (whether the field has been changed or not). Often used for field validation. |

### D.1.2 Block triggers

| Trigger | Description |
| --- | --- |
| Pre-query | Fires when a query has been initiated (by [*Execute query*] or [*Count query hits*]) and before the query is executed. Often used to modify details of the query. |

| Trigger | Description |
|---------|-------------|
| Post-query | Fires once for each record retrieved by a query as the record is displayed. Often used to calculate totals or other statistics. |
| Pre-delete | Fires once for each row to be deleted just before deletion. Often used to enforce referential integrity. |
| Post-delete | Fires once for each row after deletion. Often used for auditing. |
| Pre-insert | Fires once for each record to be inserted just before insertion. Often used for special validation. |
| Post-insert | Fires once for each inserted record just after insertion. Often used for auditing. |
| Pre-update | Fires once for each updated record just before update. Often used for record validation. |
| Post-update | Fires once for each updated row just after update. Often used for auditing. |
| Pre-record | Fires when the cursor moves into a record, before the pre-block trigger and before the pre-field trigger. Often used for coordinating the contents of different blocks. |
| Post-record | Fires when the cursor leaves a record as a result of cursor movement, deleting the record or clearing the record. Often used for cross-field validation. |
| Pre-block | Fires as the cursor moves into a block. Often used for controlling access to a block. |
| Post-block | Fires as the cursor leaves a block and after post-field and post-record triggers. Often used to correlate data across several records. |

## D.1.3  Form triggers

| Trigger | Description |
|---------|-------------|
| Pre-form | Fires just before the form is entered. Often used to control access to the form. |
| Post-form | Fires as the form is exited, after post-field, post-record and post-block triggers and after committing any changes. Often used to tidy up global variables etc. |

## D.1.4 Key triggers

| Trigger | Description |
| --- | --- |
| KEY-CLRBLK | [*Clear block*] |
| KEY-CLRFRM | [*Clear form*] |
| KEY-CLRREC | [*Clear record*] |
| KEY-COMMIT | [*Commit/accept*] |
| KEY-CQUERY | [*Count query hits*] |
| KEY-CREREC | [*Insert record*] |
| KEY-DELREC | [*Delete record*] |
| KEY-DOWN | [*Down*] |
| KEY-DUPFLD | [*Duplicate field*] |
| KEY-DUPREC | [*Duplicate record*] |
| KEY-ENTQRY | [*Enter query*] |
| KEY-EXEQRY | [*Execute query*] |
| KEY-EXIT | [*Exit*] |
| KEY-Fn | Programmable function keys 0 to 9. |
| KEY-HELP | [*Help*] |
| KEY-LISTVAL | [*List of values*] |
| KEY-MENU | [*Block menu*] |
| KEY-NXTBLK | [*Next block*] |
| KEY-NXTFLD | [*Next field*] |
| KEY-NXTKEY | [*Next primary key field*] |
| KEY-NXTREC | [*Next record*] |
| KEY-NXTSET | [*Next set of records*] |
| KEY-PRVBLK | [*Previous block*] |
| KEY-PRVFLD | [*Previous field*] |
| KEY-PRVREC | [*Previous record*] |
| KEY-SCRDOWN | [*Scroll down*] |
| KEY-SCRUP | [*Scroll up*] |
| KEY-STARTUP | A notional key implicitly pressed when the form is activated. |
| KEY-UP | [*Up*] |

## D.2   Macro functions

The following is a list of the macro functions. They are invoked with #EXEMACRO. Many of the functions have the same effect as an operator pressing keys on the keyboard. Note that when such functions are executed, the effect is that of the key as it was originally set up and does not reflect any changes in the key definition as the result of other triggers.

| Function | Description |
|---|---|
| ABTQRY | [*Abort query*] |
| BELL | Sounds the terminal bell or buzzer. |
| CALL formname | Suspends the current form and executes the form specified. The original form will be resumed when [*Exit/cancel*] is pressed or when the called form executes the EXIT function. |
| CALLINPUT | Suspends execution of current macro to accept operator input. The macro is resumed when [*Exit/cancel*] is pressed. |
| CALLQRY formname | Suspends the current form and executes the form specified for queries only. The original form is resumed when [*Exit/cancel*] is pressed or when the called form executes the EXIT function. |
| CHRMODE | [*Insert/replace*] |
| CLRBLK | [*Clear block*] |
| CLRFLD | [*Clear field*] |
| CLRFRM | [*Clear form/rollback*] |
| CLRREC | [*Clear record*] |
| COMMIT | [*Commit*] |
| COPY source INTO dest | Copies constants or field values |
| CQUERY | [*Count query hits*] |
| CREREC | [*Create record*] |
| DEFAULT val INTO var | Sets up a variable and gives it a default value. If the variable already exists, gives it a value if it is currently null. |
| DELCHR | [*Delete character*] |
| DELREC | [*Delete record*] |

| Function | Description |
|---|---|
| DERROR | *[Display error]* |
| DKEYS | *[Display function keys]* |
| DOWN | *[Cursor down]* |
| DUPFLD | *[Duplicate field]* |
| DUPREC | *[Duplicate record]* |
| ENDSTEP | Ends the current trigger step. Parameters define whether to return success or failure and an optional message. |
| ENDTRIG | Ends the current trigger. Parameters define whether to return success or failure and an optional message. |
| ENTER | Validates the data in the current validation unit. |
| ENTQRY | *[Enter query]*. Parameters define the behaviour when the query is executed: whether all records are to be retrieved and whether to reserve the records for update. Both of these options can be expensive in machine resources. Use with care. |
| ERASE | Erases a global variable which is named as a parameter. |
| EXEQRY | *[Execute query]* Parameters define the behaviour when the query is executed: whether all records are to be retrieved and whether to reserve the records for update. Both of these options can be expensive in machine resources. Use with care. |
| EXETRG trigname | Execute a user-named trigger. |
| EXIT | *[Exit/cancel]* |
| GOBLK blockname | Moves the cursor to the first field in the named block. |
| GOFLD fldname | Moves the cursor to the named field. If the field is not in the current block, it is specified in the form of blockname.fldname. |
| GOSTEP | Branches to the trigger step named as a parameter. |
| HELP | *[Help]* |

| Function | Description |
|---|---|
| HOST | Executes a host operating system command line, optionally clearing the screen and returning. Parameters: the command; whether or not to clear and return. |
| LISTVAL | [*List field values*] |
| MENU | [*Menu*] |
| MESSAGE | Displays a message on the message line of the screen. The message is supplied as a parameter. |
| MOVLEFT | [*Cursor left*] |
| MOVRIGHT | [*Cursor right*] |
| NEWFRM formname | Suspends the current form and executes the named form. [*Exit/cancel*] will not resume the original form. |
| NOOP | No action; an 'Unrecognized Command' message is displayed. |
| NULL | No action. |
| NXTBLK | [*Next block*] |
| NXTFLD | [*Next field*] |
| NXTKEY | [*Next primary key field*] |
| NXTREC | [*Next record*] |
| NXTSET | [*Next set of records*] |
| PAUSE | Suspends execution of the macro until the operator presses any key. |
| PRINT | [*Print*] |
| PRVBLK | [*Previous block*] |
| PRVFLD | [*Previous field*] |
| PRECREC | [*Previous record*] |
| REDISP | [*Redisplay screen*] |
| SCRDOWN | Scrolls down the records displayed in a block by about 80%, fetching new records if necessary. |
| SCRUP | Scroll up the records displayed in a block by about 80%. |

| Function | Description |
|----------|-------------|
| SYNCHRONIZE | Updates the screen to resynchronize the display with the internal state of the form. |
| UP | Navigates the previous instance of the current field in the previous record (the one with the next higher sequence number). |
| UPDREC | Locks the current record. |

# D.3  System variables

| Variable | Description |
|----------|-------------|
| SYSTEM.CURRENT_FIELD | Holds the name of the current field if invoked at field level. Null when invoked at higher levels. The field name does not have a block name prefix. |
| SYSTEM.CURRENT_VALUE | Holds the value of the current field. |
| SYSTEM.CURSOR_BLOCK | Holds the name of the block where the cursor currently is. |
| SYSTEM.CURSOR_FIELD | Holds the name of the field where the cursor currently is. |
| SYSTEM.CURSOR_VALUE | Holds the value of the field where the cursor currently is. |
| SYSTEM.MESSAGE_LEVEL | Holds the value of the message severity level used to govern error message output. |
| SYSTEM.TRIGGER_BLOCK | Holds the name of the current block when a trigger was activated. Null for **pre-** and **post-form** triggers. |
| SYSTEM.TRIGGER_FIELD | Holds the name of the current field when a trigger was activated. Null for **pre-** and **post-record, pre-** and **post-block** and **pre-** and **post-form** triggers. The field name has the block name as a prefix. |

# SQL*Report: reference information

## E.1 Example RPT programs

### E.1.1 A tabular report for Statement of Account

```
.REM ********************************************
.REM
.REM    An example of an RPT program to produce
.REM    a Statement of Account in a tabular format.
.REM
.REM    File Name: TABRPT.EX
.REM
.REM ********************************************
.REM
.REM    Define Tables and print title
.REM
#DT 1 13 73 #
#DT 2 1 5 9 28 32 39 42 49 52 0 #
#PAGE 6 58
#T 1
#S 4
#CUL "    STATEMENT           OF    ACCOUNT  " #
#S 2
.REM Prompt for the Customer Number
.&askcust
.ASK "Enter Customer No: " customer_number
.IF "&customer_number <= 0" THEN askcust
.IF "&customer_number IS NULL" THEN askcust

.REM ********************************************
.REM    Declarative Section: Declare all variables and
.REM    initialize as required.
.REM ********************************************
.DECLARE statement_date a9
.DECLARE customer_number 99999
.DECLARE item_no 099
.DECLARE registration a8
.DECLARE miles_used 999999
.DECLARE charge 9,999.99
.DECLARE balance 99,999.99
.SET item_no 0
```

```
.REM *******************************************
.REM    Define the SELECT macro
.REM *******************************************
.DEFINE selcust
    SELECT TO_CHAR(SYSDATE,'DD-MON-YY'),
        registration, miles_in - miles_out,
        rental_period * 150
    INTO    statement_date, registration, miles_used,
        charge
    FROM    bookings
    WHERE   cust_no = &customer_number
..


.REM *******************************************
.REM    Define BODY macro
.REM *******************************************
.DEFINE body
.REM    Print each column variable and proceed to
.REM    next column
    .IF "&miles_used IS NULL" THEN nocharge ELSE
        charge
    .&nocharge
    .SET miles_used 0
    .SET charge 0
    .&charge
    .ADD item_no item_no 1
    .PRINT item_no
    #NC
    #CEN
    .PRINT registration
    #NC
    .PRINT miles_used
    #NC
    .PRINT charge
    #NC
    .ADD balance balance charge
    .PRINT balance
    #NC
..


.REM *******************************************
.REM    Define the HEAD macro
.REM *******************************************
.DEFINE head
    #CUL TO
    .PRINT statement_date
    #
```

```
       #S 2
       #CEN CUSTOMER NO: \ \
       .PRINT customer_number
       #S 2
       #T 2
       ITEM #CEN NO #NC
       #CEN CAR #  #N  #CEN REGISTRATION #  #NC
       #R MILES #N USED #NC #N
       #R CHARGE #NC #N
       #R BALANCE #NC
       #S 2
.REM    Execute the body macro to print the first
.REM    row
    .body
..


.REM ********************************************
.REM     Define the FOOT macro
.REM ********************************************
.DEFINE foot
    #TE
    #S 5
    #CEN COMPANY \ \ CONFIDENTIAL #
..


.REM ********************************************
.REM    The Procedure Section
.REM ********************************************
.REPORT selcust body head foot
#TE
.STOP
```

## E.1.2  A nested report for car maintenance

```
.REM ********************************************
.REM
.REM    An example of an RPT program to produce
.REM    a nested report.
.REM
.REM    File Name: NESTRPT.EX
.REM
.REM ********************************************
.REM


.REM ********************************************
.REM    Declarative Section : Declare all variables
.REM    and initialize as required.
```

```
.REM *********************************************
.DECLARE car_group a2
.DECLARE registration a8
.DECLARE model a8
.DECLARE cost 999,999
.DECLARE maintenance_interval 99999
.DECLARE miles_to_date 999999
.DECLARE min_mileage 999999
.DECLARE max_mileage 999999

.REM *********************************************
.REM    Define the SELECT macros
.REM *********************************************
.REM    Select the Car Group information
.REM
.DEFINE cargroup
   SELECT DISTINCT car_group
   INTO   car_group
   FROM   cars
   ORDER BY car_group
..
.REM
.REM Select the cars within a group
.DEFINE selcars
   SELECT registration, model, cost, maint_int,
   miles_to_date
   INTO registration, model, cost,
       maintenance_interval, miles_to_date
   FROM cars
   WHERE car_group = &car_group
   ORDER BY registration
..
.REM
.REM Select car group summary information
.DEFINE groupsum
   SELECT min(miles_to_date), max(miles_to_date)
   INTO min_mileage, max_mileage
   FROM cars
   WHERE car_group = &car_group
..

.REM *********************************************
.REM    Define Procedural macros
.REM *********************************************
.REM
.REM    HEAD macro for the Car Group report
.DEFINE grouphead
   .REM This macro processes the first row returned
```

```
        .REM for the Car Group report. This is required
        .REM because a foot macro is specified in the
        .REM .REPORT statement.
        .groupbody
    ..
.REM
.REM    BODY macro for Car Group report
.DEFINE groupbody
.REM Print heading for Car Group
    #NP
    #S 2
    #CEN ************** #
    #CEN \ Car Group:
    .PRINT car_group
    #
    #CEN ************** #
    #S 2
.REM Process every car within this group
    .REPORT selcars carbody carhead carfoot
    ..
.REM
.REM    FOOT macro for Car Group report
.REM
.DEFINE groupfoot
.REM Print end of report message
    #S 4
    #CEN ** End of Car Maintenance report ** #
    #TE
    ..
.REM
.REM    HEAD macro for Car report
.DEFINE carhead
    #T 2
    #S 1
    #CEN CAR # #N  #CEN REGISTRATION #  #NC
    #CEN MODEL # #NC  #CEN COST # #NC
    MAINTENANCE #N  #CEN INTERVAL # #NC  MILES TO
    #N \ \ DATE #NC ------------ #NC #CEN ----- #
    #NC #CEN ---- # #NC ----------- #NC -------- #NC
.REM Set up right justification for the
.REM "miles to date" column
    #NC #NC #NC #NC #R #NC
.REM Execute body macro to process first row
.carbody
    ..
.REM
.REM    BODY macro for Car report
.DEFINE carbody
```

```
      #CEN
      .PRINT registration
      #   #NC   #CEN
      .PRINT model
      #   #NC   #CEN
      .PRINT cost
      #   #NC   #CEN
      .PRINT maintenance_interval
      #   #NC
      .PRINT miles_to_date
      #NC
..
.REM
.REM   FOOT macro for Car report
.DEFINE carfoot
.REM Print minimum and maximum mileage for this
.REM car group
      .EXECUTE groupsum
      #TE
      #T 3
      #S 2
      Car Group Summary
      #NC #NC
      Min. Mileage:
      .PRINT min_mileage
      #NC
      Max. Mileage:
      .PRINT max_mileage
      #TE
..

.REM ********************************************
.REM     Main Section of Report
.REM ********************************************
.REM
.REM     Define Tables
#DT 1 13 73 #
#DT 2 1 12 14 22 24 31 33 44 52 59 #
#DT 3 1 20 25 45 #
#PAGE 6 58
#T 1
#S 4
#CUL   CAR MAINTENANCE REPORT   #
#S 1
#CUL BY Car Group     #
.REPORT cargroup groupbody grouphead groupfoot
.STOP
```

## E.2   RPF switches

Switches are used to control the execution of RPF. They are specified on the command line, in any order, without spaces in between and preceded by a single minus sign.

| Switch | Effect |
|--------|--------|
| A | The whole report will be printed in boldface. Relevant only with Diablo-type printers. |
| B | Underlined sections of the report will be printed in boldface. Relevant only with Diablo-type printers. |
| D:D | Output is to go to a Diablo-type printer which supports bi-directional and boldface printing. |
| D:V | Output is to go to a VT100 (or compatible) terminal. Underlined text is converted to reverse video. |
| F | Pages in the output are separated by form feed characters rather than by a number of blank lines. |
| I | The report will start with a blank page. |
| P:n:m | Where *n* and *m* are page numbers. Produces a selective print of only page *n* to page *m* (inclusive) of the report. If *m* is omitted, page *n* to the end of the report will be printed. |
| R | For underlined text, print the underline first before the backspace and the text character. Normally, RPF prints the text character first, then the underline. Use of this switch results in the correct text appearing on devices which do not allow overstriking. |
| S | Report is to be sent to the system spooler for later printing on a system printer. |
| U | All alphabetic characters will be printed in upper case. |
| W | Printing is suspended at the end of each page of the report. Printing restarts after any key is pressed on the terminal. This switch is only relevant in conjunction with the D:D or D:V switches. |

## E.2.1 RPT switches

Switches can be used to control the execution of RPT. They are specified on the command line, in any order, each preceded by a minus sign and separated by a space.

| Switch | Effect |
|--------|--------|
| –An | Specifies the number ($n$) of rows to be retrieved in one fetch. |
| –Nm | Specifies the number of data cursors to process SQL statements. Default is 5. More cursors improves the efficiency of SQL processing at the expense of store occupancy. |
| –? | Causes RPT to display its version number when invoked. |
| –X | Causes RPT to continue execution even if errors are found in the command file. |
| –O | Allows RPT to run command files containing old-style format masks. Only used to run old RPT programs. |

# Index